ITALIAN DYNASTIES

ITALIAN DYNASTIES

**The Great Families of Italy
From the Renaissance to the Present Day**

Edward Burman

First published 1989

British Library Cataloguing in Publication Data

Burman, Edward
Italian dynasties: the great families
of Italy from the Renaissance to the present day.
1. Italy. Dynasties, ca 1500-1987
I. Title
945

ISBN 1-85336-005-8

Equation is an imprint of the Thorsons Publishing Group,
Wellingborough, Northamptonshire, NN8 2RQ, England

Printed in Great Britain by Butler & Tanner Limited,
Frome, Somerset
Typeset by MJL Limited, Hitchin, Hertfordshire

1 3 5 7 9 10 8 6 4 2

CONTENTS

INTRODUCTION

Most of the family names of the dynasties that form the subject of this book — the Visconti, the Sforza, the Medici, and others — are well known in the twentieth century. Because of their exceptional role as sponsors of humanism and the arts these dynasties are part of the European cultural heritage. Some claimed descent from Roman emperors, and some still survive today; thus their collective history spans two thousand years. Yet without exception they reached the peak of their wealth, power, and fame within a relatively short period from about 1350 to 1550.

In the thirteenth century the Italian peninsula was the terrain of a power struggle between the Holy Roman Empire and the papacy. From his stronghold in the Kingdom of Sicily, the Hohenstaufen Emperor Frederick II sought to bring central and northern Italy under his sway while successive popes resisted him — and more than once excommunicated him. Many cities and local rulers openly sustained one of these forces. Yet many others managed to achieve neutrality and even independence — either temporary or permanent — and instead fought against one another in order to achieve local supremacy. During the interregnum of 1250–73 that followed Frederick II's death the political situation changed dramatically. As the empire disintegrated local rulers sought to extend their lands by seizing towns and regions. Revolts against Rudolf of Habsburg, after his election as Holy Roman Emperor in 1273, continued this process. The situation was further complicated by the political parties known as the Guelphs and Ghibellines — who supported papacy and Emperor respectively. The process was again accelerated by the transfer of the papacy from Rome to Avignon in 1305.

These independent cities or territories were often ancient feuds, but also included amongst their number recently built towns and cities. In that turbulent century they were more often than not at war with their neighbours, and, as their wealth and power grew, were able to employ mercenary soldiers to fight their battles. Thus,

Opposite *The Wise Men travelling to Bethlehem with Lorenzo the Magnificent, by Gozzoli.*

Detail from Gozzoli's painting: Piero the Gouty, Galeazzo Maria Sforza and Sigismondo Pandolfo Malatesta.

as the fourteenth century opened, a small number of them had managed to achieve political solidity as despotic rulers, while in some cases the mercenaries themselves rose to become rulers. The dynasties which became celebrated during the early part of the Renaissance sprang — with the single exception of the Medici — from these two sources: each one traced the origins of its power either to a feudal ruler or to a great *condottiere*. The former include the Visconti of Milan, the Este of Ferrara, and the Colonna of Rome; the latter include the Sforza of Milan, the Gonzaga of Mantova, the Montefeltro of Urbino, and the Malatesta of Rimini.

Once they were securely established in their states and duchies, increased Mediterranean trade — and Italy's position as ideal middleman between the Holy Land and northern Europe — provided the means for these dynasties to perpetuate their names through large-scale patronage of arts and letters. Thus, during the fourteenth century these families sponsored both the new humanism and the beginnings of the Italian Renaissance.

It is significant that most of the dynasties came to real power, a stable political situation in which they were able to build or rebuild their cities and devote patronage to the arts, after 1350. Even more remarkably, the most renowned men and women who bore these names lived in the second half of the fifteenth century. From the Peace of Lodi in 1454 to the invasion by Charles VIII of France in 1494 there was an unparalleled period of peace and stability in Italy. In this single half-century cities like Florence, Mantova, Ferrara, and Urbino flourished; figures like Lorenzo the Magnificent, Isabella d'Este, Lodovico Sforza, Federico II da Montefeltro, and Sigismondo Malatesta ruled; artists like Botticelli, Mantegna, Donatello, Piero della Francesca, Ghirlandaio, and Leonardo da Vinci were at the height of their powers; buildings like Palazzo Rucellai and Palazzo Strozzi in Florence, the Ospedale Maggiore in Milan, and the Palazzo dei Diamanti in Ferrara were built, while the Doges' Palace in Venice was completed and the new town plan of Rome instigated. With the single exception of Venice, all these works were carried out under the direct or indirect patronage of the dynasties cited here.

Many of these families intermarried in the perennial search for political alliances. The more spectacular marriages were those between sons and daughters of ruling lords: for instance between Lodovico Sforza and Beatrice d'Este, or between Francesco Gonzaga and Isabella d'Este. Yet through the centuries there were matrimonial connections between other families which would make a broad-based genealogical table horrifyingly complex. Members of the Colonna family, for instance, in the course of seven centuries have married into all the families treated in this book with the single exception of the Visconti. In the case of the Sforza and Gonzaga families, these Colonna marriages occurred on no fewer than five separate occasions for each family. In the late fifteenth century the links between the Gonzaga, Este, and Montefeltro families were particularly close, for instance when Isabella d'Este, who was married to Francesco Gonzaga, provided a home in exile for her sister Elisabetta, Duchess of Urbino.

Although some of these families are of much more ancient lineage, they represent the single flowering of a truly Italian culture which was unified by the constant

Equestrian portrait of Sir John Hawkwood in Florence cathedral, by Paolo Uccello.

flux of ideas and artists between the main centres of patronage. They came into being in the power vacuum left by the German Emperors, and were then swept away by the invading French and Spanish. They are largely responsible for the 'Italian' element of the Italian Renaissance. The period between 1350 and 1550 can in fact be seen as a kind of Italian interregnum between foreign domination.

THE *CONDOTTIERI*

In military terms, this interregnum was the period of the *condottieri*—mercenary captains of adventure—without whose vital contribution many of the smaller states, wealthy but militarily weak, would not have survived. Several of the better leaders perceived this obvious weakness of their masters and founded states of their own. Each of the dynasties discussed here had at least one *condottiere* in its history; some were veritable dynasties of *condottieri*.

The word *condottiere* derives from the *'condotta'*, which was the contract between the *condottiere* and his temporary master. It was in effect a guarantee of his loyalty or good conduct (*'buona condotta'*). The forms of contract were manifold, but consisted of two main types: the *'condotta a soldo disteso'* — or full pay — in which a *condottiere* agreed to fight a battle or war on behalf of a city or lord; and the *'condotta a mezzo soldo'* — or half pay — in which the *condottiere* was part of a larger army and at the command of a general. In the latter case the pay was less in proportion to the risk.

From the earliest times, the *condottieri* organized their troops in groups of three, each group being called a lance. The lance consisted of a mounted soldier, his squire, and a lancer either on foot or mounted on a jade. Thus a city putting out a contract for an imminent battle would ask for three hundred 'lances' rather than nine hundred men. In this way he was sure to get three hundred cavalry, with the necessary logistical support. Since these soldiers were mercenaries the problem for employers was to obtain loyalty. Many wars and battles changed course dramatically as the result of a better offer of pay from the 'enemy', and success was rewarded with grants of money, land, and castles. In some cases the *condottieri* were further privileged by monuments in their honour, as in the case of the Englishman John Hawkwood whose tomb in Florence cathedral was painted by Paolo Uccello. The lances who frequently changed commander were known as 'free-lances', a term which has survived until today with almost the same meaning.

The fragmentation of states, absence of regular armies and unwillingness of merchants to fight made the employment of professional soldiers a necessity. The means existed to pay them, and an ample supply of men from the so-called free companies of northern Europe guaranteed sufficient men. Recruits were also found in foreign armies which invaded or attacked Italy. In particular the fluctuating Hundred Years War (1338–1453) between England and France provided recruits during the lulls in warfare. Men such as Hawkwood began their careers in Italy following the Peace of Bretigny in 1360, when the first phase of the Hundred Years War ended.

Fanciful portrait of the condottiere *Francesco Sforza between Julius Caesar and Hannibal, from an illuminated manuscript.*

It is likely that many of his men were born during the French campaigns, and therefore although they were 'English', they had neither a home nor the possibility of employment in England.

The *condottieri* organized their men into companies, some of which were famous throughout Italy. The troops were well disciplined and battle-trained. At first many of them were German, as in the Grand Company formed by the Montreal d'Albarno, a *condottiere* from Provence. But throughout the fourteenth and early fifteenth centuries one of the main reserves of recruitment was the tough warrior caste of Emilia Romagna. The case of Sir John Hawkwood was exceptional, since he arrived with his company already formed from the wars in France. His legendary meticulous care over weapons earned his men the name of the White Company, because each evening they were required to clean and polish their weapons so that they shone in the sunshine. His tactics and courage were celebrated, and he fought for many of the cities and states of the time. But he finished by serving Florence for the unusually long period of twenty years, after which he was given a villa in the hills near the city and a pension. He and his fellow mercenary captains were largely responsible for creating the peaceful conditions in which the Florentine Renaissance could take place.

But service with one of the leading *condottieri* in a kind of apprenticeship was the usual way to begin. The famous Company of St George, led by Alberico da Barbiano, served as a training for several of the generation of *condottieri* who came to the fore towards the end of the fourteenth century. Two of the greatest *condottieri* once fought side by side in this Company as young men: Muzio Attendolo and Andrea Braccio da Montone, known as Sforza ('Strength'), Fortebraccio ('Strongarm') respectively. This reflects the common practice of attributing nicknames to *condottieri*: Erasmo da Narni was Gattamelata or 'the Tabby Cat', Muzio's constant rival Tartaglia was 'the Stammerer', and Francesco Sforza's main rival was Niccolo Piccinino, 'Tiny'. At one time the whole of Italy was divided into the supporters of Sforza or Braccio: the Sforzeschi and Braccheschi, as the two parties were known.

The shrewdest of these men were able to see that the rulers for whom they fought could not manage without them. If that were the case, they reasoned, they could fight for themselves and carve out a small territory or take a city — their native city or any other. The best *condottieri* did in fact make this move towards independent lordship, often with very great success — though some, like Braccio da Montone, failed badly and died in the attempt. Muzio Attendolo's son Francesco Sforza became Duke of Milan and founded the second great dynasty of that city. The Malatesta, Montefeltro, and Gonzaga dynasties were also founded by *condottieri*. Others achieved almost equal fame by being represented by the greatest artists of the time: for example, the splendid equestrian sculpture of Gattamelata by Donatello outside the church of S. Antonio in Padova and that of Bartolomeo Colleone, who came from Bergamo, made by Donatello's pupils Andrea del Verocchio outside the Venetian church of SS. Pietro e Paolo.

The importance of the *condottieri* faded towards the end of the fifteenth century as the political situation changed and small cities and states which employed them were incorporated into larger political units. Moreover their fighting methods were useless against the new techniques and weapons of the huge armies of France, Spain, and Germany which then began to contest Italy. But by that time they had made their mark on Italian history and culture.

THE MERCHANT REPUBLICS

The wealth which enabled the new rulers to purchase the trappings of power, to finance the building of great cities, and provide patronage to the artists who in turn immortalized them, derived from the position of Italy as middleman to international trade. This was the historical legacy of the country's position in the Mediterranean Sea, and the consequence of a near monopoly of the trade which developed between Europe and the East during the preceding two hundred years.

Venice, Pisa, Amalfi, and Genova had been quick to establish trading communities in the Latin Kingdom of Jerusalem after the First Crusade established a Christian base in 1100. Venice in particular grew into one of the largest and richest of all cities, and in 1338 had a population of 120,000. From Ancona, Rimini, and Venice, merchandise was transported overland to Rome and Florence, or on to northern Europe. Cities such as Milan and Florence derived much of their wealth from strategic importance in trading and their function as bankers. Behind the great cities such as Venice, which produced virtually no agricultural produce, others such as Ferrara and Mantova were able to exploit their fertile territories in supplying the rich Venetians with food. Payment for military services together with trade created the wealth which made these dynasties possible.

It is a striking fact that almost the entire thrust of the early Renaissance should come from a small group of tyrants and pseudo-republics. Furthermore, the interesting individual patrons of great importance come exclusively from dynasties within their cities: there are no parallels to be found in Venice or Genova for individuals such as Lodovico il Moro in Milan, Isabella d'Este in Mantova, and Lorenzo the Magnificent in Florence. Conversely, it is no surprise that the wealth of these cities, and consequently the patronage and power of the dynasties which ruled them, declined as the focus of trade passed from the Mediterranean to the Atlantic during the sixteenth century. The wealth of the Americas flowed into Spain, while the role of middlemen in international trade passed to the English, the Portuguese, and the Dutch. The centre of gravity of new discoveries passed north from Italy: in painting to the Netherlands, and in science and philosophy to England.

FOREIGN INVASIONS

Southern Italy had been constantly under foreign domination: the Kingdom of Naples was ruled directly by Spanish monarchs until 1501, after which it was ruled by Spanish viceroys for two centuries. But by the end of the fifteenth century the minor states and republics of the Renaissance became anachronistic and failed to resist the armies which began to overrun northern Italy. As the two great powers of France and Spain began a protracted struggle for control over the fragmented states of Italy, principalities like Rimini, Ferrara, Urbino, and Mantova found they could no longer survive as independent entities. Even Florence and Milan eventually succumbed.

Whereas Milan had often made war against Venice, Florence against Pisa, Rome against Florence, and the many smaller states almost incessantly against one another, the new invasions were on a scale which traditional fighting methods could not resist. *Condottieri* were matched against cannon, hastily gathered militia against huge armies of well-trained soldiers, and Italy became the battlefield in a struggle for continental supremacy.

The French began the rout. King Charles VIII (1470-98) entered Italy in 1494 with the intention of presenting his claim to the throne of Naples, which had been an Anjou fief until it was subdued by Alfonso V of Spain in 1442. France was strong and had a highly experienced army after the end of the Hundred Years War. Charles managed to take Naples the following year, but was forced to return to France almost immediately when Milan, Venice, the pope, and Austria formed the League of Venice against him. He died in France after an accident, while he was preparing a new Italian campaign. His successor was Louis XII (1462–1515), who had fought under Charles on the previous campaign. Unlike Charles, whose sole objective was Naples, Louis aimed to subjugate Milan — basing *his* claim on the fact that his grandfather Louis, Duke of Orleans, had married Valentina Visconti. He succeeded in taking the city briefly, but was soon forced to retreat. The most tangible sign of his presence in Italy was through his daughter Renée, who married Ercole II d'Este and became Duchess of Ferrara.

Louis, in turn, was followed by Francis I (1494–1547), a much greater soldier and more dangerous opponent, who destroyed Sforza power and imprisoned Lodovico il Moro in France. He had opposed Charles V in the 1519 election of the Holy Roman Emperor, and was from that moment the Spanish king's sworn enemy. In 1515 he had already led an expedition to conquer Milan, where he won the reputation as the most powerful prince in Europe at the Battle of Marignano. A later expedition failed when he was captured by the troops of Charles V. While he failed in his overall ambition, he was shrewd enough to take back with him what was best in Italy. He continued the tradition of princely patronage by employing Leonardo da Vinci and Benvenuto Cellini, and came within a hair's breadth of convincing Michelangelo — which would have deprived us of such works as *The Last Judgement*. Cultivated Italians like the splendid Cardinal Ippolito Il d'Este were welcome at his court in Fontainebleau.

The French were in turn expelled by Francis's enemy, Charles V of Spain (1500–58). This remarkable king succeeded to the Spanish throne (as Charles I) in 1516, and was then made Holy Roman Emperor in 1519 after an election which included both his major rivals, King Francis and King Henry VIII of England. He succeeded his grandfather Maximilian I in this new role, and thus united in

his person the forces of Habsburg Germany and Spain. With such military might he was able to destroy French hopes forever at a battle near Pavia in 1525 in which Francis I was captured. After that there was no force capable of stopping the Emperor. The climax of his expeditions may be said to have been the Sack of Rome in 1527, when his angry, unpaid army moved south from Lombardy and ransacked the entire city. That event marked the beginning of a long period of Spanish and Habsburg dominance in Italy and a long-term effort to control the whole of Europe.

In 1529 Francis and Charles signed the Peace of Bologna, after which Italy began to assume its modern political configuration: Milan was given to Francesco II Sforza; Florence was returned to the Medici after the short-lived Republic; Genova was nominally independent under the Doria family; and the remainder of Italy was under the control of Charles V. For the next thirty years there were only minor changes to this distribution. In that period Siena disappeared as a separate state, while Milan was absorbed into the Spanish Empire. The only new feature was the creation of the Duchy of Parma and Piacenza, made to measure for the ambitious nephew of Pope Paul III, Pier Luigi Farnese. A few years later Charles abdicated in favour of Philip II — England's great enemy — and a system of governors and viceroys was set up to rule Palermo, Naples, and Milan. Then in 1559 the Peace of Cateau-Cambrésis brought the long conflict between France and the Habsburg Empire to a conclusion, and Italy was completely ruled by the Spanish.

None of the major Italian dynasties produced its most important figure or enjoyed great power after that date. Some of them were already in irreversible decline and those who continued to rule did so with Spanish connivance. The portraits of the Colonna, Gonzaga, and Farnese in the late sixteenth century show men in Spanish costumes, with Spanish armour and hairstyle. They had often been educated in Spain. The distinctly Italian nature of the culture of the peninsula was suffocated by Spanish fashions and ideas, and an efficient Roman Inquisition.

NOBLE HOMES IN THE RENAISSANCE

The early members of the dynasties to be discussed dismissed comfort as super-fluous. They were essentially warriors and farmers whose priorities might be described as primitive: weapons, power, food, and shelter. These men were admired for the quality of the horses they rode and their ability in warfare. We shall see in the case of the founders of the Sforza family that they spurned domestic comfort almost as a point of honour. Such men desired space rather than comfort: large cold rooms with little in the way of furniture beyond chests, benches, tables, and simple trestle beds. There were no carpets and no protection for windows, except perhaps a hanging linen soaked in oil.

But as they achieved political stability and established permanent roots in the

Opposite *Charles V of Spain, by Titian.*

newly acquired cities, they began to devote more care to the decoration of their palaces. Painters were called in to fresco the walls, tapestries were commissioned from the great looms of Tuscany, and luxury began to dominate the concept of prestige. The ducal palaces of Mantova and Urbino still survive almost intact and give an excellent idea of life in this second stage of the history of the great dynasties. Yet even these huge structures pale beside some of the family palaces of the six-teenth century, especially the vast Roman constructions of papal families such as the Farnese.

Courtly life was organized about the person of the prince. At the period of their greatest power, the Sforza dukes maintained as personal staff forty chamberlains and ten assistant chamberlains, plus innumerable servants in kitchens, halls, gardens, and stables. There were cooks, table setters, falconers, dog handlers, court singers, and artisans as well as the more obvious staff, and anything up to a thousand merce-naries directly dependent on the court. The stables themselves held eight hundred horses and mules for the exclusive use of members of the court. This entourage of men, women, and animals had a sole purpose: to serve the duke or prince. On a princely whim they could earn a fortune or lose their lives, however important or well related they might be. Many of the courts — at Ferrara, at Urbino, and at Mantova — were ultimately ruined by the cost of maintaining an extravagance beyond their means. Only the absence of money curbed the grandiose imagination of such men, and when there was no limit on the amount of expendable cash the extravagances were astonishing. In the case of the Sforza or the Este these were temporary, but when a later type of dynasty realized that infinite expenditure could be sustained, there was no restraint. This happened when the great papal families gained access to the limitless coffers of the Church, fuelled by Spanish gold and perpetually replenished.

The great Roman palaces of the papal families are immense even by modern standards. The family palace of the Doria Pamphili, whose wealth derived mainly from the papacy of Innocent X (1644–55), was until the nineteenth century inhabited by about a thousand people. The fact that life in some of the great Roman palaces continued on the Renaissance pattern into modern times allows them to serve as models for this system.

Rigid rules governed these patriarchal palaces up to recent times. The main floor was inhabited by the head of the family and his wife, and consisted of bedrooms, a study, a private dining-room, a state dining-room, a ballroom, and a picture gallery which might have occupied an entire wing. The succession of antechambers, cham-bers, and reception rooms were ordered according to ancient Roman household organization, where the vestibule was followed by the atrium, the atrium by the peristyle and so on. The second floor of the palace would be occupied by the first son, and the third floor by the second son. If, for example, a family member were a cardinal an entire wing might be allocated, while further sons, daughters, cou-sins, uncles, and aunts would each receive an apartment somewhere in the building.

Domestic organization was equally rigid. The cook worked under a contract to the chief steward to provide a certain number of meals per day for a fixed number of persons. If a member of the family required something extra during the day, or demanded a separate meal apart from the main family dinner of twenty to thirty people, then it was charged to his account and deducted from his allowance when accounts were checked. In the case of daughters-in-law these amounts could be deducted from expenses specified in the dowry. Clothing, use of horses and carriages, occasional drinks and snacks were all accounted for in this way. The novels of the American writer Francis Marion Crawford, who was born in Italy and lived in Rome for many years, provide excellent descriptions of this life, for instance in the opening chapters of *Saracinesca* (1892) — first published in *Blackwood's Magazine*. This is the first volume of a trilogy concerning a great Roman princely family — the fictional Saracinesca — and is full of details which had not changed for centuries.

A small book entitled *Concerning the Management of a Roman Nobleman's Court*, published in 1542 under the auspices of the Farnese pope Paul III, provides a vivid picture of what the author considers a 'sufficient household' for a less grand family. This 'minimal' staff included two chief chamberlains, an estate manager, a chief

The Battle of Pavia (tapestry).

steward, four chaplains, a master of the horse, a secretary and assistant, an audi-tor, a lawyer, four 'letterati', six gentlemen of the chambers, a chief carver, ten waiters, pantry butler, wine butler, six head grooms, a purchaser and assistant, a storekeeper, a cellarer, a chief cook and assistants, chief scullery-man, water-carrier, sweeper, and doctor. It is noteworthy that this establishment is for a single person, with no female family members or staff, and that many of the senior staff would themselves have servants. Thus this minimal staff could easily have been between fifty and a hundred in number.

The major dynasties to be discussed here clearly exceeded such minimal stan-dards, and often included painters, architects, and writers whose stipends were far superior to the ordinary household servants.

PAPAL DYNASTIES: THE NEW WEALTH

As the fortunes of the merchant republics which stimulated the Renaissance declined, and the new political situation ended an era in which it was possible to earn large sums through mercenary warfare, a new source of wealth arose in Italy. The Roman Catholic Church enjoyed an increase in revenues with the gold and silver which came to Europe from the Americas via Spain. At the same time the Counter-Reformation brought a new authority to the Roman Church by placing it once again at the centre of Catholicism. The dynasties which began in the sixteenth and early seventeenth centuries were different in character, although in fact based upon a despotic power just as the earlier dynasties. The only way for a new man to achieve the immense wealth necessary for artistic patronage on the grand scale was through the newly enriched papacy. This was the source of wealth of the Farnese.

Ambitious families had always aspired to the papacy. The Counts of Segni had three popes in the thirteenth century, and Renaissance families such as the Medici, the Borgia, and the Della Rovere all managed to place at least one member of the family on the throne of St Peter. But the new wealth and power of the Church created a different phenomenon: rather than great families exercising their influence to obtain the Holy See, men from relatively poor or unimportant backgrounds became pope and then used the position to enrich their families. That was the case of the Farnese dynasty, which owed its initial wealth and power to Pope Paul III. Extant Roman noble families such as the Borghese, Barberini, Pamphili, Pallavicini, Ludovisi, Aldobrandini, and Rospigliosi also owe their initial rise to wealth and power to a pope.

With the decline of the great Renaissance dynasties and their successors within the Church, Italy ceased to be the centre of art patronage and the centre of innova-tion in art. Local traditions were maintained, and artists worked for the various foreign invaders — Spanish, French, Austrian — but their work was not distinctly Italian. It is an ironic truth that Italian culture was at its peak when the peninsula was most fragmented; when the minor states and duchies were grouped into larger political units, and eventually into a single state, culture languished. This is because the main thrust of Italian culture had always derived from the patronage of individuals or great families, which is why the dynasties presented here played such a vital role in the history of Italian culture and especially in the Italian Renaissance.

1

THE VISCONTI

For centuries the Visconti name was synonymous with cruelty and ruthlessness, only being displaced in the sixteenth century by Machiavelli. Yet the earlier identification was more accurate. In fact the dynasty first entered history with a bloody instance of the methods for which they became notorious.

Legends attributed the origins of the family to the time of St Gregory the Great, who was pope from 590 to 604, and the Longobard King Desiderius. But as with many of the Italian dynasties, these legends were part of a conscious or unconscious attempt to legitimize despotic power by providing noble or even imperial origins. Yet the Visconti were in no sense parvenus even when they did come to the fore. They formed part of the feudal nobility at least from the tenth century, and probably attained the office of Viscounts of Milan early in the eleventh century. They were in fact one of the many minor feudal families which moved into the vacuum created by the death of Frederick II. The crucial step towards the later eminence of the family was made when Ottone Visconti was appointed Archbishop of Milan in 1262, twelve years after the Emperor's death.

Milan was then dominated by a Guelph family known as the Torriani, who prevented the new Ghibelline archbishop from occupying his palace and assuming his pastoral functions. Under their leader Napoleone della Torre, known as Napo, the city flourished while the archbishop remained in exile near Lago Maggiore. Great palaces were built and roads paved, and feasts and public displays of extravagance were not infrequent. Illustrious guests such as the Kings of England and France paid visits to the city and admired its new buildings. But while a small number of citizens lived well under successive members of the Torriani, there was also widespread discontent over the heavy taxes they were forced to pay. That is the reason why loyalties were quickly shifted to Ottone, and he was immediately accepted as the Lord of Milan, when he at last managed to defeat Napo and enter the city.

Opposite *The Certosa (Charterhouse) at Pavia.*

The stalemate continued for fifteen years, until Archbishop Ottone eventually decided to resolve the situation in his own ruthless manner. On 21 January 1277 he and his supporters approached the headquarters of the Torriani, at Desio about twenty kilometres from Milan, under the cover of night. Paid traitors expected him there, and opened the town gates so that the Visconti's attack was totally unexpected. The consequence was a massacre rather than a fight, with Napo and his brother Francesco della Torre, and their men, taken half-dressed and completely unprepared for battle. Francesco was killed almost immediately and his body brutally trodden into the mud; one of the Visconti infantrymen cut off the head, thrust it onto his lance, and paraded through the town with his prize. For the few survivors of the bloody assault there was no respite. They were forced into wooden cages like animals and despatched to a remote fortress near Como together with their leader Napo. In a single night, the archbishop destroyed a family which had controlled the city of Milan and its satellites for two generations. Napo died after nineteen months of captivity in his cage, consumed by filth and lice, and constantly insulted and spat upon by the people. This bloody slaughter initiated nearly two hundred years of Visconti rule of Milan.

Ottone was installed as archbishop and acclaimed as ruler by the populace the next day. They were so delighted to be freed from the tyranny of the Torriani that few of them questioned whether the new tyranny might not be greater. The homes of the Torriani and their supporters were razed to the ground, while Ottone's spies and observers ensured that any political opposition was stifled as soon as it arose. Arrest, imprisonment, and torture were commonplace in those early days. In fact Visconti power was not to be consolidated for many years, and Ottone himself — who was already in his sixties at the time of the massacre — soon left active politics and in 1287 assigned the role of captain of the city to his great-nephew Matteo. The ageing archbishop left Milan for the comfort and peace of his palace at the Cistercian monastery of Chiaravalle just south of Milan, where he died at the age of eighty-eight in 1295. It was left to future generations of historians and panegyrists, working under Visconti patronage, to provide the portrait of the archbishop as a a lover of peace, an exemplary bishop, and much-loved governor of the people.

During his brief rule there was a curious case of witchcraft which had unexpected repercussions forty years later. Around the middle of the century there was a woman called Guglielmina who was famed as an astrologer, healer, and witch. She also seems to have belonged to the more profound heretical tradition deriving from the Calabrian priest Joachim da Fiore, who had advocated a mystical interpretation of the scriptures and developed a concept of history divided into three successive phases: the age of the Father, the age of the Son, and the age of the Holy Ghost. In this last age, a period of love and freedom, the knowledge of God would be revealed directly to the hearts of men. Guglielmina's heresy derived from her utter conviction that she herself was the Holy Ghost incarnate. This conviction led to her avowed duty to convert all sinners, Jews, and Muslims to the Holy Catholic faith. At a certain point this strange woman even announced her future resurrection and nominated another woman known as Manfreda to be her vicar on earth.

Manfreda was a Visconti; her precise relationship to Ottone is impossible to establish, but he and other members of the family accepted it as fact. She believed totally in her teacher and took her own duties seriously, working towards the implementation of the audacious ideas of Guglielmina. These included the overthrowing of the pope and subsequent installation of Guglielmina as pope, and the renovation of Christianity as a matriarchy. Nothing came out of this project, but Manfreda continued to propagate these ideas. The unfortunate consequence was to draw the attention of the popes upon her and the Visconti family, who tried without success to cover up the scandal and conceal their relationship to her.

This was important in an epoch when members of a witch's family were themselves suspected of witchcraft, and successive popes were instigating inquisitorial activities against witchcraft and heresy in an unprecedented manner. The Cathars, who were being so effectively eliminated throughout south-western France, had their equivalents in the *patarini* of Italy, whose strongholds were Florence and Milan. The fury of the Church fell upon Manfreda Visconti, but only later were the full implications of the scandal to come to light.

MATTEO I
(1250–1322)

Matteo was forty when he came to power, a patient and careful man, more reluctant than his great-uncle the archbishop to use the sword to achieve his aims. His first success was to obtain the title of Imperial Vicar of Milan from the Emperor Adolf of Nassau. This provided some legitimacy to his rule, and he was able gradually to establish his sons in key positions in Milan and its territories as if they were a personal family property. When the imperial eagle was emblazoned on his escutcheon beside the traditional Visconti symbol of a viper devouring a Saracen, his power seemed to be consolidated.

Milan was then a city of some ninety thousand inhabitants, second only in Italy to Venice. The Milanese writer Bonvesin de la Riva provided a detailed account of the city in his 'Wonders of Milan', written in 1288 just after Matteo Visconti came to power. While his figures may be exaggerated to give an impressive picture of his city, the details of the way of life are probably reliable. Judiciously avoiding all mention of the political situation he provides a wealth of fascinating detail about life in his city under the early Visconti.

It was a wealthy city sited on one of the principal trade routes from the Italian peninsula — and especially from the great trading port of Genova — to northern Europe, surrounded by fertile agricultural land which provided food for its inhabitants. The hundred and fifty hotels and thousand hostelries, cited by Bonvesin, indicate the flux of travellers and visitors. He writes of continual arrivals of carts carrying cereals, meat, wine, wood, and spices for the population. There were artisans in their workshops and factories, money-changers, and contacts with foreign countries. The people ate well, favouring capons, beef and pork in pepper sauce, *salame*, and the breaded cutlets which are still today one of the classical dishes of Milan. They also enjoyed themselves at great feasts, and it seems that the noblewomen of Milan turned Sunday church attendance into a spectacle which might be compared to today's fashion shows.

But Bonvesin de la Riva's almost idyllic description of the city must be corrected by the violence, sackings, bloody vendettas, and proscriptions which characterized Milan at the turn of the fourteenth century. Matteo himself was exiled from the city after a revolt in 1302 instigated by surviving members of the Torriani. He was able to return only eight years later under the protection of the Holy Roman Emperor Henry VII. But he was a patient, sage ruler who had been content with his secondary role under Ottone and now knew how to manoeuvre with consummate skill between the varying factions both within Milan and in the whole country. A man of native political intelligence, unscrupulous but at the same time moderate in the means he employed, he was more than a match for his enemies. Rather than lose his control in bloodthirsty vengeance or mere shows of cruel strength, he paved the way for the succession of his five sons, working with far-sightedness towards the future consolidated power of the Visconti Lords of Milan.

For a long time his ambitions were thwarted by a dispute with Pope John XXII (1316–34) concerning the title of Imperial Vicar. Matteo was excommunicated and accused of heresy. But the pope's real motivation was his fear of the increasing power of the Visconti and the legitimacy of the title of the Imperial Vicar, and at that time the accusation of heresy and witchcraft was the most efficacious of accusations for the speedy removal of a political rival. Less than a decade earlier the Knights Templar had been destroyed in similar fashion. Moreover, in the matter of the Visconti there was the unfortunate precedent of Manfreda to taint the reputation of the entire family.

Twenty-five accusations were made against Matteo Visconti by Pope John, each clearly aimed at undermining his power and most of them as manifestly absurd as the charges against the Templars. Matteo and his son Galeazzo I were charged by the ecclesiastical court with invocation and sorcery, specifically an attempt to kill the pope by image magic. Matteo was further accused of denying the resurrection of the body, and to have lain with enough young girls to have filled an entire convent. Most serious of all, he was accused of celebrating mass in front of the heretical and excommunicated tyrant Ezzelino da Romano. Yet such accusations were commonplace then, and need not be taken too seriously. In 1317 Hugues Gérard, Bishop of Cahors, had been burned at the stake for a supposed attempt on the life of the pope by means of sorcery. In the same year Matilda of Artois was tried for using sorcery to kill Louis X; two years later Jeanne de Latilly was accused of the same crime against Charles of Valois.

Pope John XXII was himself notorious for his interest in magic: he used a curved horn against evil spells, thrusting it into his bread at table surrounding it with salt. It was this sincere belief in the power of sorcery which created a paranoia in him. Thus the whole affair of Manfreda, Matteo, and the accusations of heresy were typical of the period, when accusations of witchcraft became a common political weapon. As a matter of fact, in the succeeding years John XXII used the same accusations against the allies of Federico of Montefeltro. They too were charged with idolatry, heresy, and invocation in what were clearly politically motivated charges.

In the end Pope John both won and lost: Matteo resigned his role as direct ruler, but only in favour of his son Galeazzo — who managed to conserve family power. At the time the cities under Visconti rule included Como, Bergamo, Piacenza, Tortona, Alessandria, and Pavia.

VISCONTI RULE
(1322–54)

The period of thirty years after Matteo's death was one of consolidation of the power obtained by Archbishop Ottone and Matteo himself. No dominating personality, or ruler of equal stature, appeared during these years. Matteo's son Galeazzo was succeeded by his own son Azzo and then by two of Matteo's younger sons, Luchino and Archbishop Giovanni. The territory of Milan was expanded in this period, as were the private Visconti properties. Under Archbishop Giovanni such important cities as Bologna and Genova came temporarily into the orbit of the state of Milan.

From his birth, Galeazzo I (1277–c.1328) possessed all the qualities normally associated with the Visconti. For he was born on the same day that Ottone defeated the Torriani at Desio, and his mother was heard to say that he screamed like a cock during the delivery. Where his father preferred diplomacy, Galeazzo preferred the sword. The family emblem of the serpent was probably used originally to represent the classical allusion to a deity or guardian spirit, but it also bore the biblical significance of subtlety and cunning, which derives from the Book of Genesis. His marriage to Beatrice, daughter of Obizzo II d'Este, paved the way for the grandiose dynastic marriages of future centuries, though in 1300 the Visconti had neither the stability nor the wealth to equal later celebrations. As the result of this alliance, Galeazzo was the natural choice of heir for Matteo. But for the Visconti that was no guarantee, since family members always considered their own personal power as more important than family ties. That is why in the two centuries of Visconti rule there are more instances of murder and suspected murder within the family than in any comparable dynasty. In fact, one of Galeazzo's first tasks was to build a prison at Monza for potential political opponents and rebellious family members. Ironically, he himself was later to spend eight months as a prisoner inside his own building.

His son Azzone (1302–39), who ruled for ten years from 1328, was possessed of a courtliness and grace which his predecessors had lacked. Long before Galeazzo's death he had become genuinely popular amongst the people of Milan as the result of several successful military missions in central Italy. Although opposed by his uncles Marco, Stefano, Luchino, and Giovanni — the first two of whom he probably murdered, while the second two succeeded him — the younger man managed to establish his power quickly. He was blond-haired and gentle in aspect, not over tall but well built, and spoke in a friendly manner, with genuine concern for his listeners. Moreover, he was as devoted to the city of Milan as its citizens, and embarked on a building programme which inaugurated the expansion that made Milan one of the greatest capitals of Renaissance Italy in the next two hundred years. He began by building new city walls. Then he developed a network of roads, canals and bridges, and a sewer system which was remarkable for its time. He also built the church of San Gottardo. Milan was later fortunate to have one of history's greatest architects, Leonardo da Vinci, work on its canal and irrigation systems under the Sforza family, but Azzone Visconti was a worth ancestor of the later city plans.

Within the new city he built himself a palace in which he could reign as a king, with all the accoutrements of royalty. It stood on the site of the much later royal palace now used for museums and temporary exhibitions. The immense size and luxury of Azzone's palace, with an enormous number of frescoed rooms, represented a new spirit after the austere traditions of medieval Milan. The Lord of Milan ruled there with a genuine court in which writers and artists played an important role. He introduced a new coinage in his own name, breaking the medieval tradition in which Milanese money was minted in the name of the Emperor. He even allowed himself the luxury of exotic gardens filled with rare plants and birds, and rare fish swimming in pools and fountains. He represented something distinctly new and almost 'Renaissance' in the life of Milan and the Visconti, and was much loved for the prosperity which allowed his subjects to prosper with him. Yet no Visconti was completely good, and Azzone's career was tainted by the extremely plausible accusations that he had been directly responsible for the murder of his *condottiere* uncle Marco. Another uncle, Stefano, who had schemed against Azzone together with Marco, also died in mysterious circumstances.

When Azzone Visconti died of gout at the early age of thirty-seven the citizens of Milan mourned him with sincere grief — unlike the forced show of mourning shown to earlier members of the dynasty. For over a decade they had come to identify the fortunes of their city with that of the young ruler. He left to his uncles Luchino and Giovanni a well-administered, wealthy city with a loyal army and a clergy which was completely under the control of Giovanni himself, the Archbishop of Milan. The Visconti dynasty had achieved Archbishop Ottone's dream of sixty years before: a hereditary Visconti state.

Archbishop Giovanni (1290–1354) worked for the dynasty with a subtle under-standing of the need to prepare for the future by creating alliances with their most powerful neighbours. To this end he arranged for the marriages of the two sons of his murdered brother Stefano: Galeazzo II married Bianca of Savoy, sister of Duke Amadeo VI of Savoy — who ruled both French Savoy and Italian Piedmont and thus controlled the vital trade route over the Alps to France; Bernabò married Regina della Scala, daughter of the Lord of Verona Mastino della Scala, who ruled the lands immediately to the east of Milan's territory. This latter marriage had an unforeseen consequence many centuries later: when Regina gave birth to a son by Bernabò, a church called Santa Maria della Scala was built in her honour and to give thanks for a safe birth. When, in 1778, an opera house was built on the site of the church it was given the name of the church, and is today one of the great opera houses of the world. Regina's son was less fortunate: he was killed by poison in prison by his cousin Gian Galeazzo Visconti when the latter reunited Visconti power after Galeazzo II's death.

These alliances allowed the Visconti to expand southwards with no fear of attack from their flanks. To the north, their lands were protected by the natural frontier of the Alps. Thus on Archbishop Giovanni's death — and after the one-year rule of their elder brother Matteo II, who probably died the traditional Visconti death at the hands of his two brothers — the entire dominions of the Visconti were divided between Galeazzo II and Bernabò. These lands then included Milan, Lodi, Piacenza, Parma, Bologna, Cremona, Brescia, Bergamo, Como, Novara, Alessandria, Vercelli, Alba, Asti, Genova, and Savona. Furthermore, alliances and agreements with local rulers virtually amounted to control of Tuscany, Umbria, and the Marches.

BERNABÒ (1323–85) AND
GALEAZZO II (*c*.1320–78)

From 1354 to 1378 Bernabò ruled from Milan and Galeazzo II from nearby Pavia. They were independent in theory, but in practice their policies were closely co-ordinated as they sought to maintain and increase Visconti power.

These brothers have often been considered the archetypes of the Renaissance despot. Bernabò in particular is accused of subordinating affairs of the state to his love for hunting wild boar, so that the people of Milan were forced to maintain his pack of five thousand boar-hounds and were immediately tortured and put to death if they in any way interfered with his amusement. Adjectives such as cruel, arrogant, and bitter appear in any description of him, and even in his own lifetime his name became a byword for brutality and violence. He can be seen in his contemporary equestrian portrait in the Museum of the so-called Castello Sforzesco in Milan, which was in fact orginally built by Bernabò's own brother Galeazzo. He towers above the viewer with more than a suggestion of the arrogance he must have displayed in life. He is erect and powerful, holding his riding crop with the firmness of infinite confidence. His face is proud, his lips tight and commanding, and enormous strength and calm seem to issue from the eye sockets. The statue provides interesting confirmation of the physical presence of Bernabò as perceived by his subjects.

Galeazzo II was no less ruthless, a complex figure whose character veered dangerously and often unpredictably from great generosity, charm, and learning to avarice, suspicion, and hatred. His vision of the Visconti dynasty exceeded that of Archbishop Giovanni in its ambition: his son Gian Galeazzo was married at nine years old to Isabelle of Valois, daughter of King John II of France; his daughter

Pavia in the Renaissance, with Visconti Castle, by Lanzani.

Violante was married to Lionel of Clarence, son of Edward III of England. He himself lived in great luxury and extravagance in his castle in Pavia, one of the largest in Europe, with exotic animals in the park and a fashionable court of writers and artists. A sense of his ruthlessness is perhaps best conveyed by the celebrated 'Lent' of Galeazzo II, which was a forty-day programme of torture, judiciously interposed with days of 'rest' so that prisoners would be able to appreciate the next stage. Beginning with alternate days of strappado and repose, it built up through enforced drinking of water, then salt rubbed into flesh left exposed by removing strips of skin, to the gradual removal of eyes, hands, feet, limbs, and finally sexual organs. If by chance any man were to survive this 'Lent', on the forty-first day he would be carried to the wheel for his last torture.

Yet the concept of cruelty is both a relative and a modern one. With a subtlety which modern organizations against political torture would not appreciate, Machiavelli, writing a century later, distinguishes between cruelty used well and cruelty used badly. In a passage from *The Prince* of relevance to many of the dynasties discussed in this book he explains that cruelty is employed well when it is used to protect one's own safety and for the good of the prince's subjects. On the other hand, it is employed badly when its use becomes increasingly more frequent and persistent, so that instead of disappearing it becomes more evident in the state. The crucial point is that cruelty of some kind is considered by Machiavelli to be inevitable, not because he was the devil later critics often made him out to be, but because it was a simple matter of fact at the time he wrote.

Moreover, while the Visconti streak of cruelty was evident in both of them, Bernabò and Galeazzo II were for seven years patrons to the greatest and most sensitive writer of the age and one of the fathers of humanism, Francesco Petrarca (1304–74), who had come to Milan during the last year of Archbishop Giovanni's rule. A brilliant and cultivated man known today above all for his sonnets to Laura, and in England for his influence on sixteenth-century poets such as Sir Thomas Wyatt, Sir Philip Sidney, and William Shakespeare, he was then known as a man of letters who wrote — in Italian and in Latin — philosophy, epistles to important persons, and biographical sketches of great Romans. Already famous and contested between the courts of Italy, he was to apply himself to many formal tasks for both Bernabò and Galeazzo II as a valued member of their courts during this sojourn. He was sent as ambassador to Venice and Prague, wrote official elegies on the deaths of members of the Visconti family, wrote letters to monarchs and other rulers, and negotiated the contract for the marriage of Gian Galeazzo and Isabelle of Valois. Although he was criticized by his friends, including the author of *Decameron*, Giovanni Boccaccio, Petrarch was paid well for his services and seems to have understood his value well. He left Milan for Padova during the great plague of 1361, which decimated the population of the city, and never returned.

Despite what seem to us to be his failings, Bernabò was in fact well liked by his citizens. This was largely the result of his openness of character, natural grace, and generosity with gifts of money — qualities which must have weighed heavily with Petrarch too.

GIAN GALEAZZO
(1351–1402)

Gian Galeazzo, the greatest of the Visconti, succeeded his father in 1378. Precocious in paternity, battle, and diplomacy, he had already produced his first son by his child-bride Isabelle when he was fourteen. His innate political skill was evidenced in the coup with which he later usurped his uncle Bernabò, and brought the Visconti lands and power once again under a single person. He was already by that time a widower and managed to strengthen the new unity by marrying his own cousin, Bernabò's daughter Caterina.

At first he lived a reserved life in his castle at Pavia, which is now a fascinating museum. Almost every Visconti succession had involved vicious infighting until the new political and military hierarchy was established, with no holds barred in the process. But Gian Galeazzo used a different strategy. Well protected in his own castle from attempts by uncles and cousins to poison him, for seven quiet years he waited and planned. With diabolical cunning he feigned obedience to Bernabò, and created the image of a weakling, cowering before the physical strength of his uncle and regularly attending mass in order to appear pious. His life was noticeably free of the womanizing and court extravagances of his ancestors. Bernabò came to perceive his nephew as a rather stupid and bigoted man, and dismissed him as an incompetent and innocuous ruler.

Then in the spring of 1385 Gian Galeazzo sent a message to his uncle to the effect that he was planning to make a pilgrimage to the sanctuary of Santa Maria del Monte, some eighty kilometres west of Milan near Varese. Since he would pass through Milan on his way, he courteously requested to be received by Bernabò and to pay homage to his uncle. It must have seemed a reasonable request to Bernabò, who in his enormous pride was probably delighted that this nephew should be seen to treat him with such obsequiousness. On 6 May of that year, Bernabò met Gian Galeazzo near the ancient church of Saint Ambrose, the fourth-century Bishop of Milan and the city's patron saint. Several of his sons accompanied him. Suddenly, with such rapidity of action that Bernabò and his sons barely knew what had happened to them, they were surrounded by Gian Galeazzo's soldiers, handcuffed and taken off to prison in the castle of Trezzo. Seven months later Bernabò died in his own prison: some said from the humiliation suffered, others that his nephew had him poisoned.

Whatever the cause, Gian Galeazzo was then undisputed ruler of Milan. As if in conscious penance for the dramatic usurpation and imprisonment of his uncle, one of his first actions was to order the construction of a great cathedral to equal those of the most important cities of Europe. The only part of the present cathedral which dates from this period is the apse, while the façade was finally completed only in the nineteenth century. But the original plan bears witness to the grandiloquence of his gesture. The finished building measures 167 by 92 metres, and includes over three thousand statues — mainly on the elaborate exterior. The proverbial phrase 'as long as the building of the cathedral' is used in Milan for anything which never seems to come to an end. Yet now that it is completed, it ranks as the largest of all Gothic cathedrals, and the third in size in the world. It is thus a fitting monument to the megalomaniac visions of Gian Galeazzo.

In the same year, his second wife Caterina was responsible for instigating the foundation of an equally famous building, the consequence of a vow made during childbirth. Half way between Milan and Pavia they founded the Certosa di Pavia, one of the most splendid buildings in Europe. Yet as in the case of the castle, the real merit belongs to a later age, for it was the Sforza family which completed and embellished the Certosa when they succeeded the Visconti as Dukes of Milan. Lodovico il Moro, the greatest of the Sforza and patron of Leonardo da Vinci — who worked on the Certosa — built the tomb for himself and his equally famous wife Beatrice d'Este inside the main church of the monastery. But in his short rule Gian Galeazzo also fortified the castle in Pavia, and in 1361 founded the University, which still retains its medieval aspect and is one of the most prestigious universities in Italy.

In keeping with this megalomania were his diplomatic manoeuvres to obtain the title of Duke of Milan, which he finally succeeded in doing in 1395. The event was the occasion for one of the great feasts for which the Renaissance princes remain celebrated. The diplomacy necessary before the feast took place was extensive and expensive — both in practical expenses and in gifts of money to the Emperor Wenceslas of Bohemia. When at last the imperial diploma of investiture arrived in Milan, there was a grand ceremony presided over by the then Bishop of Novara, later Pope Alexander V, who used all his rhetorical powers in praising Gian Galeazzo and the 'sublime honour of the Duchy'. Gifts of gold and jewels were exchanged, and then the banquet took place.

When the guests' hands had been cleansed in scented water, the dishes, each announced by a fanfare, began with marzipans decorated with the stems of the Visconti and the Emperor and served with white wine in gold cups, followed by individual baby chickens in a red sauce with gold-coated bread. Taillevent, the head cook of Charles VII of France, was to insist on the use of gold and gilt, since dishes should not only be palatable but pleasing to the eye: cooks of his school made the celebrated soup dorée, and made such dishes as a swan served whole on a bed of green pastry, with its wings opened, its beak gilt and its body silvered. It was presented on a table covered with silk, announced by a fanfare and designed to astonish. The food was spicy and highly flavoured, using the full range of spices and products recently introduced from the East. At this Visconti feast two whole gilt pigs and two gilt calves were presented, followed by huge silver dishes of veal, mutton, beef, whole young goats, a ham, and sausages. These meats were accompanied by imported Greek wines — probably the then fashionable Malmsey which in fact came mainly from Cyprus, whence the Portuguese later discovered it and successfully transplanted it to their newly discovered island of Madeira.

There followed two further goats, two large hares, six large pigeons, and four rabbits. Then, as a kind of climax, four stuffed peacocks, the most regal and praised of medieval dishes, an entire gilt deer, two golden bears cooked in lemon juice, four pheasants for each guest, roebucks in gelatine, quails and partridges in green sauce, and gilt trout-shaped meat with cooked pears. Then, after more scented water for the hands, silvered bread, syruped lemons and roast fish were brought in, followed by jellied lampreys and sturgeon. The feast ended with giant cakes, fresh almonds, malvasia wine, and various highly decorative and multicoloured sweets.

From that moment, worthy of a royal prince, Gian Galeazzo was in effect the sovereign of a hereditary state which was part of the Holy Roman Empire, with a motto coined by no less a person than Petrarch — who, it is pleasant to believe, may have perceived its fine irony: *a bon droit*. At forty-five years of age, strong both physically and politically, Gian Galeazzo Visconti now looked capable of achieving ambitions far beyond those of his forebears. It was said that he aspired to become King of Italy.

Had he been allowed sufficient time, he might well have succeeded in this ambition, which entailed bringing his two greatest rivals, Florence and Venice, under his control. The papal states were in a condition of absolute weakness and confusion after the Schism of 1378, and presented no threat.

He began by centralizing the government of Visconti territories and reforming the administration, aiming at a state ruled by a 'natural prince' as his humanist scholars and friends in Pavia counselled him. Although it was not to survive long under the Visconti, the duchy which he reorganized with genuine care and concern lasted for centuries. It was definitively destroyed by Napoleon when he became commander of the army in Italy, and defeated the Austrians so that France obtained control of Lombardy, in 1786. That Milan had become the undisputed leader of the Lombard cities was the most significant legacy of Gian Galeazzo Visconti. In the seventeen years of his rule he was noted for solitary walks, intense discussion, and conversation with scholars rather than the hunting, hawking, and gambling associated with other Visconti.

Ironically, given the violent deaths of so many of his family and even his own early opponents, his ambitions were truncated just as they reached their acme by a death which in this context is almost ridiculously peaceful. In 1402 he managed to bring Pisa, Siena, Perugia, and Bologna under Visconti influence and could plausibly consider seizing Florence. He then ruled over Milan, Pavia, Bergamo, Brescia, Como, Lodi, Cremona, Novara, Vercelli, Alessandria, Valenza, Tortona, Piacenza, Parma, Reggio, Pontremoli, Verona, Vicenza, Feltre, Belluno, Assisi, Lucca, and Genova beyond the cities mentioned above. It was at this moment of success, following the sighting of a comet which his astrologers held was an omen of disaster, that he died of a fever at the age of fifty-one. It was such an absurd and unexpected death that many people refused to believe it. The chroniclers' accounts of great thunderstorms, winds, and rains on the night of his death probably belong to the rhetorical tradition. It was never fully explained, but does seem to have been non-violent; it was most likely some form of malaria or the plague. The city of Florence was described as experiencing the delight of being liberated from the coils of a serpent.

No other Visconti was ever to approach such supremacy. Within a decade of his death the principal line of the Visconti dynasty was to consign its power to the Sforza family.

Building of the Certosa (detail from 'Christ and the Carthusians'), by Fossano.

GIOVANNI MARIA (1389–1412) AND
FILIPPO MARIA (1392–1447)

The two sons who in turn succeeded him could not have been more different from their father. They were born of his incestuous marriage with his first cousin and possessed all the Visconti faults in concentrated doses. Each was exceptionally cruel and of a nervous disposition which bordered on madness.

Giovanni Maria (1402–12) is best remembered for his mastiffs; but he was also generally believed to have murdered his own mother, Caterina. The most notorious legend concerning this duke is that he fed the flesh of his enemies to the hounds that he owned. It may be that the stories of him and his keeper of the hounds, Squarcia Giramo, roaming the streets of Milan to hunt passers-by are exaggerated. But the fact is that this reputation for tyranny and cruelty rendered the legend credible to his subjects. While earlier Visconti such as Bernabò had kept large numbers of hunting dogs, Giovanni Maria chose ferocious guard dogs. His wiser father-in-law Carlo Malatesta exhorted him in letters to be less savage to his enemies and to encourage his subjects to venerate him as a just ruler, but he continued to act with violence and impulsiveness throughout his brief rule. He ordered executions on the slightest whim: once he was said to have executed two hundred people because they had shouted 'Peace, peace' as he passed; he then proclaimed that fresh mention of the same word would be punished by the gallows.

Another story concerned the twelve-year-old son of one of his old enemies, Giovanni Pusteria, who had been murdered some time before. When the boy was brought before him, the duke ordered that he should be given as food to a particularly ferocious dog called Guercio. But the dog simply sniffed his feet. Squarcia Giramo was ordered to bring another mastiff, which also refused to eat him. Furious with his dogs, Giovanni Maria ordered Squarcia to kill the boy. Such behaviour obviously did not endear him to his subjects, so that when a group of conspirators assassinated him in the church of San Gottardo on 16 May 1412 the event was met by universal indifference. But the conspiracy which stimulated the assassination failed, since the *condottiere* Facino Cane, who had taken Pavia and aspired to rule Milan, died on the same day.

Whatever the truth of the legends about Giovanni Maria and his hounds, it is difficult to believe that in this case the act of political assassination was not justified. During his rule many of the cities laboriously brought under the Visconti serpent by Gian Galeazzo had rebelled, so that the dominions of the family had shrunk considerably. It seemed to make no difference to Giovanni Maria, who, contrary to most of his ancestors, never appears to have given a thought to the future but to have indulged himself in the vicarious pleasures of the present.

Filippo Maria immediately opened his rule by punishing his brother's assassins

Opposite *Certosa di Pavia: cloister*

Medallion with Filippo Maria Visconti, by Pisanello.

with as refined a display of torture methods as any Visconti ever employed. At the same time he was more prudent than his brother and governed with some success until his death thirty-five years later. Yet continued success entailed employing military support from a man who was eventually to usurp the Visconti and establish himself as Duke of Milan. For he turned for assistance to the greatest *condottiere* of the time, Francesco Sforza.

The last Visconti duke was notorious for the physical ugliness which led him to appear in public as rarely as possible. We have no means of judging for ourselves, since his ugliness went together with vanity and he never allowed his portrait to be painted. He spent his time closed inside the great Castello di Porta Giovia, now know as the Castello Sforzesco in the centre of Milan. Decades of this reclusive life and an obsession with privacy eventually drove him into paranoia. His suspicious nature became such that if a general or courtier was fortunate enough to be admitted to his presence he would have to be careful not to stand near a window, since Filippo Maria would then suspect him of sending messages to someone outside. He was also superstitious and terrified of thunderstorms; a special room sound-proofed with double walls was built in the castle for him to take refuge in during storms. It is also said that his marriage was never consummated. As a result of extreme obesity he was incapable of riding into battle, so he was forced in spite of his doubts to call upon Francesco Sforza to fulfil the role of military leader.

Filippo Maria exemplified the ruthlessness of the Visconti in at least one interesting episode. At the time of his brother's murder, the *condottiere* Facino Cane had been attempting to found his own independent tyranny, and chose the Visconti city of

Pavia for this purpose. As we have seen, however, he died of severe sickness on the very day that Giovanni Maria was murdered in Milan. In order to take advantage of Facino's excellent and well-trained army, now leaderless, Filippo Maria married the *condottiere*'s widow Beatrice Tenda — who was twice his age. This move was vital to his plan of recovering Visconti domination of their traditional territories, but he soon tired of the old widow. In a typical Visconti plot, Beatrice was accused of adultery with one of her pages, confessed under torture, and was then executed together with the page and all of her maids. Such a story was the very stuff of Romanticism, and it is no accident that Beatrice fascinated writers and composers of the early nineteenth century. Following the success of historical operas like Donizetti's *Anne Boleyn*, the composer Vincenzo Bellini (1801–34) wrote his melancholically beautiful and little-known opera *Beatrice da Tenda* a year before he died from consumption.

Thus Filippo Maria had gained his army, and then disposed of the means by which he gained it with customary Visconti treachery. His next marriage, to Maria of Savoy, was just as clearly a marriage of political convenience and perhaps for this reason never consummated. As he dithered and plotted, the duchy slipped inexorably out of his control and into the hands of his captain-general, who skilfully planned the transfer of power and married Filippo's illegitimate daughter Bianca Maria.

Francesco Sforza, son of Muzio Attendolo, the first of the Sforza dynasty, was an exemplary military leader who was tough and aggressive himself. He insisted upon great discipline and the attention to detail shown by many great commanders,

*Reverse of medallion by
Pisanello.*

and had a magnetic personality which gained the loyalty of his men. He was friendly with Cosimo de' Medici in Florence and Federico da Montefeltro in Urbino, who both financed his enterprise in usurping the Duchy of Milan; the former wished to maintain trade routes through the Alps to Florence, while the latter preferred that Francesco Sforza should gain the lands he was clearly destined to gain far from Urbino and Romagna. Filippo Maria Visconti himself was caught in an impossible dilemma: he knew that he would never hold Milan without the *condottiere*'s help, yet must have suspected Sforza's ambitions. Nevertheless he gave his blessing to the marriage alliance which was to prove of enormous importance to Sforza and provided a continuity between the Visconti and Sforza dynasties.

Prolonged discussions concerning the inheritance were not completed when Filippo Maria died in 1447. Francesco Sforza himself was not in Milan at the time, and the duchy was abolished by popular acclaim when the so-called 'Ambrosian Republic' was created. But it was to last a matter of months. When Francesco eventually entered Milan he was enthusiastically acclaimed duke inside the new cathedral by the same people who had instituted the Republic.

THE LATER VISCONTI

The direct male line of the Visconti descending from Matteo I ended in 1447, since Filippo Maria left no male heir. But a second Visconti line has survived until the twentieth century, descending from a brother of Matteo's called Uberto (d. 1315). This Uberto was sent — as was normal with the younger brothers of these dynasties — to fill the post of *podestà* of Vercelli and Como. His descendants were granted the title of Counts of Lonate Pozzolo in 1541, and became Marquises of Vimodrone in 1690. It is from this title that their present family name, Visconti di Modrone, derives. Carlo Visconti di Modrone became Imperial Chamberlain of France, and was made duke in 1813, a title which was later reconfirmed by Austria when the Duchy of Milan again changed hands. The present Duke Uberto di Modrone (b. 1927) has no male heir, and since the later titles of Marquis and Duke can be transmitted only by male primogeniture they will become extinct with his death.

There is, however, another branch of this secondary line, known as the family 'dei Duchi di Visconti di Modrone', which bears the title of Counts of Lonate Pozzolo. The family continues to this day to live mainly in Milan. The most illustrious member of this family was the film director Count Luchino Visconti (1906–74), the third son of Count Giuseppe Visconti, uncle of the present head of the family Count Ruggero dei Duchi Visconti di Modrone (b. 1906). A further minor branch of the family, already considered distinct from the main Visconti line when Archbishop Ottone commissioned a list of Milanese noble families in 1277, known as the Visconti di Oleggio Castello, resides mainly in Tuscany.

The Visconti name thus continues even though the most direct ducal line is about to be extinguished. Although he was not the last descendant of Matteo Visconti, it is in many ways fitting that the last Visconti of international repute should have been Luchino Visconti. His sensitive portrayals of the decline of great noble families, and the decadence of the European nobility just before the First World War, bear the stamp of authenticity which derived from his aristocratic background. He brought an innate sense of period taste, social etiquette, and appropriate gesture to such magnificent films as *The Leopard* and *Death in Venice.*

2

THE ESTE

When Marquis Obizzo d'Este seized Ferrara and made it the base of family power in the later twelfth century, his ancestors had already ruled the much smaller town of Este in the hills near Padova for centuries. They had been members of the Carolingian nobility and therefore form one of the most ancient Italian dynasties. But the true greatness of both the dynasty and its city, which survives in the architecture and character of the city today, was achieved in the fifteenth century. The unusual aspect of this family history is that two of the most celebrated members were women. They were to play a prominent role in the history of the Sforza of Milan and the Gonzaga of Mantova. Indeed, Isabella d'Este, Duchess of Mantova, is in her own right one of the three most fascinating personalities of the entire Italian Renaissance. Other members of the family married into the houses of Malatesta, Borgia, and Aragon.

The legendary history of the Este was celebrated by the sixteenth-century epic poet Torquato Tasso (1544–95) — who became secretary to Cardinal Luigi d'Este — in his *Jerusalem Delivered*. In a strange scene of Canto XVII the semi-legendary warrior Rinaldo finds a magic shield in which he can watch, as if in a film, the adventures of the ancestors of the Este. He sees Azio, descended from Roman warriors; Caio, who fought against the Barbarians after the fall of the Roman Empire; and Foresto, who defended Italy against Attila the Hun and is described as 'the Hector of Italy'; and many other heroic warriors. The deeds of these men, expressed with evident sycophancy by a poet who was in the pay of the Este family, illustrate the desire also seen in other Renaissance families to trace their origins to Roman antiquity.

While to a modern reader a family history of several centuries would seem sufficient, matters of precedence made such matters vitally important to these Renaissance princes — and, as we shall see, survived into the twentieth century with

Opposite *Alfonso, first Este Duke, by Titian.*

the bitter millennial rivalry of the Colonna and Orsini in Rome. In fact, the origins of the Este family can be traced to a certain Boniface I, a knight of Longobard descent who came south into Italy with Charlemagne and who was in 813 both Count and Duke of Tuscany.

This provides a dynastic explanation of the long-standing and bitter rivalry between the Este and the Medici of Florence, whom the Este tended to look down upon as vulgar upstart merchants. To them, the matter of precedence was of vital importance, and became particularly visible during the sixteenth century. On the memorable occasion when the two families paid their respect to the Spanish Emperor Charles V and Pope Paul III at Lucca in 1541, together with Italy's greatest princes, the Este were seen to come off better: when Charles rode through Lucca he invited Ercole II d'Este to ride on his right and Cosimo I de' Medici on his left. Similarly, when Pope Paul III celebrated Christmas Mass that year the whole peninsula rang with gossip about who had been in the front row and who on the left or right — like commentators at a modern royal wedding. Once again, the Este came off best. Years later, when the two families were marrying their sons to the daughters of the Austrian Emperor Ferdinand I at Trento in northern Italy, Cardinal Luigi d'Este threatened to smash down the doors of the chapel where the weddings were to be celebrated if his nephew were not first. This long-standing dispute was partially resolved in 1586 with the marriage of Cesare d'Este to Virginia de' Medici.

Yet beneath these apparently frivolous arguments lay more serious matters of political importance. Just as today the nearby city of Bologna is the vital nerve centre of Italy's road and rail network, so Ferrara — situated on the River Po and sandwiched between Venice to the east, Milan to the west, and the papal states to the south — was of great strategic value. The ancestor to whom the Este themselves always looked with reverence was Alberto Azzo II, who was said to have lived over a hundred years from 996 to 1097. The reason for this is pertinent: Azzo transferred the seat of family power from Tuscany to the hills around Este, forming the first nucleus of feuds which enabled the family eventually to take Ferrara, Modena, and Reggio and establish themelves as rulers of that vital passage through the valley of the Po.

The Emperor Henry III granted the fiefs to Azzo II, and made him a Marquis of Italy by investing him as a Margrave of the Empire. He also became Duke of Milan. One of his sons became Duke of Bavaria and began a German line of the family, while the Italian line slowly gravitated towards Ferrara. By the end of the thirteenth century they were Lords of Ferrara, but it was with Niccolò III that the family became firmly established.

NICCOLÒ III
(1383–1441)

For three decades the proverbial amatory excesses of Niccolò III produced enough sons and daughters to guarantee the Este line. He married three times and was said to have had more than eight hundred mistresses in this time, giving birth to the incredible total of three hundred illegitimate children. Following the generous contemporary practice of recognizing bastard offspring, twenty-two male children were officially legitimized. In a charming popular acknowledgement of his adventures, the people of Ferrara and its surrounding countryside sang the verses:

> On this and that bank of the Po,
> They're all children of Niccolò.

The same rhyme is used in Milan for Bernabò Visconti. A physically tough, bull-necked, and arrogant man, Niccolò had larger-than-life appetites. His life was devoted to fighting, spending, and loving, and his activities spawned legends of the erotic life of Ferrara which lasted for centuries. Still today, the idea that Ferrara is the most sensual of Italian cities persists.

But extra-marital adventures did nothing to dispel his intense jealousy, which resulted in the incident for which Niccolò is most remembered today. In 1418, when he was thirty-five, Niccolò married the beautiful fifteen-year-old Parisina Malatesta — who was compared by one chronicler to Phaedra for her sparkling eyes and bold lasciviousness. Some sources suggest she had once been promised to Niccolò's son Ugo, who was the same age. In any case it was reported that the young bride was having a secret affair with Ugo whenever her husband left Ferrara on hunting trips. At first Niccolò refused to believe the stories, but repeated rumours aroused his jealousy. He drilled a hole in the ceiling of her chamber and waited until he caught the lovers *in flagrante*. Up to this point the many versions of the story disagree, but there is no doubt about the terrible conclusion. After a summary trial in which Niccolò refused to listen to the supplications of his courtiers, Parisina and Ugo were beheaded in the prison of Ferrara on 21 May 1425. As if to justify to his own conscience such a brutal punishment, the greatest adulterer of the Renaissance then ordered that all the adulterous women of Ferrara should suffer the same fate. The result was a massacre.

It was Niccolò who in 1385 began the construction of the massive moated castle which symbolizes more than any other building in Ferrara the Este power. It was completed and decorated by his successor Leonello, who included drawbridges over the moat and fortified corridors linking it to the Este palace opposite the cathedral. At that time it marked the city boundary, and the famous Tower of the Lions protected one of the four city gates. Later, under Ercole I, the city was extended and the castle now stands in the centre of the old town.

Through his many children, Niccolò assured the continuity of the Este line and achieved important alliances for the future. His bastard son Leonello married Margherita Gonzaga and later Maria of Aragon; Ercole married Eleonora of Aragon and established the main line of the family; his daughter Ginevra married Sigismondo Malatesta. One of his other bastard sons, Borso, was a celebrated *condottiere*.

LEONELLO
(1407–50)

Son of one of Niccolò's favourite mistresses, who had the picturesque name of Stella dell'Assassino, Leonello was very much a learned and humanist prince. In both senses of the word humanist Leonello was an examplar — in his belief in the educational value of the Greek and Latin authors, and in his faith that man's intellectual and spiritual resources were sufficient to achieve knowledge and resolve moral problems without ecclesiastical intervention. The laws he established in Ferrara were based upon a rational understanding of the best available principles, whether their origin be in a Christian writer like St Paul or in a Roman dramatist like Seneca. His quiet, rational approach to political problems and disputes foreshadowed the later perfection of the same method by Lorenzo de' Medici. Yet it is worth remembering that even Leonello served his military apprenticeship with the celebrated *condottiere* Braccio da Montone.

He married twice, once for love and once out of political necessity. His first wife was Margherita Gonzaga, to whose father Niccolò was indebted for money

The Este Castle at Ferrara.

46

Leonello   d'Este,   by Pisanello.

loaned towards the building of a new castle. Yet it seems to have been a romantic marriage, with the attractive and intelligent duchess we see in the portrait by Antonio Pisanello (*c.* 1395–1455) bringing grace and learning to the court at Ferrara. Unfortunately, she died after only three years of happy marriage. Leonello contracted a second and more powerful alliance by marrying Maria of Aragon, daughter of King Alfonso I of Naples, in 1444. This marriage, celebrated in grandiose and extravagant style as befitted the status of the bride's father, was destined to last only a little longer than the first. At forty-two Leonello was twice a widower, and he himself died the following year, in 1450.

Under such a wise and educated ruler, Ferrara was one of the most interesting courts of the time. In 1429 Niccolò had offered the court tutorship at Ferrara to one of the day's leading teachers and humanists Guarino Guarini (1370–1460). Guarini held the position for seven years, and his school became the basis for a *studium generale* or university in which he was then professor of rhetoric for the remainder of his life. He was an excellent scholar who translated many works from Greek, including Strabo's *Geographia*. His son Battista, who succeeded him, wrote a book entitled *On the Order and Method of Teaching and Reading Classical Authors*, based upon his father's experience. Apart from information concerning the teaching of grammar, with specific examples, this book contains enlightened advice on teaching method, emphasizing the use of kindly, persuasive teaching methods rather than physical coercion. Rather than an abstract text on humanistic ideals he provided a practical everyday teacher's guide with advice on problems of classroom management and hints for using the educational methods proposed in the best possible way. He included tips on preparation and presentation of lessons from the teacher's point of view, on note-taking, on marking both grammar and reading exercises, and on grading pupil progress from the student's point of view. The Este children were indeed fortunate to have such an exceptional private tutor.

These examples illustrate the seriousness with which education was approached at the court of Ferrara, and explain how members of the family such as Leonello and his celebrated nieces Beatrice and Isabella gained their impressive learning. They also go a long way towards explaining Ferrara's reputation as the centre of great poetry, for such fundamental works for European literature as Ariosto's *Orlando Furioso* and Tasso's *Jerusalem Delivered* were written under Este patronage.

Since Leonello's first wife Margherita Gonzaga was brought up in the equally illuminated court school of Mantova, in which as we shall see Guarini's predecessor Vittorino da Feltre set educational precedents which were destined to survive the Renaissance, we may imagine their household as quite different from those of the Visconti. Scholarship and learning predominated, with decisions conditioned by classical authors. Leonello's portrait by Pisanello suggests a quiet, powerful, and intelligent man, with none of the violent traits of many contemporary rulers.

BORSO
(1413–71)

Yet not all Niccolò's children were scholarly in taste and rational in temperament. Neither were the Este of this period more than partially enlightened despots: they killed as readily as their contemporaries, and exacted exorbitant taxes from starving subjects to sustain the grandeur of their court. They employed ruthless methods with little thought for other human lives. Niccolò himself had not been slow to behead his young wife Parisina and his son Ugo when they betrayed him; Alfonso I later sentenced his brothers to perpetual imprisonment.

Although he was born of the same mother, Borso was in fact quite different from his brother Leonello — whom he succeeded as Lord of Ferrara. He is said to have remarked to his father that life held nothing more fascinating than death on the battlefield, and dedicated himself with enthusiasm to a military career. Unfortunately, his enthusiasm was not matched by success.

At eighteen, he was sent with a hundred lances to gain experience fighting for Venice with the *condottiere* Carmagnola. From the beginning, his career was marked by failure. He was lucky to escape death when Carmagnola himself was killed, and a few years later made an ignominious escape from the Battle of Imola. He was involved in a curious example of diplomatic duplicity when his father continued to insist that he fight with the Venetians. In 1439 Venice and Florence joined forces in attacking the Visconti of Milan. While Niccolò III assured the Venetians that Borso would join them with his army, he secretly ordered his son to fight for the Milanese and publicly blamed this apparent change on Borso. In this war Borso again failed to achieve great honour, and retired from his military career after having barely saved himself and his men at the battle of Soncino in 1440.

He adapted himself to a princely life at the court of his brother Leonello, hardly thinking that he would soon inherit the city. But when he did, he adapted to the new role with voracious enthusiasm. He always appeared in public dressed in rich

*Borso d'Este, by
Baldassare d'Este.*

costumes, covered in delicate embroidery and expensive jewels. In 1452, a mere
two years after his succession, this ambitious man agreed to pay 4,000 ducats a
year to the Emperor Frederick III for a ducal title, in addition to the gift of a
bejewelled collar worth 40,000 ducats. Some idea of the worth of this gift will be
given by the fact that a skilled artisan of the time might have expected to earn between
15 and 20 ducats a year.

The imperial fiefs of Modena and Reggio were thus raised to a duchy and Borso
became the first Duke d'Este. The reckless expenditure involved in purchasing the
title was, if anything, exceeded by the extravagance of the pageantry when Borso
made his triumphal entry into Reggio to receive the homage of the city. He was
met at the gate by an enormous cart on which St Prospero, the patron saint of the
town, appeared to float. The saint was shaded by a baldachin supported by angels.
Below him was a revolving disk with eight singing cherubs, two of whom received
from the saint the sceptre and keys of the city, which they then delivered to the
duke while saints and angels sang his praise. Then a chariot drawn by concealed
horses came forward, bearing an empty throne behind which stood a figure of Justice
attended by a genius. Further decorated floats followed these in procession through
the city to the cathedral.

But even this show of wealth was belittled when Borso travelled to Rome in 1471
to receive the papal investiture as Duke of Ferrara from Paul II. The procession,
consisting of a train of over five hundred mounted noblemen dressed in silver or
gold brocade, with hundreds of liveried servants and 150 pack mules, took twenty
days over the journey. Borso distributed silver coins to the inhabitants of each town

they passed, at the entrance to and departure from the towns. But in spite of this apparent grandeur and generosity, Borso's life is best viewed as something of a failure overshadowed by immense ambitions. He did not equal the wisdom of his brother Leonello, and his twenty years of rule cannot be compared with those of his younger brother and successor, Ercole I. Beyond these extravagances and some limited building activity, his rule left nothing to show beyond the acquisition of the ducal titles.

Yet he was much loved by the people of Ferrara, and his passing was lamented. He was always ready to hear complaints and resolve problems. Each morning he walked in the city accompanied by secretaries, counsellors, and judges. There, in the streets and squares of the city anyone was free to approach him, explain their problems or simply talk to him. This popular form of 'democracy', together with his generosity towards citizens and nobles alike, helped to make him a popular duke in spite of the heavy taxes he imposed in order to sustain his extravagance. The rich frescoes of Duke Borso preparing for a hunting expedition, at the country palace of the Este, strongly suggest a joyous atmosphere of common pleasure and relaxation.

ERCOLE I
(1421–1505)

Borso was succeeded in 1471 by his half-brother Ercole, whose rule marked the highest point of Renaissance Ferrara. As the third legitimized son of Niccolò, he probably never expected to succeed to the dukedom and spent most of his early life as a soldier. He had been sent as page to the royal court at Naples, where he received his military training. At the Battle of Ricciardina in 1467, fighting under the great *condottiere* Bartolomeo Colleoni for Venice against the Florentines, he was wounded by a shot in the leg which rendered him lame for the rest of his life. Thereafter, like many *condottiere*, he was known by his nickname 'Ciotto', the Lame.

He was quick to adapt to the new importance of his role as Duke of Ferrara. Two years later he married Eleonora of Aragon, daughter of King Ferdinand I of Naples, partly in reparation for an earlier offence but also to increase family prestige. From that moment he sought throughout his rule to increase his political and diplomatic role as mediator between the greater powers. The marriages of his celebrated daughters Isabella, to Francesco II Gonzaga, and Beatrice, to Lodovico Sforza, and his son Alfonso's two marriages to Anna Sforza and Lucrezia Borgia were part of his scheme.

Even as duke, he continued his activity as *condottiere*, fighting for Florence and Milan against Naples and the Papal State. This was an ambiguous role, since the commander of the opposing army, Alfonso of Calabria, was his own brother-in-law. Then from 1482 to 1484 he was engaged in a war that developed between Ferrara and Venice for commercial reasons concerned with the Venetian monopoly of the salt trade. At the same time he was engaged in a potentially more serious

Isabella d'Este,
by Leonardo.

struggle with Pope Sixtus IV (1471–84), who was pursuing every possible means to create a new state for his nephew Girolamo Riario. At one point, Ferrara itself was under siege. It seemed that a combination of plague, famine, and Ercole's own illness would combine to dictate the end of Ferrara as an independent duchy, but the situation was saved by the last-minute intervention of forces sent by the King of Naples — which demonstrated the wisdom of Ercole's policy of marriage alliances. After this dangerous adventure, he devoted himself to his duties as Duke of Ferrara, creating one of the finest of all Renaissance courts.

His ambitions are best seen in the extraordinary urban development of Ferrara, which was inspired in part by dynastic ambition and in part by the need to build stronger defences against future wars with Venice. Between 1490 and 1500 Ferrara saw a rapid expansion which included one of the first coherent urban plans of any European city. Much of the old city was restored and a new suburb called the 'Addizione Erculea' created from scratch. Ercole's brother Sigismondo built the Palazzo del Diamanti there, so-called from the thousands of diamond-shaped stones on its façade, and many of the noble families of Ferrara built large palaces which still exist today. There were twelve new churches, and two broad streets running through the city. Older buildings such as the Palazzo Schifanoia and Palazzo del Paradiso, built at the end of the fourteenth century by Niccolò III's father Marquis Alberto, were restored and decorated. This rebuilding and embellishment made Ferrara into an attractive capital, and was the physical basis for its sixteenth-century greatness. The teachings of Guarini and his son and other pupils, together with the new university, had prepared the nobles of Ferrara for the boom in letters during which three major poets like Boiardo, Tasso, and Ariosto were resident in the city. They had also cultivated an interest in art; some of the period's best painters decorated town and country palaces, for example the magnificent frescoes of hunting scenes in

51

the ironically named Palazzo Schifanoia (Palace of Boredom). The theatre was also enjoyed by the people of Ferrara, whose taste ranged from the classical dramas of Plautus and Terence to religious plays and curious comic representations of battles, in which one group of actors 'besieged' with vegetables and rotten fruit another group defending a wooden castle.

While not equalling the legendary exploits of his father, Ercole maintained the Este reputation for womanizing and erotic pastimes. He was a fun-loving duke, whose greatest pleasure was to be with his court fools, and with a group of boon companions celebrated for their drunken sprees. One such friend, know as Moschino, could easily have been a model for Falstaff. When he died, the people observed that they would have to plant fewer vines in future years.

Under Ercole I the financial administration of Ferrara was brought to a fine art. The city was now a modern capital with fine public and private buildings, thriving commerce, and a political freedom which made it attractive for refugees from the whole of Italy. Taxes were high, but basic foodstuffs were guaranteed in times of severe need. Likewise, the dukes were proud of the fact that both soldiers and university professors received their salaries punctually. The dukes would make an annual *andar per ventura*, or tour of the wealthy citizens, visiting their people and collecting what were named euphemistically 'presents', often in the form of produce. Other money entered from the practice of selling government offices, all of which were assigned prices in proportion to their importance. Thus judges, notaries, bailiffs, and even the tax officials paid for their positions, just as their masters had paid for the dukedom. It was generally believed that huge sums of cash were kept in the Este castle inside its citadel.

Duke Ercole I made Ferrara into one of the most magnificent cities of Italy, which can still be reconstructed in the eye of the imaginative visitor today. He patronized scholars and painters, created a fine library, and lived in one of the most civilized courts of the time. The extraordinary atmosphere which dominated Ferrara during his rule was never repeated by his successors. But perhaps the best testimony to this great duke is the legacy he left the Italian Renaissaince in his two remarkable daughters Beatrice and Isabella, who exported the Este model to Milan and Mantova.

ALFONSO I
(1476–1534)

When Alfonso I became the third Duke of Ferrara in 1505, it might have seemed that his chances of a long rule were slight. His brother Ferrante, less than a year younger, lamented the bad luck that made him second son and was determined to do something about it. Two other brothers, Giulio and Cardinal Ippolito, were also fiercely ambitious. His more moderate sisters Beatrice and Isabella lived in the courts of their husbands. Although their childhoods were spent in Ferrara, they both married young — Isabella was betrothed at six and married at sixteen — and

Fresco of Borso d'Este rewarding his fool, in Palazzo Schifanoia.

achieved renown in their adopted cities. Their lives and history therefore form part of the history of the Sforza and Gonzaga families.

Events were not long in coming to a head, and illustrate in a long drawn-out tussle the violence and ruthlessness for which the courts of Renaissance Italy were notorious. The duke's brothers Giulio and Cardinal Ippolito were both in love with Angela, the eighteen-year-old sister of his wife Lucrezia Borgia. Angela became pregnant and then expressed her preference for Giulio. One day, after meeting her outside Ferrara, Giulio was accosted by his brother Ippolito who was in a wild fit of anger which contrasted with his normally cautious behaviour. Giulio was severely beaten with staffs. Furthermore, the cardinal threatened to tear out the eyes which had caused him to fall in love with Angela. He was left bleeding and half blind, to be succoured by passers-by. But he did nothing to retaliate. For his part, Duke Alfonso did not wish to anger Pope Julius II and so allowed Ippolito to go unpunished. It was he who persuaded Giulio to do nothing.

Rancour smouldered within the offended brother. Soon after this event he joined the jealous and ambitious Ferrante in plotting the deaths of both Duke Alfonso and Cardinal Ippolito. But duke and cardinal were saved by the incapacity of their mistrustful brothers to agree on means, place, and time of this double assassination. The more they prevaricated, the more chance there was of their plot becoming known; and, indeed, it came to the ears of Duke Alfonso. They were brought to trial together with their fellow conspirators, in 1506. The latter were immediately hung, drawn, and quartered, while the two Este had their death sentences commuted to perpetual imprisonment. Ferrante died in prison over thirty years later; Giulio survived and was finally pardoned in 1559 when he was 81 years old.

Alfonso's second wedding was no less dramatic than these events. Just as Pope Sixtus IV had sought to create a state for his nephew, so Alexander VI (1492–1503) desired the same end for his nephew Cesare Borgia. To this purpose he had arranged for his own daughter Lucrezia to marry Duke Ercole's heir Alfonso in 1502. The daughter of Alexander's long-standing mistress Vannozza Catanei when he was still Cardinal Rodrigo Borgia, Lucrezia had been involved in a series of diplomatically based betrothals since the age of ten, and was later divorced from Giovanni Sforza, and widowed by Alfonso of Aragon. It seems she was eager to leave the intrigue of Rome, and genuinely pleased to travel to Ferrara. Certainly her life had been far from pleasant up to that moment. Daughter of the most irrepressibly licentious of all popes, sister to one of the cruellest men of the Renaissance, witness to the messy attempted murder of her second husband, she was later charged with committing triple incest with her brothers and her father the pope. She has been denigrated ever since both in history and in literature as one of the most abominable of all women. Yet it is also true that these stories belong to the early, Roman, phase of her life when the machinations and corruption which her family engaged in necessarily embroiled her in intrigue. In the event, she turned out to have been a wise choice.

Alfonso's brothers Ippolito, Ferrante, and Sigismondo travelled to Rome in great pomp to collect Lucrezia, whose marriage had been celebrated by proxy in Ferrara. Her brother Cesare rode to the city gates with an escort of four thousand men to greet the groom's brothers, who rode with over one thousand five hundred nobles, trumpeters, and soldiers, and were now led into Rome by two hundred Swiss guards. After formal greetings and orations, Pope Alexander performed a second ceremony in St Peter's. Lucrezia was dressed in gold brocade and crimson velvet trimmed with ermine, with sleeves which fell to the floor. On her golden hair she wore a beautifully contrasting black ribbon set off by a stunning string of pearls in which was mounted a large pendant consisting of an emerald, a ruby, and a pearl. This ceremony was followed by a carnival lasting for days, with processions of decorated floats, drinking, dancing, and singing. Then, fifteen days after the arrival of Cardinal Ippolitio, Lucrezia departed for Ferrara.

Representatives of the city of Rome and the Roman nobility including Francesco Colonna and members of the other great Roman families, were appointed to accompany her. A special escort of two hundred men was financed by her brother Cesare — together with musicians and clowns to amuse her during the journey. Lucrezia's personal retinue consisted of a hundred and eighty people, and a hundred and fifty mules to carry her trousseau. There were new carriages and carts, and a special French sedan-chair. Once the final payment of the dowry was made to the Ferrarese ambassadors, this immense cavalcade was able to leave. The wedding party was preceded by papal letters commanding the towns *en route* to provide suitable hospitality. The terrified recipients quickly prepared triumphal arches and festivities, even though they might well be ruined by the expense. The journey took twenty days, partly because it was mid-winter, and partly as the result of Lucrezia's lack of experience in travelling. A Ferrarese ambassador wrote to Duke Ercole that 'Donna Lucrezia is of a delicate constitution and, like her ladies, is unaccustomed to the saddle, and ...does not wish to be worn out when she reaches Ferrara'. In fact she insisted on travelling from Bologna to Ferrara by boat in order to avoid the discomfort of overland travel. Charmingly, before arriving at Ferrara, she stopped for an entire day to prepare her hair. At the city gates she was met with even greater drama than at Rome, and escorted through festive streets to the marble steps of the ducal palace.

In Ferrara she gained the reputation of a charming, graceful, and happy duchess. A contemporary chronicle describes her in this way: 'She is of medium height and slender figure. Her face is long, the nose well defined and beautiful; her hair a bright gold, and her eyes blue; her mouth is somewhat large, the teeth dazzlingly white; her neck white and slender, but at the same time well rounded. She is always cheerful and good-humoured.' It is interesting to see how in seventeen years of regular correspondence, her sister-in-law Isabella gradually came genuinely to like her after initial doubts. The people of Ferrara took to her immediately. In fact the elaborate wedding celebrations, lasting six days, showed off the elegant Lucrezia at her best at banquets, balls, and theatrical events. She was an excellent dancer and extremely graceful, and lost no opportunity to demonstrate her skill in the latest French dances. Duke Ercole himself had been personally responsible for erecting a temporary theatre complete with eleborate scenery and the capacity for three

View of Villa d'Este at Tivoli, by Muziano.

thousand spectators. There were serious plays, including Plautus, each evening, but also comedies, music, and popular dances. When the festivities had ended Alfonso and Lucrezia took up residence in the castle.

When his duchess died seventeen years later, Alfonso wrote movingly and with obvious sincerity in a letter to his nephew Federico Gonzaga of 'the illustrious lady, the duchess, my dearest wife' stating that 'I cannot write this without tears, knowing myself to be deprived of such a dear and sweet companion. For such her exemplary conduct and the tender love which existed between us made her to me'. This letter and the general esteem in which she was held present Lucrezia Borgia as totally different from the black picture usually portrayed of her; yet it seems unlikely that a Duke of Ferrara — belonging to a dynasty which thought nothing of decapitating an adulterous Marchesina — would condone the crimes with which she had been accused if he believed there was any truth in them.

Like many others of the Este family, Alfonso had been sent by his father to train as a *condottiere*. One of the lessons he learned from this experience was the importance of artillery in modern warfare. So when he refortified Ferrara he added new and more efficient cannon which were to play a vital role in future battles. His interest in the design and production of weapons was extremely practical, to the extent that he enjoyed working in the forge. He was said on several occasions to have personally cast the cannon which were to be installed on the castle. He also performed experiments with metals, trying to achieve new alloys or stronger materials for weaponry. Thus it was that he acquired the nickname 'Gunner'.

One of his military exploits was occasioned by his feud with Pope Julius II (1503–13). In spite of the care he took during the case of Giulio and Cardinal Ippolito to maintain cordial relations with the pope, Julius was determined to destroy the power of the Este. The new pope was the nephew of Sixtus IV, who had combated Ercole in order to create a state for his nephew Riario. He bore a bitter, inherited grudge against the Este, and was driven to one of the most remarkable episodes in the history of the papacy when at the age of sixty-six he took the field in full armour and led the papal army into battle against them at Mirandola in 1511. The spectacle of a pope encouraging his soldiers in battle and promising booty was unique even then. This totally fearless man, who had commissioned a tomb from Michelangelo of which the Moses is a mere fragment, was not discouraged even when shot from Alfonso's cannon fell on the room where he was sheltered and killed his servants. During the battle he narrowly escaped being kidnapped by an Este lieutenant. He eventually succeeded in taking Mirandola, but failed both in dislodging the Este from Ferrara and in creating the new state of his dreams.

In the last twenty years of his rule Duke Alfonso I concentrated on maintaining Este power through diplomatic manoeuvres in the complex shifts of power and allegiances following the arrival in Italy first of King Charles VIII of France and then of the Emperor Charles V of Spain. When diplomacy failed, he resorted to buying back territory the family had lost — as in the case of Modena and Reggio. He never married again after the death of Lucrezia Borgia, and was survived by five of their children. His son Ercole succeeded him after his death in 1534, while Ippolito II became a Cardinal of the Church renowned for his wealth and artistic taste.

ERCOLE II
(1508–59)

The fourth Duke of Ferrara was less fortunate in his choice of consort. While it might have been expected that Lucrezia Borgia would bring difficulties because of the stories which surrounded her family and her own reputation, the opposite was the case of Ercole's wife Renata, daughter of King Louis XII of France. Ercole married a quiet, royal princess and later found himself with a devout Calvinist who threatened to turn the court at Ferrara into a vigorous centre of Protestantism in the heart of Spanish dominated Catholic Italy. She was not especially beautiful, but maintained an intelligent and informed interest in philosophy, history, and astrology. It was presumably this rational intellectual streak which drew her to the thought of John Calvin.

Ercole II's rule as duke covered almost exactly the period of Church history known as the Reformation. The corruption of such popes as Alexander VI, Ercole's own grandfather, and the selling of papal indulgences created a willing audience for the ideas of such as Martin Luther. The reformers rejected the authority of the pope, the doctrine of transubstantiation, and the adoration of the Virgin and the saints. The first rational explanation and justification of the new ideas was provided by the Frenchman John Calvin from Picardy, who became the intellectual leader of the Reformation even though many Protestants rejected his concept of predestination. His ideas inspired the French Huguenots, but his main early following was in his adopted city of Geneva.

The Duchess Renata always remained ostentatiously French, creating a kind of mini-state within Ferrara with nearly two hundred servants and followers brought from Paris. Within this intimate circle she offered shelter to Protestant refugees from her native country and enjoyed discussing theological questions with them. Calvin himself was among these refugees for a short period in 1536, disguised as a certain 'Charles d'Heppeville'. For many years Duke Ercole sought without success to prevent the formation of this Protestant enclave, apparently being forced to trade off his extra-marital affairs against this 'weakness' of his wife. Finally he managed to confine her to a villa in the country, where a theologian was sent to purge her of heretical ideas. She feigned reconversion in order to gain her freedom. But when Duke Alfonso died she returned to France, to her castle of Montargis — which became a centre for the Huguenot fugitives she protected.

Duke Ercole II's rule was characterized by a period of peace and stability which was mainly due to the foundations laid by the diplomacy of his father. Ferrara's greatest glory was its food, and the banquets offered by its duke; its greatest scandal lay in the religious tendencies of his wife Renata. In terms of lasting cultural achievement and historical importance his younger brother Ippolito is a far more interesting personality.

CARDINAL IPPOLITO II
(1509–72)

The second son of Duke Alfonso I and Lucrezia Borgia, Ippolito was elected Archbishop of Milan at the age of ten in place of his uncle Ippolito I, and was made cardinal before he was thirty. Had it not been for the constant opposition of the Spanish cardinals, he would certainly have become pope in one of the five enclaves during his cardinalship. But although he was a cardinal, he was introduced to all the worldly pleasures wealth could provide. He studied Latin and Greek, but also hunting, fencing, and shooting. He was not averse to secret love affairs. As a young man he was known for the quality of his library, jewels, and gardens. For many years he resided at the brilliant French court of King Francis I as ambassador for Ferrara; in that Italophile court, where Benvenuto Cellini and Leonardo da Vinci worked, Ippolito was in his element. He became Archbishop of Lyons and built himself a palace near the king's favourite residence at Fontainebleau. It was after Francis I's death in 1547 that he returned to Italy.

Although he was also a contender for the Holy See in his own right, Ippolito was one of the main supporters of Giovanni Del Monte in his election as Pope Julius III in 1550. One of the new pope's first decisions, as a consolation, was to appoint Ippolito to be governor of Tivoli, visible on the first slopes of the Alban Hills east of Rome where once emperors had built their summer palaces. In deciding to restore and enlarge his official residence, the cardinal created one of the most splendid of all Renaissance villas, whose fountains and sculptures make it one of the few essential sights outside Rome even for the transient visitor.

The enormous main building of the Villa d'Este at Tivoli, built by the architect Pirro Ligorio, was finished within a decade. But the gardens and their fountains took another ten years to complete. Two new aqueducts were constructed to provide water for the fountains, pools, and grottoes which provided both musical pleasure and an effect of water-sculpture. Hundreds of fountains, elaborate stairways, and terraces are set into the hillside amidst cypresses. The avenues are lined with antique sculptures excavated in the vicinity. The Oval Fountain and Path of the Hundred Fountains still stun today, as they inspired Franz Liszt into writing *Les Jeux d'Eau à la Villa d'Este* after residing often in the villa during the last twenty years of his life. He would have enjoyed the water-operated organ which was one of the celebrated features of the garden in the sixteenth century. The Fountain of the Owl and the Birds once emitted alternately the calls of an owl and ordinary bird-song.

Of all the many palaces, gardens, and castles in Italy which still bear the Este name, this Villa d'Este is the best known and most spectacular. Cardinal Ippolito II spent most of his life far from the court at Ferrara, but was in many ways its most brilliant representative. As grandson of the Borgia pope and the greatest of Este dukes, and nephew of Beatrice and Isabella d'Este, he maintained the tradition of patronage. He surrounded himself with writers like Tasso and composers like Palestrina, commissioned the famous gold table service from Cellini, employed the best artisans, and also collected mosaics, paintings, sculptures, and manuscripts. In many ways he was the apotheosis of Este culture, and his garden at Tivoli remains one of the key monuments of the Italian Renaissance. Rarely does such a famous monument reflect so well the personality of its creator.

ALFONSO II
(1533–97)

Duke Alfonso II was the fifth Duke of Ferrara. After the legendary procreation of Niccolò III and satisfactory achievement of the other Este dukes, Alfonso's apparent lack of ability to produce an heir was considered a problem even before he he became duke in 1559. The conditions of Este rule over Ferrara and the ducal title itself were specific: that in the case of absence of a male heir, their right to the vicariate of Ferrara would cease and direct control would revert to the papal state.

His first marriage was little short of disastrous. Engaged to marry Maria de' Medici, she died before the wedding could be celebrated and he accepted her younger sister Lucrezia instead. She, child-duchess at fifteen, died at seventeen. The worried Duke Alfonso obtained a horoscope from the French astrologer, Nostradamus, whose prophecies have since become famous, and was relieved to learn that he would indeed bear a male heir but only with his third wife. Thus, while expecting — and receiving — no child from his second wife he busied himself attempting with innumerable young girls provided by the desperate courtiers of Ferrara, in whose own interests it was vital that the line be continued. In such lax days, the mother was of little importance and any male child could have been quickly legitimized. Each of the girls was provided with a dowry and married into a good Ferrarese family; but no heir was forthcoming.

The sterile duke never lost hope. Believing that Nostradamus' prophecy would be right, he married yet another sixteen-year-old girl when he was in his late forties, this time the attractive Margherita Gonzaga. Finally, when even he must have accepted the fact of his sterility, he devoted himself almost exclusively to dancing, drinking, and celebrating — ironically — the lack of an heir which had frustrated his entire life in spite of every possible remedy and cure attempted.

When it became obvious that he would never have a male heir, Alfonso arranged for the Este titles to transfer to his illegitimate cousin Cesare, who was the descendant of an unrecognized son of Duke Alfonso I. He had been the Este male chosen to marry Cosimo de' Medici's daughter Virginia in a vain attempt to create an alliance with the Medici and heal old wounds. On his 'succession' Cesare attempted vainly to maintain Ferrara, but was forced to relinquish both the ducal title and the city within a year of his cousin's death. After three centuries of Este rule in Ferrara, he established his ducal capital in Modena. Thus began the centuries of gradually reducing power which led inexorably to the final extinction of the Este power and name.

THE LATER DUKES

Duke Francesco I (1610–58) made a hopeless attempt to regain Ferrara for the Este, and Duke Rinaldo I (1655–1737) renounced his role as cardinal in order to save the dynastic aspirations of the house. But the people of Modena and Reggio lived in much reduced circumstances, and Modena was said to have the atmosphere of a large monastery. The male ducal line ended with the death of Ercole III in 1803. He died in ignominious exile in Treviso where the activities of Napoleon had forced him to seek refuge. Thus the line which probably began with Boniface I under Charlemagne in 813 lasted almost exactly a thousand years.

But Ercole's daughter, Maria Beatrice, married the Archduke Ferdinand Charles Habsburg, and gave birth to Francis IV (1779–1846), who was recognized as legitimate ruler of Modena and Reggio. With ambitions worthy of both sides of his family, Francis's aim was to create an Italian kingdom in opposition to French power. His son, Francis V (1819–75), in turn nurtured a dream of an Austro-Italian confederation. In 1859 however he was forced to flee from Modena, and the last vestige of Este rule vanished with him. With his death in 1875 the titles which came with the Este name passed to the Archduke Francis-Ferdinand, heir to the Habsburg thrones, whose assassination at Sarajevo in 1914 sparked off the First World War.

Thus ended what Byron in *Childe Harold's Pilgrimage* memorably and accurately called in an apostrophe to Ferrara:

> . . .the antique brood
> Of Este, which for many an age made good
> Its strength within thy walls, and was of yore
> Patron or tyrant, as the changing mood
> Of petty power impelled. . .

The phrase 'changing mood of petty power' conveys perfectly a sense of the abrupt changes and vicissitudes which characterize the history of the Este dynasty and many other local rulers.

Fresco of hunting scene, Palazzo Schifanoia.

3

THE COLONNA

The Colonna family still lives today in the Roman palace they have inhabited for nearly a thousand years. Their roll of honour includes Pope Martin V, twenty-one cardinals from the twelfth to the eighteenth centuries, twenty-five senators of Rome, and six Viceroys of Spain in the Kingdom of Naples. Guests of the family through the centuries have included Petrarch and Rabelais, while the friendship of the poetess Vittoria Colonna and Michelangelo is one of the most celebrated in Italian literature. The family art gallery may still be visited and contains fine works such as Giorgione's portrait of Sciarra Colonna, twelve landscapes by Poussin, and paintings by Tintoretto, Paolo Veronese, and Annibale Carracci. But this dynasty is an interesting example of one in which patronage was mainly of literature rather than the visual arts. The results are to be seen in the prose and poetry of Petrarch and Michelangelo, and the sonnets of Vittoria Colonna herself.

Above all the Colonna were warriors. Their history reads like a list of regimental battle honours. Stefano Colonna the Elder appears in most of the interesting episodes at the end of the thirteenth century; several members of the family won renown as *condottieri* in the fourteenth and fifteenth centuries; Marcantonio II was one of the greatest generals of the sixteenth century. A myriad of minor Colonna maintained the dynasty's military tradition.

Piero, son of the Count of Tusculum, in the Alban Hills east of Rome near Frascati and today little more than a hill, was the first to bear the name Colonna, taken from a castle that he inherited in the mid-eleventh century. But the Counts of Tusculum had ruled the area since the fall of the Roman Empire, so that the real origins of this family are shrouded in the mists of antiquity. Two prevalent legends demonstrate this. The first shows how the counts were descendants of Julius Caesar, since their lands corresponded almost exactly with the property of Caesar's family; the Emperor's own villa on the Via Labicana belonged to the Colonna dur-

Opposite *Members of the Colonna family in 1581. Detail from a painting by Scipione Pulzone.*

ing the Middle Ages, and the site is still part of their land. The second legend links the family with the Emperor Trajan, and even further back to the Egyptian Osiri, the builder of Cairo. It is probably apocryphal, although there is an obvious romantic fascination in the derivation of the family name from the Column of Trajan, which stands a stone's throw from their palace in Rome.

That the Colonna family is one of the most ancient of Italian families is however beyond doubt. The first documented occurrence of their name was in a diploma dated 1 January 1047, naming Piero as 'Signore della Colonna'.

From that moment a series of warrior Colonnas fought for feudal control of Rome and the entire Lazio region, while a series of cardinals gradually acquired diplomatic and political status. The first was the Giovanni Colonna elected in 1193, who won distinction through his friendship with St Francis of Assisi. Cardinal Giovanni was instrumental in obtaining permission for the foundation of the Order of St Francis in 1210. He died in 1216, but in the following year Pope Honorius III elected another Giovanni Colonna as cardinal. At the end of the thirteenth century three other Colonna cardinals were active in Roman politics and Pope Nicholas IV (1288–92) was so much their man that he may as well have been a Colonna. The family largely controlled the papal elections until the papacy was transferred to Avignon in 1305. But even the French Pope John XXII at Avignon promoted another Colonna to the purple. With this combination of secular power and ecclesiastical influence, by the mid-thirteenth century the Colonna were one of the four families who controlled Rome, established in their fortified palace in the heart of Rome near the present Piazza Venezia. Their main rivals were the Orsini, the Gaetini (or Caetani of Sermoneta, Roman branch of an ancient Sicilian family), and the Massimo families — all of which still survive today.

STEFANO THE ELDER
(c.1265–1349)

None of the medieval Colonna was more fascinating than Stefano Colonna, Count of the Romagna, who for over half a century was intimately involved with the politics of Rome in one of the most turbulent periods of the city's history. He appears as a key figure in such varying episodes as the contest between Church and King Philip the Fair of France and the short-lived Republic of Cola da Rienzo forty years later. A great soldier, he was also the intimate friend and patron of the man whom contemporaries considered the supreme man of letters, Francesco Petrarca.

Pope Nicholas IV had been bishop of the Colonna town of Palestrina. One of his first actions as pope was to bestow the title Marquis of Ancona on the head of the Colonna family Giovanni, and that of Count of Romagna on Giovanni's son Stefano, known later as the Elder. Stefano was cousin to Cardinal Giacomo and uncle to Cardinal Pietro, both created by Nicholas IV, the latter of whom left his monument to posterity in the façade of the great Roman basilica of Santa Maria Maggiore. Stefano's years in the Romagna interacted with the family fortunes of the Malatesta and Montefeltro families, since he needed to depose Malatesta da

Verrucchio and Corrado, son of Taddeo of Montefeltro, in order to claim the lands the pope had assigned him. He succeeded briefly, but after a series of battles and diplomatic squabbles the lands were reclaimed from him. Ironically these losses made the Colonna more powerful nearer home, for in compensation Giovanni and his sons Agapito, Stefano, and Giacomo were granted several feuds in the Abruzzi. Giacomo was made a Roman senator, and managed by negotiation to end further violent wars and bring Perugia, Narni, Terni, and Rieti under Roman rule.

Stefano had already been the first of the line to achieve international notoriety, although in a paradoxical sense his power was merely local. This was explained by the fact that local power in Rome implied power over the Church, and therefore to a certain extent over Christendom. One of the most famous — and far-reaching — diplomatic incidents in the history of the Church began when Pope Boniface VIII (1294–1303) first promised to raise the French King Philip the Fair to the status of Emperor, and then passed him over in favour of Rudolph of Habsburg. In retaliation King Philip expelled the papal legate from his kingdom and made an alliance with Stefano Colonna, who was at that time in France and presumably accepted because Boniface belonged to the rival Caetani family.

The pope immediately excommunicated Stefano, expropriated all Colonna land, and razed their castle to the ground. In a venomous letter dated Ascension Day of the third year of his pontificate, he referred to Giacomo Colonna and his nephew Pietro as men 'who entered the Church in the guise of sheep but then showed themselves to be rapacious and troublesome wolves' who aimed at destroying the unity of the Church. He counted them amongst the party of 'heretics, schismatics, and blasphemers'. From their role amongst the greatest nobles of Italy, Stefano and his brothers were reduced to the status of landless exiles. One of many stories concerning this episode provides an interesting insight into the personality of Stefano Colonna, and the pride bordering on arrogance which typifies this and many other such families. He was once stopped on the road and asked to declare his name; when he did so, the soldiers derided him and asked him where his castles were, since he had lost his major stronghold in Palestrina. Colonna, undetered, lay his hand on his heart and replied proudly: 'Here!' Another time, on being surrounded by brigands outside Rome and ordered to identify himself, he replied as simply as a proud ancient Roman would have done: 'Stefano Colonna, a Roman citizen'.

In the long run, the Colonna had the better of Boniface. King Philip sent his legal adviser and Keeper of the Seals, Guillaume de Nogaret, to Italy. Together with Giacomo Colonna and Stefano's brother Cardinal Pietro, usually known as 'Sciarra', De Nogaret openly attacked Boniface at his summer residence in Anagni, south of Rome. Sciarra Colonna is said to have struck the pope in the face, and then humiliated him by making him ride out of the town sitting backwards on an ass. Soon after this the Colonna regained their lands and rebuilt their palaces and castles. For a family of such ancient tradition it was a minor incident.

When the Frenchman Pope Clement V (1305–14) was elected to the Holy See at Avignon under the influence of Philip the Fair, the Colonna fortunes rose again. Clement revoked the excommunications against them, named Stefano a senator, and gave him permission to rebuild their castle at Palestrina. A courageous, restless, and powerful man, it was he who then consolidated Colonna power, increased their lands and made them a major force in early fourteenth-century Italy. For much of his career he was involved in local power struggles with the Orsini and other great Roman families, which sometimes brimmed over into brief but violent warfare. In 1312 he was severely wounded in a particularly violent battle for the Capitoline hill, in which he fought with his brother Sciarra for the Emperor Arrigo VII — who wished to become King of Rome, as Pope Clement had promised him. The attempt failed, and after an ignominious imprisonment in Castel Sant'Angelo the Colonna were sent to their castles and ordered never again to enter Rome. 'Never' is however a dangerous word for a temporal power to use of such a dynasty as the Colonna, who already counted their history in centuries.

In 1326 he was again at the head of a force attacking the Capitol against the papal Vicar and Governor of Rome, who was unpopular both with the nobles and with the people. In the short-lived republic of the following year, a paradoxical situation developed in which the pope pleaded with Stefano to help the Church against the rebels while the people themselves unanimously demanded that Sciarra be their leader. King Ludwig of Bavaria was invited by Sciarra to accept the crown of Rome: when he set out on his ceremonial procession to St Peter's to accept the crown he departed from Palazzo Colonna. From this event dates the Colonna family's right to use a crown on the column in their escutcheon. The pope naturally excommunicated King Ludwig, but no one dared to mention the fact in Rome. Stefano's son, Jacopo, courageously defied the Bavarian king by reading the excommunication aloud in front of a large crowd. It was as a result of this action that Ludwig, furious with the Colonna and unable to attack them in their stronghold at Palestrina, named Pietro Randaccio as the anti-pope, giving him the name Nicholas V (1328–30).

But the day after King Ludwig departed from Rome, Stefano Colonna and his long-time adversary Bertoldo Orsini took the city in the name of the legitimate Pope John XXII. This episode was followed by a period of relative peace between the powerful Roman families. Yet it was while Stefano Colonna was away on a mission to obtain food supplies for the city in May 1347 that one of the strangest characters in Roman history, Cola da Rienzo, took advantage of his absence and declared Rome a republic with himself as Tribune. A convincing orator and reader of the Roman classics, the plebeian Cola sought to reinstate the ancient greatness of Rome. Beyond that, in a flash of prophetic genius which makes his short and blazing career one of the most exciting moments of the age, he proposed a union of all the states of Italy which could restore its ancient glory. Such fiery rhetoric, harnessed to a dictatorial desire for personal power, made him a dangerous enemy; and the combined forces of both Empire and papacy were soon ranged against him.

As it happened, the return of the nobles he had rebelled against was enough to ruin him. When Stefano came back to Rome he attended a banquet offered by Cola, at the end of which all the Roman patricians present were imprisoned. Condemned to death, they were reprieved at the last moment, probably after Cola was warned of the possible consequences of executing such powerful and popular men. With hindsight, it is clear that this was Cola's biggest error, since the patricians then attacked Rome with a force of seven hundred cavalry and four thousand foot soldiers led by Stefano Colonna in the name of the pope. The battle was lost, and Stefano's son Stefanello and grandson Giovanni were killed. Pietro Colonna, Lord of Gennazzano and nephew to Stefano, was killed by troops who followed the Colonna to Palestrina. But in a sense the war was won, since Cola da Rienzo's Republic soon came to an end. Stefano himself died the following year, supposedly as a result of the sorrow he felt for this loss of his son and grandson. But it is worth recalling that this remarkable man must have been in his eighties at the time.

Although much of his life was spent in exile or in internecine warfare with his Roman enemies, Stefano Colonna was no simple soldier. He must have been a man of considerable learning to have won the lasting esteem of Petrarch. Furthermore, he laid the basis for future Colonna power both through his military and diplomatic activity and in siring thirteen children by his wife Calceranda de' Insula.

THE COLONNA AND PETRARCH

The links between Petrarch (1304–78) and the Colonna family were of profound importance for the poet and humanist's life. It was probably during his period in Bologna from 1320 to 1326 that he came to the attention of Cardinal Giovanni Colonna and Bishop Giacomo Colonna. In 1326 he returned to his 'home' in Avignon where he had passed his childhood with his exiled Florentine father. He tells us in his *Letter to Posterity*, written many years later in 1373, that he was 'first courted by that very distinguished and noble family' the Colonna. Giacomo Colonna, then Bishop of Lombez, who took him to Gascony to participate in the summer conversations of his court.

Then Petrarch was taken up by Cardinal Giovanni Colonna, who employed him as household chaplain. In his own words we may see how this family was regarded by the man universally acknowledged as the first man of letters of his age:

> . . . I passed many years in the house of Giacomo's brother, Cardinal Giovanni Colonna, not as if he were my lord and master, but rather my father, or better, a most affectionate brother — nay, it was as if I were in my own home. . . On my return from that journey [to Paris] I went to Rome, which I had since my infancy ardently desired to visit. There I soon came to venerate Stefano, the noble head of the family of the Colonna, like some ancient hero, and was in turn treated by him in every respect like a son.

This close relationship with the Colonna family was to last for the remainder of his life.

In 1335 he travelled to Italy by sea with Giacomo Colonna, landing at Civitavecchia and staying first with Agnesina Colonna at her estate in Capranica, north of Rome. Stefano the Younger provided an armed escort into Rome through the troubled area. Then, on 8 April 1341, Petrarch was crowned Poet Laureate on the order of King Robert the Wise of Naples. The king had failed in his attempt to convince Petrarch to accept the honour in Naples, so the ceremony took place in Rome. He was decorated with laurels in a special ceremony at the Capitol. The crown should have been posed by the great Stefano Colonna, but as he was unable to be in Rome his son Stefanello performed the task. The younger Colonna also recited an oration in honour of the guest, and afterwards offered a sumptuous banquet for the poet at Palazzo Colonna — which in those days was visible from the Capitol.

The following year Pope Benedict XII died in Avignon, and was succeeded by Clement VI. The Romans had been attempting for decades to have the papacy returned to their city from France, and on this occasion it was Stefano Colonna and Petrarch who travelled to Avignon as ambassadors of the Roman people. But even the rhetoric of the world's greatest living writer failed to convince the new pope to transfer his seat. He did however nominate Stefano Colonna as his Vicar in Rome. When Colonna left to begin his return journey to Rome, Petrarch wrote a sonnet to honour him in which he develops the play on words between family and an architectural column:

> Glorious Colonna, on whom rests
> Our hope and great Latin name;

In another sonnet, written during one of the frequent wars with the Orsini family, Petrarch encourages Stefano not to leave his sword but to follow fortune. In this way, he argues, prophetically as it turns out, Stefano Colonna will achieve lasting fame and honour through the centuries. Other sonnets and verse letters were dedicated to Giovanni and Giacomo Colonna, while Giacomo was one of the many contemporaries who replied to Petrarch in sonnet form.

POPE MARTIN V
(1417–31)

Oddone Colonna was born in 1365 in Gennazzano, near Rome, grandson to Pietro, the senator who was killed by Cola da Rienzo's troops. He became Pope Martin V two years after the end of the Great Schism which had seen the existence of a double papacy, with claimants in both Rome and Avignon. As member of a prominent Roman family, and descendant of Stefano, he had for years sustained the policy of bringing the papacy back to Rome.

Throughout the fourteenth century the aristocratic families of Rome were engaged in a futile power struggle, while the city deteriorated around them. The internecine strife between the Colonna, Orsini, and Frangipani turned city and province into a permanent battleground. When the popes built a palace in Avignon, artists and courtiers went there in search of patronage while Rome was in decline physically as well as spiritually. Churches were pillaged and huge palaces left to decay. The schismatic Roman popes did little to glorify their city, since their energy was absorbed by the struggle with Avignon. During that century King Ladislas of Naples plundered the city and did as he pleased, while the anti-pope John XXIII was so corrupt that he was accused of incest, sodomy, and murder and could not be expected to serve as an example.

This decline was halted by Martin V. He became pope at the Council of Constance, resisted attempts to move the papacy back to Avignon or even to Germany, and after two years in Florence managed to restore it to Rome in 1420, after more than a century. Nine years later he obtained the definitive renunciation of the anti-pope Clement VIII, ending the Schism.

He administered both Church and Rome well, but above all, through a combination of his own personality and the prestige of his family name, he brought peace to the city. As robberies and violence were curbed, the population slowly increased. Above all, with the return of the papacy came the pilgrim trade which was vital for the Roman economy. With economic improvement merchants and international traders also returned. The turn-about was not perfect, and corrupt popes following Martin — like the Borgia pope Alexander VI — threatened to undo what had been

Tomb of Oddone Colonna, Pope Martin V, in St John Lateran, Rome.

done. Yet in an important sense the process of revival was started by this pope from an indigenous patrician dynasty, and the Rome of the Renaissance that students and travellers today recognize began to take shape. Within a century much of the city had been rebuilt, with new streets and such achievements as the Sistine Chapel and plans for the new St Peter's. Popes from other Italian dynasties like the Della Rovere, Medici, and Farnese brought new prestige to the papacy. The popes were neither scholars nor saints, but worldly-wise politicians and excellent administrators.

Martin V himself managed to do little more than refurbish some of the Roman churches, establish a customs house for new trade, and restore aqueducts — including the one which takes water to the Trevi Fountain, where he built an earlier fountain long since destroyed. At that time the Vatican had become virtually uninhabitable, so he established the papal residence in Palazzo Colonna. He also increased Colonna power by rational distribution of their lands between family members. Similarly, he encouraged them to strengthen their castles by exempting them from the prohibitive salt and hearth taxes he imposed to raise money for rebuilding the city.

In the portrait in the Galleria Colonna in Rome he seems to be an arrogant and unpleasant man, while in the huge statue made for the cathedral in Milan his strength — perhaps more idealized — seems benign. By all accounts he was a kind and gentle man, humble in his bearing and modest in his habits. The inscription on his tomb in the basilica of S. Giovanni in Laterano is a just recognition of his revival of the Roman papacy and preparation for the glories of Renaissance Rome: *temporum suorum felicitas* — his were times of happiness. He is remembered as the restorer of the papacy, but is reproved by historians for missing the opportunity to do more in the way of reforms which might have avoided the trauma of the following century.

THE COLONNA *CONDOTTIERI*

While the Colonna family did not gain their original power from *condottieri* like so many other Italian dynasties, they did produce many well-known *condottieri* in the course of centuries.

Giovanni Colonna (*c.*1350–1417), of the line of Palestrina, fought with other Colonna against Boniface VIII but then fought for the Ghibellines against members of his own family. His son Ludovico (*c.*1390–1436) fought for Naples under Braccio da Montone against Muzio Attendolo Sforza. It was he who took Braccio's body to Rome after the disastrous battle at L'Aquila recounted in the history of the Sforza dynasty. Later he also fought for Filippo Maria Visconti, and was murdered by a soldier in the pay of the family enemies, the Orsini. A less well-known Colonna *condottiere* was Giovanni's nephew Lorenzo (*c.*1410–*c.*1450), who was excommunicated together with Braccio da Montone by Pope Eugenius IV. It is interesting to see how he raised an army under extreme pressure in 1436 by the simple expedient of taking one able-bodied man per house from the Colonna feuds in and near Palestrina.

Members of the family who came to the fore in the late fifteenth and early sixteenth century were engaged in the struggle for possession of the Italian peninsula which engaged the French and Spanish kings. Of these the most important were Prospero, son of Antonio, Prince of Salerno of the principal line of Paliano, and his cousin Fabrizio, son of Odoardo Count of Celano and Duke of Amalfi.

PROSPERO
(1425–1523)

Prospero was born near Velletri, south of Rome, and gained his first military experience fighting against the Orsini family in defence of family possessions. The story of the constant reversals of fortune in his life is symptomatic of the endemic insecurity of Italy at that time. He first became involved in the civil war which resulted from Pope Sixtus IV's ambitious nephew Girolamo Riario's attempt to take Romagna as his personal fiefdom. As the result of his opposition to Girolamo his lands and castles in and near Rome were confiscated by the pope, like many Colonna before him. But before he lost everything Sixtus IV died and he was able to recover his lands.

But it was with Pope Alexander VI (1492–1503), Rodrigo Borgia, that Prospero's real problems began. He had been an ally of Alexander's mortal enemy, Cardinal Giuliano della Rovere — the future Pope Julius II and patron of Michelangelo — and was consequently declared a rebel and imprisoned in the papal prison at Castel Sant'Angelo. Finally, with his cousin Fabrizio and the troops of Charles VIII of France he entered Rome as victor in 1495. He then followed the French king in the conquest of Naples but risked losing all his lands once again as the new pope attempted to create a state for his notorious nephew Cesare Borgia. This brought the two Colonna cousins closer to the Neapolitan king, until Naples itself was taken by Louis XII of France and both Prospero and Fabrizio again finished in prison — this time in Naples. As soon as he learned this, Pope Alexander confiscated their castles near Rome.

When Alexander died, Cesare Borgia feared the return of the Colonna and Orsini to Rome and contrived an ambiguous alliance with Prospero, who thus regained his Roman property. His triumph was completed a few years later when the Spanish viceroy Consalvo de Cordova arrested Cesare Borgia and charged his 'ally' Prospero Colonna with the duty of escorting him to Spain. Legend states that he refused to look his prisoner straight in the face for fear of humiliating him.

Julius II tried to pacify the Roman families, first by giving his niece Lucrezia Gora in marriage to Prospero's nephew Marcantonio I, then by arranging a *Pax Romana* between the disputing families in 1511. Prospero's career, at the age of sixty, had been less glorious than that of his cousin Fabrizio, and did not improve when he joined the army of Maximilian Sforza as Captain-General of the Milanese forces. He lost several opportunities to achieve success, leading the contemporary historian Guicciardini to describe him as a soldier who tried to 'defend his position without exposing himself to the danger of battle unless it was absolutely neces-

Stefano Sciarra Colonna, by Bronzino.

sary'. But he had one notable victory when he took Milan from the French in 1521, with the help of the Marquis of Pescara, Vittoria Colonna's husband. Old age brought new successes, but did not manage to remove the stigma attached to his name by Guicciardini. While most *condottieri* were renowned for their fearlessness in attacking, Prospero stands out as a *condottiere* who avoided all risks. Yet his career conforms to the reality of war more than the legendary exploits of the earlier *condottieri*. It is interesting to speculate whether Prospero's apparent 'failure' to measure up to exacting standards is a reflection of the larger amount of documentary evidence available.

Prospero is pictured with an exceptionally high forehead, denoting great sense of strength, a pallid face, thick arching eyebrows, and a short pointed Spanish-style beard. His eyes were said to move slowly but menacingly, and although he was of a great family it was thought that his gifts were personal rather than inherited.

FABRIZIO
(*c.*1450–1520)

Fabrizio was originally destined by his family for the Church, but rebelled and fought with his cousin Prospero in the perennial wars with the Orsini. He soon gained an impressive reputation, but was still under pressure to assume his ecclesiastical career. In order to avoid this destiny, in 1481 he travelled south to fight against the Turks at Otranto for King Alfonso of Aragon. Soon after this he passed into the service of Charles VIII against the Aragonese, a move which was the key to his future career since his life was intimately bound up with the Spanish kings and their viceroys in Naples.

Fabrizio married Agnese Montefeltro of the ruling family of Urbino, but established his home in Naples when he associated himself with the Spanish rulers of the city, and became a close friend of the Spanish general Alfonso d'Avalos, Marquis of Pescara. It was to cement this allegiance that marriage was arranged between Fabrizio's daughter Vittoria and Alfonso's nineteen-year-old son Ferrante (who later became Marquis of Pescara) at the end of the same campaign. Fabrizio's loyalty was repaid by King Ferdinand with the high office of Grand Contestabile. He died in 1520, and was buried with full honours in the family tomb at Paliano. The Emperor Charles V paid his family the special honour of elevating his son Ascanio to the same official position in Naples 'for the affection and loyalty which he and his family have shown towards our crown'.

MARCANTONIO I
(c.1480–1522)

The Colonna were at that time divided into three major branches: the princes of Paliano (from whom the present Colonna descend), Palestrina, and Zagarolo. Marcantonio belonged to the Zagarolo line. He too was excommunicated by the Borgia pope Alexander VI, but managed to evade the persecutions inflicted upon the Colonna by Cesare Borgia. He learned the soldier's trade with the Spanish viceroy Consalvo of Cordova and first came into prominence fighting under Fabrizio. From that moment he undertook an independent career, and at the age of twenty-six was fighting for Florence as a *condottiere* with seventy men under his command.

His courage and ferocity are apparent in the portrait in the Galleria Colonna, dressed in full Spanish armour. But his military career was short and tragic, demonstrating once again the facility with which *condottieri* of this period were able to change sides. In fifteen years he fought for Spain against Naples, for Florence against Pisa, for Pope Julius II against Ferrara, for the Emperor Maximilian against the French and Venetians, and finally for Francis I against Milan.

His fighting life was truncated by a tragic misunderstanding which resulted from these constant changes. While combating under his uncle Prospero against the French, he was taken prisoner and was so struck by the good treatment he received that he decided to fight for the French King. He was sent on a reconnaissance mission to spy out the enemy's defences and was struck by a culverin, a kind of primitive hand-gun. The irony in his death was that the shot was fired by his own uncle Prospero, who was naturally shocked by his inadvertent action. Marcantonio was succeeded by four daughters, one of whom, Lucrezia, built a chapel in honour of the Assumption in the church of Trinità dei Monti at the top of the Spanish Steps in Rome. It contains a curious and little-known painting of the Assumption by Daniele da Volterra, a pupil of Michelangelo — who himself appears in the painting.

VITTORIA
(1492-1547)

This tenuous link between the Colonna and Michelangelo was made solid and indelible by the friendship of Vittoria Colonna and the artist. She was the daughter of Fabrizio Colonna, and the only woman for whom Michelangelo seems to have approached the feeling of profound love. She was married to Ferrante d'Avalos as part of her father's policy of alliance with the Spanish viceroy. Both were children at the time — she was two — so the marriage was actually celebrated in 1509. She seems to have lived a happy life as Marchesina of Pescara until her husband's death, which she mourned in some moving poems, in 1525. From then on she spent much of her time in spiritual retirement in convents at Orvieto, Viterbo, and Rome. Throughout her life she remained in close contact with the court of her Montefeltro mother at Urbino. Even in the formal portrait in the Colonna Gallery in Rome her eyes are piercing and intelligent and suggest her strong character.

She was a fine poetess, leaving about three hundred poems, mostly sonnets, at her death. Although her poetry is often considered monotonous taken as a whole, there are many good sonnets and some passages of excellent poetry in them. Before meeting Michelangelo she maintained literary friendships with Pietro Bembo, the foremost literary figure of the day, the poet Giovanni Guidiccioni, and also Baldassare Castiglione. She was celebrated as an intellectual hostess in early sixteenth-century Rome. It was due to the visit of the little-known Portuguese artist Francisco d'Ollanda to a Sunday meeting arranged by her that we have a unique record of the informal conversation of Michelangelo. Such statements as 'I dare affirm that any artist . . .who has nothing singular, eccentric, or at least reputed to be so, in his person will never become a superior talent' provide interesting insights not only into his own personality but into ideas about artists at the time.

They met in 1536, when he was a famous artist of sixty-one about to begin his fresco of the Last Judgement and she was forty-four. Their 'love' was profound and reciprocal but almost certainly platonic. She was a deeply religious woman, and used her influence as a Colonna in an attempt to reform the Church at a time when other forces were working in the same direction. She is thought to have influenced Michelangelo's ideas about religion, which shifted from the neo-Platonism of earlier works like the Sistine Chapel ceiling to the more specifically Christian, dramatic, and horrifying images of the *Last Judgement*. Both of them had been influenced by the fiery preaching of Savonarola. Although the two fresco masterpieces of Michelangelo are in a single and relatively small building, they have little in common and might appear to have been painted by different men. Giorgio Vasari tells us in his *Lives of the Artists* that she often travelled from Viterbo, where she lived, to visit Michelangelo.

Michelangelo made three paintings for her and wrote some of his finest sonnets. Of the approximately three hundred sonnets, madrigals, and verse fragments we know of, thirty-seven were certainly inspired by or dedicated to Vittoria Colonna. In one of the sonnets written on the occasion of her death he refers to her verse

Vittoria Colonna, by Pontormo.

as 'sweet, light, and sacred inks'. One of the best known of all Michelangelo's sonnets is '*Non ha l'ottimo artista alcun concetto*', dedicated to her. It is given here in the translation by John Addington Symonds:

> The best of artists hath no thought to show
> Which the rough stone in its superfluous shell
> Does not include: to break the marble spell
> Is all the hand that serves the brain can do.
> The ill I shun, the good I seek, even so
> In thee, fair lady, proud, ineffable,
> Lies hidden: but the art I wield so well
> Works adverse to my wish, and lays me low.
> Therefore not love, nor thy transcendent face,
> Nor cruelty, nor fortune, nor disdain,
> Cause my mischance, nor fate, nor destiny;
> Since in thy heart thou carriest death and grace
> Enclosed together, and my worthless brain
> Can draw forth only death to feed on me.

The assertion that beauty exists somehow imprisoned within the marble is central to an understanding of Michelangelo's sculpture.

Apart from those devoted to the death of her husband, her own sonnets were as religious in inspiration and theme as we may imagine the lady herself to have been. In one supremely beautiful sonnet she likens herself to a hungry fledgling in search of the divine sun of God. It is written in the Petrarchan style, with the delightful word of Provençal origin *augellin* which 'bird' does not really convey. The syntax is complex but clear and always in perfect control as the argument develops in this translation by L.R. Lind:

> Like some small hungry bird that sees and hears
> Its mother's wings beat round about him when
> She brings him food, and he who loves her then
> And food as well, perks up with joy, and cheers,
> And in his nest he chafes and struggles, peers
> About, desiring to follow the good hen,
> Singing his thanks when she flies off again,
> As if his tongue might talk he then appears;
> So I whenever the warm and living ray
> Of the divine sun, where I feed my heart,
> Shines out with more than its accustomed light,
> I move my pen urged on love's inward way;
> Without perceiving quite in whole or part
> The things I say, the praise of love I write.

This fine expression of religious feeling, reaching a level of mysticism in verse which may be compared to more celebrated mystical poets like St John of the Cross, is the best possible testament to the character of Vittoria Colonna.

MARCANTONIO II
(1535–84)

Ascanio Colonna, the surviving son of Fabrizio and brother to Vittoria, lost his own son Fabrizio when he was only sixteen years old. Thus his second son Marcantonio became sole heir to the Colonna family name and lands. In order to guarantee the line and to achieve an alliance with the family's long-standing rivals and enemies the Orsini, he was — against his own desire — married to Felice Orsini in 1552.

He was one of the greatest soldiers of his age, and was publicly praised by such men as Duke Cosimo de' Medici and the Emperor Charles V during the Tuscan campaigns of 1554. Yet he was a humane and loving father, whose greatest distress came from the unhappy marriage of his daughter Costanza to Francesco Sforza, Marquis of Caravaggio. In a desperate plea to her father which portrays sixteenth-century women as anything but weak and fatalistic, Costanza wrote 'If you don't free me from this house and [my husband] I shall kill myself and not care whether I lose my soul with my life'. Marcantonio supplicated his friend Cardinal Borromeo to intercede with the pope in order to bring the marriage to an end. These letters, and the cardinal's replies to the Colonna family, present the plight of Costanza in a humane and quite extraordinarily modern light. Unfortunately, however, the only legal means to dissolve the marriage was by claiming nonconsummation, and while negotiations went ahead Costanza became pregnant. Thus she was condemned to remain with the Marquis, who, it seems, treated her better in later years.

On another occasion, Marcantonio Colonna was thought to have saved Rome. When Cardinal Giovanni Pietro Carafa was elected to the Holy See as Paul IV (1555-9) he strengthened the new Roman Inquisition — founded by the Farnese Pope Paul III at his own instigation — in order to reform the Church. He invented the celebrated Index of printed books. He had Inquisition informers spy on the private behaviour of prominent Roman families and insisted on quick and exemplary punishment for the slightest deviation from doctrine. Thus he alienated men of learning with the Index, the clergy with his harsh reforms, and the people with his fanatical zeal and cruelty. This unpopularity resulted in popular riots when it became known that the ageing pope was on his deathbed. Prisoners were released by storming citizens from both city and Inquisition prisons. A note in the Vatican Secret Archives describes the scene as follows:

> At this hour, that is, midnight, a courier arrived with news of the death of the Pope. This has given great joy to all. Those who had had statues made of him were to break them into pieces as soon as they knew he was dead. Then they set free from prison all those who were there because of the Inquisition, burning documents and court records.

Then the people moved towards the headquarters of the Inquisition at the Dominican convent of S. Maria sopra Minerva with the intent of sacking it. Had it not been for the intervention of Marcantonio there is no telling what damage they might have wrought.

Having burnt the headquarters of the Inquisition, men now arrived thirsty for blood with burning torches and swords. They were determined to burn down the church of S. Maria sopra Minerva and kill the friars inside. But as they approached the church Marcantonio Colonna appeared on horseback with four relatives. None was wearing armour, and their swords were sheathed; moreover, the people were sympathetic towards the Colonna since it was known that they had suffered as much as any family from Paul IV's confiscations. It would be interesting to know the words he used to convince them, speaking slowly and calmly. Presently they left the scene, content with what they had already done, while Colonna and his men rode through the city all night to ensure no further damage was done. Once again in the history of this remarkable family, the safety and integrity of Rome was placed before all else.

The succession of Pius IV to the hated Paul IV restored the Colonna fortunes, and Marcantonio found himself in a position of great favour. He was given honours by Pius IV, and at that time he became friendly with the papal nephews Carlo and Federico Borromeo, and married his eldest son Fabrizio to Carlo's sister Anna.

The Battle of Lepanto.

In 1560 King Philip II of Spain conferred upon him the Order of the Golden Fleece, and in the same year he became Deputy of the Kingdom of Naples. It was in 1569 that Pope Pius V issued the diploma raising Paliano to a principality in favour of Marcantonio and his first-born male descendants. From that *motu proprio* date the present titles of Prince and Duke of Paliano.

Marcantonio II's proudest moment came during the defence of Europe at the Battle of Lepanto, which was the last naval battle fought with galleys. Suleiman the Magnificent (1494-1566), who had ruled wisely and in grand style over the Ottoman Empire, had been succeeded by his son Selim. When he attacked Cyprus, Pope Pius V answered the Venetian appeal for help by demanding support from all the Christian princes. Only Philip II of Spain agreed, ordering Gian'Andrea Doria of Genova to command his navy; Pius himself was forced to improvise a navy. Marcantonio Colonna was to command it, and without waiting for the twelve Venetian galleys promised he went ahead and prepared and armed twelve ships in Ancona. Commanders of the galleys were to be Prospero and Pompeo Colonna, together with other Roman noblemen.

When they arrived in Cyprus both Nicosia and Famagusta were under siege. While Doria argued with the Colonna and suggested they retire to Sicily since the winter was coming, Selim's men attacked Nicosia, killing forty thousand and imprisoning fifteen thousand people. After retreating to Rome, the papal forces sailed again under the leadership of John of Austria. From Corfu these forces reached the Turkish fleet in the mouth of the Gulf of Lepanto on 7 October 1571. After playing an important role in the great victory over Selim's navy in his ship the *Capitana* Marcantonio Colonna distinguished himself in refusing to accept the spoils of victory. He argued that they should be given to the Church, and set sail for Messina. The victory at Lepanto was celebrated in the manner of ancient Rome. With eight days of constant drum beats, arquebus shots, and banquets.

Shortly after this Marcantonio was appointed Viceroy of Sicily by Philip II, bringing him ever closer to the Spanish throne. He died in Spain in 1584. His career, like that of the Colonna *condottieri* in earlier centuries, was exemplary and points to the paradox inherent in Colonna successes. Since their ultimate loyalty was to the city of Rome, this family was never able to establish itself in an independent state like many other Italian dynasties. In Rome it was impossible to compete with the pope, and even the pope himself had to bow before such powerful foreign lords

Map showing site and battle formations at Lepanto.

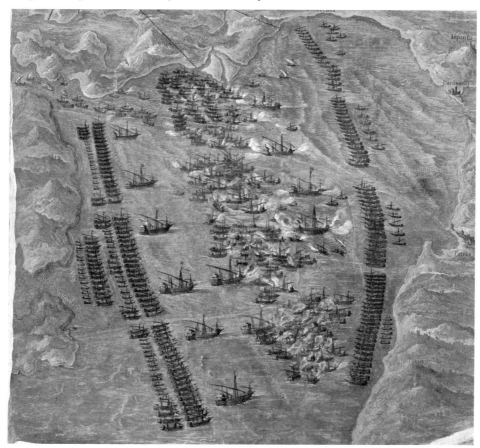

as the Spanish kings. Furthermore, successive members of the dynasty seemed unprepared to look beyond Rome, which with the temporary exception of Naples remained the emotional centre of Colonna life for over a millennium. This is perhaps the reason why the Colonna are amongst the least known of the major dynasties of Italy, although their family history is second to none.

THE COLONNA FAMILY TODAY

Ancient loyalties still govern the Colonna family, which forms part of the Vatican nobility, known in Rome as the 'black aristocracy'. Prince Aspreno Colonna was the last man to bear the title Assistant to the Papal Throne, abolished in the 1960s by Pope Paul VI when he ended the tradition of noble guards as part of an attempt to modernize the Church. This title entailed the privileges of accompanying the pope on formal occasions and receiving the incense and *pax tecum* immediately after the Vice-Chamberlain of the Holy Roman Church. The Assistants wore splendid seventeenth-century Spanish-style costumes.

Aspreno Colonna belonged to the line of the Princes of Paliano, one of the Colonna's most ancient feuds which has remained in the family since the times of Piero Colonna in the twelfth century. But two collateral lines have also survived to this day: the Princes of Stigliano, a Neapolitan branch of the family, represented by Don Lorenzo Filippo Colonna; and the more remote Barberini-Colonna di Sciarra family, whose princely title expired with the death of Don Urbano during the Second World War. He was survived by his wife and two daughters.

The bearer of thirty-four other noble titles apart from the main ones of Prince and Duke of Paliano, Aspreno Colonna died in October 1987, saddened by the double death of his wife and mother within two months of each other in 1984. His funeral was celebrated in grand style in the family church of SS. Apostoli, built onto the family palace in Rome. According to the ancient custom of placing the coffin of one who was high in life in a low position, his coffin rested on the floor *more nobilium* during the funeral ceremony, guarded by four pages in livery holding waist-high candles at the corners of the carpet on which the coffin lay. The funeral was attended by the entire Roman nobility, including representatives of two of the families who fought for power against the Colonna in the Middle Ages, the Gaetani and the Massimo. Other guests were Beatrice de Bourbon, the Infanta of Spain, the Grand Master of the Order of the Knights of Malta, and several government ministers. The ceremony included the public reading of a telegram of condolence from Pope John Paul II, who was officially represented by Monsignor Casaroli, the Vatican Secretary of State. Prince Aspreno was buried at Paliano.

In many ways Prince Aspreno Colonna's death marked the end of an era. Under the severe guardianship of his mother Princess Isabella (1889–1984), who was born Isabella Elena Sursok of the Lebanese noble family, the Colonna had maintained ancient traditions. She gained notoriety in the 1970s for her loyalty to the Church and her opposition to the members of the 'black aristocracy' who supported the heretical views of the French Cardinal Lefebvre. She presided over difficult questions of etiquette, which with so many families of ancient lineage and extreme formality has always presented problems in Rome — in no case more so than in the rivalry between the Colonna and Orsini families. It was taken so seriously that within living memory no host would dare invite the heads of these two families to dinner together, given the impossibility of deciding who should have precedence. In the early fourteenth century Stefano Colonna's son killed Bertoldo Orsini in an ambush, and the Orsini family retaliated by killing a Colonna boy on the steps of a Roman church. Thus a feud which began seven hundred years ago persisted into the twentieth century. Since the death of her husband Prince Marcantonio in 1947 Princess Isabella maintained the prestige of the Colonna family, and was regarded as the doyenne of Roman aristocratic society and arbiter of taste. Her influence may be perceived in the medieval ritual of her son's funeral, but it seems that such tradition — bordering on rigidity — is destined to fade with the new bearer of the princely title.

The present Prince Marcantonio Colonna (b. 1948) has been something of a black sheep in the family. In 1974, against the express wishes of his family, he married a tobacconist's daughter from Perugia, and has had little to do with the family since then. He was ostentatiously absent at his father's funeral, which the other three children attended dutifully. But he had already guaranteed the continuity of the line through his son Don Giovanni Andrea Colonna, born in 1975, approximately one thousand years after the first recorded Colonna.

4

THE SFORZA

The Sforza were one of Europe's greatest families, providing an exemplar of the Renaissance prince in Lodovico il Moro. We have seen in an earlier chapter how the *condottiere* Francesco Sforza managed to supplant his paymaster Filippo Maria Visconti, marry his daughter Bianca Maria and then become Duke of Milan himself. Yet Francesco was only the second 'Sforza', since the line began with his father Muzio Attendolo. Unlike many of the other Italian dynasties, there was never any attempt by the Sforza to legitimize their power or glorify family history by seeking noble or imperial ancestors in previous centuries. The name itself was new. In fact Muzio's life may serve as an example of how in the context of early fifteenth-century Italy a simple soldier was able to establish the basis for a powerful political dynasty.

He belonged to a wealthy warrior family from the village of Cotignola, north of Faenza in Romagna, a region sandwiched for centuries between the great powers of Venice, Empire, and Church and fragmented into feuds which were constantly at war with one another. This geographical and historical necessity seems often to have been harnessed with a natural propensity for warfare, and produced many of the great *condottieri*. Other dynasties of the Romagna such as the Malatesta of Rimini and the Montefeltro of Urbino also owed their original eminence to *condottieri*.

The Attendolo family was no exception. Several of Muzio's brothers achieved renown as *condottieri*, and no fewer than fifteen of the twenty-one children in his family were professional soldiers. Moreover, this war-like trait was not reserved to male members of the family, since Muzio's mother Elisa dei Petrascini was herself descended from another warrior family and was known to fight side by side with her menfolk in the case of need. From an early age, the children were prepared for the life of campaigns and battles. An early historian tells us that the walls

Opposite *Battista Sforza, by Piero Della Francesca.*

of the Attendolo home were hung with breastplates and shields, while the sons were brought up in the rough traditions of the neighbourhood, disdaining comfort and luxury.

Born in 1369, at the age of fifteen Muzio Attendolo was recruited by the *condottiere* Boldrino da Panicale. Legend has it that in order to decide he threw his axe into a tree: if it stuck in the tree, he would join Boldrino; if not, then he would stay in Cotignola. The axe stuck. After four years spent learning the trade he joined the Company of St George, led by the most famous of the early *condottieri* Alberico da Barbiano — who came from a nearby village.

In that turbulent period of Italian history, when the Renaissance was just beginning in the humanities and arts, a great *condottiere* was a man of considerable power and importance, since the welfare of the new cities vying for territorial power depended on their success. Muzio served for a dozen or more years with Alberico, learning from him the trade and secrets of warfare. At that time Braccio da Montone, who was from a village called Montone near Perugia, was also serving with Alberico. For the rest of their lives Sforza and Braccio would be rivals for the name of Italy's greatest general, and they were destined to die on the same campaign. Although his real name was Andrea Braccio da Montone he was nicknamed Fortebraccio, or 'Strong-arm', and is usually known as Braccio da Montone. Muzio's other great rival was the *condottiere* known as Tartaglia. For much of that time with Alberico they were on contract to Gian Galeazzo Visconti.

He was renowned for his personal strength and bravery, and expected that his men should follow his example. It was as a result of his strength that he gained his nickname, which was to become the family name of his descendants. He was said to be able to bend a horseshoe, and to be able to jump into the saddle fully armed. One day he was quarrelling over some booty which the Company had won during a battle, and when summoned to explain his behaviour to the leader he replied arrogantly. During their discussion it was Alberico himself who invented the nickname 'Sforza' when he made a joke about Muzio trying to 'force' him into submission too. From that moment he was always known as Sforza, the unusual fact in this case being that the nickname became the accepted family name.

In the Company of St George, Sforza fought *for* the Milanese armies of Gian Galeazzo Visconti; but when he was established as a *condottiere* and created his own band he also fought against them. On one occasion he defended Perugia from Gian Galeazzo's ambitions. However the Visconti knew how important it was to have the best men on their side, and Sforza was later persuaded to change sides again by the simple expedient of a huge salary increase. Yet both Sforza, and later his son Francesco, were recognized to be so strong that they were potential enemies, and in fact he once again turned against the Visconti after being literally kicked out of Milan.

Later he fought for Florence against Pisa, for Ferrara against Parma, and then both for and against the papacy. It was as the result of his services to Pope John XXIII that he gained the lordship of Cotignola. Finally, he saw service with the Anjou King of Naples, Ladislas (1386–1414). By then Sforza had married Antonia

Salimbeni, who had given birth to Bosio; but he had already had seven children by his mistress Lucia, who was not of noble birth. His eldest son was Francesco, who was now given to Ladislas as a hostage in guarantee of his father's good conduct. The King of Naples took a liking to the young boy and looked after him well, giving him the title of Count and the possession of several small towns. The father was less fortunate: jealousies and rivalries for the throne of Naples caused him to be thrown into prison when he was thought to be too close to Queen Joan II (1414–35), Ladislas's sister and successor.

The remainder of Sforza's career was passed in southern and central Italy, where he became embroiled in battles with his old friends and rivals, Braccio and Piccinino, in the internecine struggle between the Houses of Anjou and Aragon for the Kingdom of Naples. This dispute had lasted since the end of the Hohenstaufen dynasty in 1266: Charles of Anjou, brother of Louis IX of France, had been offered the Kingdom by the pope and had killed the last Hohenstaufen Emperor Manfred; but he never conquered Sicily, especially after the celebrated revolt known as the Sicilian Vespers in 1282. Then Peter III of Aragon had been offered the throne by the Sicilians, and for over a century the two royal houses, one French and one Spanish, had contended the United Kingdom of Naples and Sicily.

In a minor action which was ultimately part of that struggle, in 1424, Braccio da Montone, who was then serving Alfonso of Aragon and bore the new title of Prince of Capua, was besieging the city of L'Aquila in the mountains of the northern part of the Kingdom of Naples. It appears that he aimed to create for himself a new state in central Italy, possibly stretching from L'Aquila to Perugia. Other *condottieri* such as Piccinino and Gattamelata were with him on this campaign. The siege had lasted for months until the people of L'Aquila managed to send messages to the Queen, who publicly repudiated Braccio and declared that Sforza was to replace him. Sforza, together with his sons Francesco and Michele and their companies, went to the relief of the city against his old rival. In this campaign the rivalry that had divided Italy between Sforzeschi and Braccheschi for years finally came to a head with tragic results.

Braccio travelled eastwards towards the Adriatic Sea to meet Sforza, who was at that time near the town of Lanciano. The armies met there, but did not fight; they moved northwards along the coast towards Pescara. There, on 4 January 1424, in the River Aterno which flows into the Adriatic after passing through L'Aquila in the mountains, Muzio Attendolo was drowned in an absurd accident. One of his men was in distress in the water as they were fording the river, which was rough from a wintry storm out to sea, and he had bent down from the saddle to save him. Sforza himself then fell from the saddle: there was little chance of survival because he was wearing full armour. Thus, he died an ignominious death after a long career as a *condottiere*; ironically, his once-friend and later rival Braccio da Montone also died in his attempt to take the city of L'Aquila, killed by a local nobleman called Antonuccio Camponeschi.

Although Muzio Attendolo was a tough man and born soldier, brought up without the wealth and cultivation of the great princely houses of the time, he seems to have been intelligent and perceptive. Although not learned, he enjoyed reading the classical historians, and paid a translator generously to make versions of the Roman historian Sallust and of the writings of Caesar. He especially enjoyed the *Life of Charlemagne*, which he often cited as an example during conversation. He was an excellent leader of men and commanded loyalty at a time when such a quality was easily swayed by offers of money. He was generous with his friends and followers, but showed no mercy with enemies or traitors; in battle, he always tried to fight for a just cause and to avoid the more pernicious aspects of warfare such as plunder and rape. His simple rules for life are summed up in his supposed advice to Francesco, which is reminiscent of the kind of folk wisdom passed on by King Lear's Fool: never touch the wife of another man, never beat a servant or comrade, and never ride a hard-mouthed horse. He retained the simple tastes in food and clothes of his youth, and, although his grandson Lodovico excelled him in worldly fame and patronage Muzio 'Sforza' Attendolo was in many ways the greatest and most interesting of the dynasty.

Yet he remained a *condottiere*. Without the political subtlety — which handicapped him in his dealings with the Neapolitan court — and long-term vision of the men he fought for, it seems that he never dreamed of establishing his own state. It was his two sons, Francesco and Alessandro, who laid the foundations for later Sforza power and the control of the Duchy of Milan.

FRANCESCO I
(1401–66)

Francesco took the place of his father as leader of Queen Joan's army, and won the city of L'Aquila from Braccio da Montone in the summer of 1424. That victory gained him military renown throughout Italy, and for the next twenty-six years he served as a *condottiere* mainly in the army of Filippo Maria Visconti, Duke of Milan. His brother Alessandro became Lord of Pesaro, in the Marches, where his descendants continued to rule until 1512; Francesco himself was to wait much longer for his own state, which was to be the foundation of all future Sforza power and wealth.

We have seen that Filippo Maria Visconti was a physically unprepossessing and weak man, hiding himself from public view because of his ugliness and unable to mount a horse because of his gross obesity. This was a serious handicap at a time when military leadership meant physically leading troops into battle and loyalty was gained by demonstrating oneself to be superior in every sense. Thus he was forced to turn for assistance to the most renowned *condottieri* of the time, who could fulfil this military role according to his own political strategy. Yet Francesco Sforza's value was perhaps even greater than this, since he had won the friendship and admiration of such men as Cosimo de' Medici in Florence and Federico da Montefeltro in Urbino. But although his role under the Visconti was prestigious, his loyalty depended on satisfactory financial reward just like that of other *condot-*

Francesco Sforza, by Bonifacio Bembo.

tieri. He fought *mainly* for the Visconti and Milan, but also against them on several occasions. Like his peers, he was always willing to serve other masters in the complex and ever-shifting patterns of loyalties of fifteenth-century Italy if the conditions were right.

Eventually, after a decision by Filippo Maria which was to have consequences beyond his wildest imagination, Francesco married Bianca, one of Filippo's illegitimate daughters, in an alliance that was to prove of enormous importance to him and provide a continuity between the Visconti and Sforza dynasties. With the hand of his sixteen-year-old bride came the city of Cremona and the frontier town of Pontremoli as part of her dowry. The forty-year-old *condottiere* and his child-bride were married in the little church of S. Sigismond just outside Cremona, and afterwards entered the city in ceremony. Bianca Maria was a full-blooded Visconti and belongs to the remarkable Sforza tradition of viragos, which includes Muzio Attendolo's mother Elisa dei Petrascini and Galeazzo Maria Sforza's illegitimate daughter Caterina, the most celebrated of them all. She was immensely popular with both citizens and soldiers, and constantly provided moral support in his actions. In the absence of Francesco from Milan she once led the Milanese troops against Monza, and on another occasion inspired the men she was leading by killing one of the enemy with a lance. It was presumably for this reason that on the birth of the first son to Francesco Sforza and Bianca Maria, Pope Eugenius IV — who was clearly biased, since he was a Venetian by birth — referred to the event as the birth of a second Lucifer.

Despite the difference in age the marriage was a happy one, and their children formed the basis of the future Sforza dynasty; but Francesco also fathered twenty-two illegitimate children. As with most of the other prolific sires of the Renaissance — for example Niccolò III d'Este — there was no distinction between the legitimate and natural children in his mind. In fact the main surviving branch of the family descends from his illegitimate son Sforza Secondo, who became Lord of Pontremoli and took refuge there when the Duchy of Milan eventually fell. Francesco's illegitimate daughter Polissena was married to Sigismondo Malatesta, Lord of Rimini and one of his major allies. Marriage into the Visconti family was a far cry from his 1416 wedding to Polissena Ruffo, the Countess of Montalto in Calabria, where his father had taken him proudly for a ceremony which seemed then to mark their ascent into the nobility. Now, Francesco was married into one of the foremost dynasties of Italy.

Yet lengthy discussions concerning the heredity meant that the details of the succession were not completed when Filippo Maria died in 1447. Francesco Sforza was not in Milan at the time, and the dukedom was abolished by popular acclaim and the so-called 'Ambrosian Republic' created. But this innovation was to last a matter of months. Finally Francesco entered Milan amidst equally popular enthusiasm and was acclaimed duke by the same people inside the new Duomo. On 22 March 1450, at the age of forty-nine, he was formally invested as Duke of Milan on a platform erected outside the cathedral.

The long-term friendship of such refined men as Cosimo de' Medici and Federico da Montefeltro underline Francesco's remarkable qualities as soldier, diplomat, and strategist. His life was spent at war, so his accomplishments as patron of the arts and literature do not equal those of Lodovico il Moro or even his own contemporaries in Florence, Ferrara, and Urbino. He was strong and tall, personally courageous in battle, and also excelled in sports. He retained the erect carriage of a soldier into old age, slept little, and ate as simply as his father. He was the greatest warrior of the Renaissance, and achieved a prize greater than any other *condottiere*. In his way he was an honest man, often cheated by wily enemies and patrons. He was tough but not malicious, severe but not vindictive, and a good father to his many children. In the relief portrait by Gian Cristoforo Romano, which can be seen in the Bargello Museum in Florence, he appears as a strong-willed man, with the prominent nose and thin lips which are characteristic of the Sforza to this day. Confidence, if not arrogance, is sustained by the thrusting expression and bull neck, while the artist has allowed a slight smile of self-satisfaction to characterize the facial expression.

As Duke of Milan, he never gained the popular support of his citizens; such feeling as existed was more for his wife, who benefited from memories of Visconti rule. Perhaps this lack of affection on the part of his subjects was the reason why he spent much of his time at Pavia, hunting, hawking, and collecting books and manuscripts.

He rebuilt the castle of Milan on a grand scale in local red brick, but more for show than for defensive purposes since by that time artillery was accurate and powerful enough to destroy such a castle easily. It was not however completed in his lifetime, and he and Bianca Maria made their normal residence in the equally large

Bianca Maria Sforza, by Bonifacio Bembo.

castle of Pavia; in Milan they lived in the ancient and recently frescoed Corte d'Arengo, beside the cathedral, a building later demolished and replaced by the present Royal Palace. The most interesting Lombard painter of the period, Vincenzo Foppa (*c.*1430–1516) worked on these frescoes for him. But his greatest achievement in architecture was the Ospedale Maggiore, founded in 1456. This building consisted of a series of cloisters grouped round an immense central courtyard. It was built in red brick like the castle, by the Florentine architect Filarete. Inside, the wards were arranged on the plan of a cross, with an altar positioned so that patients everywhere in the ward could hear mass. It now houses the State University of Milan, and excavations carried out while renovation took place revealed several interesting features, such as the morgue, situated by the canal that ran past the Ospedale. In addition to its primary function of transporting the bricks for building, this canal was used to carry the dead away.

Duke Francesco is remembered as the man who began the ducal line of the Sforza, and who established them as one of Europe's great dynasties. The castle and hospital remain as his cultural legacy to Milan, though neither can compare in historical and artistic interest with the main monuments of the Sforza in their adopted city: the cathedral and the Certosa of Pavia. Above all, he must be remembered as the most distinguished soldier of the time. He died in 1466 just as the Renaissance was achieving its peak, and Milan was to wait nearly thirty years before his son Lodovico — at his father's death only fifteen years old — succeeded him with the grandeur and taste which the role of Renaissance prince required.

GALEAZZO MARIA
(1444–76)

The duchy passed to Francesco's eldest son Galeazzo Maria, who had been given a Visconti name on the recommendation of his grandfather Filippo Maria Visconti. Perhaps it was the Visconti blood which made him so different from his father. His jealousy was such that he once ordered that the hands of a man seen talking to his mistress be cut off. On another occasion he dislocated his barber's shoulders at a whim by means of the strappado, or pulley-torture. When the terrified barber

Galeazzo Maria, by A. and P. Pollaiolo.

was released in atrocious pain he was forced to shave his torturer. Another time he caught a poacher, and caused the man to die by forcing him to eat a hare he had caught, whole and unskinned. Although there is, in fact, little evidence against him, he was widely believed to have murdered his own mother, Bianca Maria.

Yet his ruthlessness was matched by considerable skill in the everyday management of his duchy, possibly under the influence of his wife Bona of Savoy, sister to Louis XI's wife Charlotte. Bona was by all accounts a beautiful woman, noted for her charm and excellent manners. This marriage made him brother-in-law both to the French king and to Bona's brother Amadeus IX, Duke of Savoy, a fact which certainly enhanced his ambitions and may have increased his great love of luxury. Unlike his father and grandfather he enjoyed all the luxuries available to a great prince, and converted the imposing but stern castle into a comfortable residence. In the quantity and quality of silks, velvet, and gold used in his own and his servants' clothing, he had no equal even in that extravagant age. The official visit of Galeazzo and Bona to the Florence of Lorenzo de' Medici was one of the great events of pageantry of the entire Renaissance — outdone only by his own son Lodovico, as we shall see.

He wished to be considered a generous prince and man of great learning. To this end he increased the already considerable library at Pavia and encouraged leading scholars to teach and study at the universities of Milan and Pavia. A printing press was established at Milan under his patronage and many important early books were published there, including the first book — a grammar — to be printed in Greek in Italy.

But in a sense, Galeazzo Maria's most interesting legacy was the introduction of rice-growing, a product which is today the basis of the Milanese diet and — in the form of 'risotto alla Milanese' — the main ingredient of the city's most famous dish. His despotic habits, and the harsh taxation which he imposed to finance his extravagances, resulted in Galeazzo Maria joining his Visconti ancestors in being assassinated by three disgruntled citizens on 26 December 1476.

GIAN GALEAZZO
(1469–94)

Gian Galeazzo Sforza became duke at the age of eight, in theory 'ruling' under the regency of his mother. But Francesco Sforza's former secretary Cicco Simonetta effectively ruled Milan. The four dissatisfied and ambitious uncles of Gian Galeazzo — Lodovico, Ascanio the Bishop of Pavia, Filippo the eldest but weakest, and Sforza Maria who was to become regent — soon conspired against Cicco Simonetta. Their first attempt failed, and three of them were sent into exile: Lodovico to Pisa, Ascanio to Perugia, and Sforza Maria to his duchy of Bari. Filippo remained aloof from the conspiracy and lived quietly in Milan.

Many powerful Milanese nobles secretly supported the claim of Lodovico to be regent in place of Cicco. When Sforza Maria died, Lodovico was made Duke of

Bari in his place by King Ferrante of Naples, who supported him in his designs on the duchy. In the autumn of 1479 Lodovico entered Milan in secret and was led to the private chambers of the young duke and his mother without Cicco knowing. There and then, in what must have been a masterful display of diplomacy and argument, he achieved reconciliation with his nephew. Within weeks he had Gian Galeazzo formally installed as duke, himself as guardian, Bona of Savoia exiled, and even his own brother and supporter Ascanio sent away so that he could not be tempted to intervene. Cicco Simonetta was first imprisoned in Pavia and later beheaded.

Thus Lodovico Maria, Duke of Bari, took control of the city, although he did not become Duke of Milan until Gian Galeazzo's death in 1494. Gian Galeazzo was formally pronounced to be capable of governing, and the twelve-year-old boy began signing papers which his uncle placed before him. In 1480 he was invested as Duke of Milan. But there was never any doubt as to who was the real ruler of the city. In a certain sense there was justice in this destiny, since Lodovico was by far the most talented of Bianca Maria's children and his own brother Duke Galeazzo Maria had wished Lodovico to succeed him in the event that he should die without an heir. To all intents and purposes, from about 1480 Lodovico Sforza was the ruler of the Duchy of Milan.

LODOVICO MARIA
(1451–1508)

In the portrait attributed to Zenale on the so-called Sforza altarpiece in the Brera Gallery in Milan, Lodovico appears as a serene, satisfied, and confident man. The obviously dark complexion, in contrast with his pale but beautiful wife Beatrice d'Este, explains his epithet 'The Moor', or Lodovico il Moro, although alternative explanations have been put forward for this unusual name. He had been christened Lodovico Mauro when born in Vigevano in 1451, son of Francesco Sforza and Bianca Maria Visconti. His mother had later changed his second name to Maria in conformity with Visconti tradition, but he seems to have been generally known as 'Il Moro' even in his childhood.

Something of Lodovico's vanity may be guessed from the delicately embroidered blue cloth, perhaps silk, that he is wearing, and the gold collar. His thick neck and oncoming double chin suggest the immense physical power of the man, while his delicate mouth and the sensuality of the whole portrait suggest a conflict with this apparent power which reminds us of his great love for fashion, luxury, and women. In his person one can discern all the violent contradictions of an intelligent, cultivated, and talented man who led a despotic life of profound immorality and was even suspected by many people of having murdered his own nephew Gian Galeazzo in order to become the Duke of Milan.

The radiance of his wife Beatrice d'Este, which makes a striking contrast on the same altarpiece, does much to soften Lodovico's harsh image. She and her sister Isabella were the most accomplished of all Italian princesses: learned, refined, dressmaker, and lover of fine jewels, she was a woman who rode well and dabbled

Francesco, son of Gian Galeazzo, by Leonardo da Vinci.

in falconry, and was the ideal companion for this Renaissance prince and patron of the arts, literature, and trade. It was in her honour that two of the most distinguished buildings in Milan were completed and decorated: the church of Santa Maria delle Grazie where her funeral took place, with its cupola by Bramante, refectory with Leonardo's *Last Supper* and portraits of Lodovico and Beatrice; and the Chartreuse of Pavia, which is Lodovico's chief glory and in which the double tomb for him and his wife may still be seen. Lodovico had several mistresses of longstanding, but was driven into genuine despair by the loss of his wife. He replaced the Emperor's effigy in his signet by that of Beatrice, draped her room in black and referred to it as the *camera nigra*, and dedicated his energies to monuments in her memory. It seems that from her death his luck changed, his alliances began to disintegrate, and even his interest in maintaining his court began to diminish.

But this was never easy, and any despotic ruler at that time needed to keep his guard up constantly. Soon after taking power he was involved in the War of Ferrara already mentioned in the history of the Este family. In 1483 he survived an assassination attempt in the ancient basilica of St Ambrose in Milan: there were so many people in the church on the feast day of their patron saint that Lodovico was forced to enter the church by a side door and thus fortuitously avoided his assassins. They were caught armed inside the church, and the fate of one of them provides an interesting insight into the ruthlessness of these Renaissance rulers: condemned to life imprisonment, he was to be tortured annually on St Ambrose Day as a reminder of his crimes.

Lodovico soon strengthened his position by taking over the castle of Pavia, while Gian Galeazzo never showed interest in ruling. The titular duke preferred hunting and hawking on his estates, according to a contemporary chronicler: since 1480 he had been engaged to Isabella of Aragon, daughter of Alfonso Duke of Calabria, son and heir to King Ferrante of Naples. It seems that Lodovico attempted to forestall the wedding, but realized that Alfonso might soon become King of Naples and deemed it better to establish an alliance with him. Eventually it was decided that they should marry in 1488.

The wedding was important not so much for the alliance, or for the characters directly involved but because it set the tone of magnificence which has come to be identified with the Italian Renaissance. Everything about it was grandiose and extravagant, so that it became a standard against which other similar occasions were to be judged.

Already the court of Lodovico was known for its wealth and ostentation. The historian Corio wrote that 'Merrymaking and pleasure-seeking were all the rage and Jove triumphed with peace, so that everywhere there seemed to reign a stability and security never before known. The court of our princes was magnificently rich in new fashions, clothes, and pleasures'. Lodovico was a great lover of music and singing, importing musicians from as far afield as the Netherlands. It is odd to reflect today that Leonardo da Vinci, who had come from Florence hoping to be able to build some of his military inventions, was mostly appreciated at the court of Milan for his singing and lute-playing.

Accounts of the wedding overwhelm the reader with details of its magnificence. Four hundred and fifty nobles were sent to Naples to escort the bride to the city. They were welcomed and feasted on the way back at Civitavecchia, Livorno, and Genova and met by the Dukes of Bari and Milan at Tortona, near Genova, where a mythological dinner was presented: Apollo appeared with a calf he had stolen from Admetus, Orpheus came in with birds he had enchanted with his lyre, and Diana presented to the bride the stag into which she had transformed Acteon. The entertainment continued with music.

Isabella arrived in Milan with six huge barges, to be greeted by trumpets, artillery, and all the bells of the city. Then she accompanied the duke through cheering crowds to the castle. The ambassador from Ferrara reported that there was nothing to be seen anywhere except gold and silver brocade and jewels. The Florentine ambassador sent a detailed report, in which he claims to have counted five hundred horses in the wedding procession, plus thirty-six priests who preceded the court from castle to cathedral, sixty knights in gold brocade with gold chains, and sixty-two trumpeters. The whole route was carpeted with white cloth, and the walls draped and

Lodovico il Moro.   *Beatrice d'Este, Duchess of Milan.*

festooned with juniper and orange. He is, however, careful to note in this letter to Lorenzo de' Medici that 'our Piero' surpassed everybody in his dress even amidst the magnificence of the Milanese court.

The genius of Leonardo was employed to make the wedding spectacular. When the bridal couple returned to the castle, there was a display in one of the halls of the castle in which he had built a mountain with a cleft covered by a curtain. This curtain was removed dramatically to reveal a vista of the heavens with the twelve signs of the zodiac and personifications of the planets. Musicians played while the three Graces and seven Virtues praised the bride in turn. Whatever Leonardo might have thought of this, it seems to the modern mind a waste of his great talents — which were in fact never fully exploited by Lodovico. But the diplomatic and popular value of such extravagance was probably worth more to Lodovico at that time than any of Leonardo's inventions.

But Leonardo's talent was not totally misused, and the artist spent most of the best years of his life at the court of Lodovico. One interesting example of his work was the project for the ideal city. Milan was at that time a city of some 300,000 inhabitants, prosperous from the important trades of armoury and textiles and provided with food supplies by the plain to the south, towards the River Po. But in 1485 the city lost perhaps a sixth of its population in a plague. After that disaster Lodovico had removed stables and other buildings in order to widen streets and thereby improve hygiene, and it is likely that he discussed these ideas with Leonardo.

The artist's ideal city is in many ways a cleaner, better organized version of late fifteenth-century Milan, but with some original additions. He wished to build a new city divided into ten towns of 30,000 inhabitants each. It was to have streets whose width was equal to the average height of the houses, and watercourses to remove sewage and dirt. Leonardo even proposed a two-level street system, with a lower level for commercial traffic and an upper level for pedestrians. He discussed such details as the stairs connecting upper to lower level, the location of stables, and the ideal amount of air, light, and heating for individual rooms.

That Lodovico was interested in improving the lot of his subjects is shown by his long-term and genuine interest in breeding animals for food purposes. He built a model farm known as the Sforzesca near Vigevano, irrigated by a canal from the River Ticino, a tributary of the Po which joins the main river near Pavia. The farm was managed economically using scientific methods to improve breeds of sheep which Lodovico imported from France. Near the Sforzesca there was also a private hunting park stocked with game for the frequent hunting parties that he provided for his court. But even when Lodovico's motives were laudable, the methods used to achieve them increased his unpopularity — in this case with the small landowners whose property was expropriated in order to create the model farm.

Yet Lodovico does not seem to have been unusually cruel, and even the two murders often attributed to him are by no means certain. By the standards of fifteenth-century despots he was a good and kind man. But the political changes and invasions of the time brought into play forces greater than he was able to deal with. Just as the Medici lost their hold on power in the same period, so Lodovico was displaced partly as the result of his own machinations. Charles VIII of France was at least partly convinced by Lodovico to enter Italy in 1494 to lay his claim to the throne of Naples, and shortly after this Lodovico himself was invested as Duke of Milan by the Emperor Maximilian I — who had married his niece Bianca Sforza. But his plans backfired, and it was King Charles who drove him from power later in the same year.

Although he was briefly reinstated, he was soon taken prisoner by the French. He was imprisoned for four years in the castle of Lys-Saint-Georges in Berry. Then he was transferred to the castle of Loches, where he was allowed more freedom and allowed to hunt. There, after eight years in exile, the once powerful Lord of Milan died in 1508.

CATERINA
(1463–1509)

The Lady or Amazon of Forlì as Caterina Sforza is better known, was one of the most remarkable characters of the dynasty. Born of an early affair between Gian Galeazzo Sforza and the beautiful Lucrezia Landriani, she appears in her portrait by Palmezziani in the Pinacoteca of Forlì as an attractive delicate young woman caressing the wild flowers in her hand. Her hair is cut back on the forehead and curled from the ears downward in the latest fashion, and she appears a typical Renaissance princess in her castle.

Yet she was a celebrated virago, with the strength, passion, and commitment to war and her territory of her *condottiere* great-grandfather Muzio Attendolo, and of his virago mother Elisa Petrascini. When she was ten years old she was married to Girolamo Riario, the supposed nephew but probable son of Pope Sixtus IV (1471–84), whose election to the Holy See had been made possible by the support of Milan. Girolamo's control of the cities of Imola and Forlì was under constant threat from local enemies and the Medici in Florence: it was he who was behind the Pazzi conspiracy of 1478, when an assassination attempt against Guiliano and Lorenzo de' Medici was made inside the cathedral of Florence.

Caterina was said to fight like a man. When Pope Sixtus IV died in 1484, it was Caterina who held the Castel Sant'Angelo for her absent husband. It was she who helped to retain the city of Forlì when the papal nephew returned fundless to his city, and on one memorable occasion gave birth to a child after spending virtually twenty-four hours in the saddle. On another occasion, when her husband was seriously ill, she unearthed a conspiracy and had the culprits hung, drawn, and quartered. Eventually her unpopular husband was in turn murdered, perhaps one of the many attempts inspired by Lorenzo de' Medici in revenge.

This event gave rise to the most famous of stories about Caterina Sforza. She was in the hands of the rebels and her supporters were barricaded in the castle of Forlì, while messengers had ridden to Milan and Bologna for help. Totally fearless, she refused to order her castellan to open the castle. By means of a trick, she obtained a three-hour truce and managed to persuade her captors to allow her to enter the castle, the rebels being assured by the presence of her children as hostages. But as soon as she was safely inside the castle with her loyal followers, she ordered them to aim their guns at the town. Then she slept. Later, the rebels came to the castle walls and demanded that she leave the castle; she laughed at them, and they presented her children, threatening to kill them. At this, Caterina, who was wearing a nightgown, is supposed to have lifted it up so that everybody could see that she was pregnant. Then she shouted, 'Can't you see that I am already making more children?' Whether or not the story is apocryphal, it is certainly in character, for she was as happy amongst the rough soldiers of Romagna as she had been in the court at Milan as a child.

After her husband's death she became her son's legal guardian, but effectively ruled Forlì as its Countess. Together with her lover Jacopo Feo, who was later killed before her eyes, she made Forlì a force to be reckoned with in late fifteenth-century Italy. It was to her that Giovanni de' Medici was sent as Florentine ambassador in 1496, and with whom she conceived her last child, who maintained the Sforza warrior tradition and became known as Giovanni delle Bande Nere. His own son Cosimo became the first Grand Duke of Tuscany. It was also to her that Niccolò Machiavelli was sent on his first diplomatic mission for the Florentine government in 1499. But her power ended when Pope Alexander VI created a state in Romagna for his nephew Cesare Borgia. After a bitter battle and siege, Forlì was taken in 1500 and she was captured and sent off to imprisonment in Rome. A year later she was released by the French, and spent her remaining years in austere and saintly retreat in Florence.

She paid great attention to personal beauty, to her skin, hair, and teeth, so that there was a great demand for portraits of her. These qualities may, in fact, be seen in the Palmezziani portrait, where signs of the Amazon are noticeably absent. Caterina Sforza was a more than life-size woman who belongs to the heroic age of the thirteenth century and would have been an ideal companion for her ancestor Muzio Attendolo. She was honest, just, tough, and totally fearless — and a beautiful woman. She did not patronize great artists, but nevertheless remains one of the most extraordinary women of the Italian Renaissance.

MASSIMILIANO AND FRANCESCO

The male ducal line ended as ignominiously as its last true representative Lodovico. His sons Massimiliano and Francesco were brought up by their mother Bianca Maria at the Austrian Imperial court in Innsbruck. Each of them ruled Milan as a puppet-duke in brief respites from the French rule which had literally swept their father away. These periods, of no political or cultural importance, may be considered the death-throes of Sforza power.

Massimiliano (1493–1530) enjoyed three brief years as Duke of Milan when Archbishop Schinner of Sion imposed him on the people of Milan — who were glad to be rid of their French rulers — after obtaining approval of Emperor and pope. The Swiss aimed at the twin objective of removing the French influence in the city, and creating the markets which they needed for their trade. They also needed access to the food supplies of the rich plains of Lombardy. Massimiliano was more German in culture and habits than Italian, barely literate and ignorant of all things Milanese. His rule was sustained by expensive payments to the Swiss army which guarded him, and he did little beyond raise high taxes in order to satisfy his own taste for amusement.

When Francis I became King of France in 1514, one of his first aims was to take Milan again. Although money was again raised to pay the Swiss and Prospero Colonna was made leader of the Milanese forces, the French army entered Italy almost by surprise. Massimiliano surrendered his rights to Milan after defeat at the Battle of Marignano in 1515. He was awarded a pension by Francis I, and died in exile in Paris.

Seven years later Francesco (1495–1535) was put in possession of Milan by Charles V of Spain and the Medici Pope Leo X, who believed that by exploiting the Sforza name they would be able to rule Milan indirectly. It was not hard for this austere and serious young man to shine by comparison with his brother. The people of Milan were so pleased to be rid of French rule once again that they celebrated Francesco's arrival with bells, guns, and gifts, and an enthusiasm which surprised observers. But Spanish dominion was no better than that of the French, as the people of Milan soon realized to their cost. On being accused of treason, Duke Francesco was besieged in his own castle for eight months while the town was ransacked for food and money by the Spanish troops. It was when the Spanish realized that there was no further blood to be drawn from the Milanese stone that they turned south towards Rome. The notorious Sack of Rome of that year, 1527, finally demonstrated to the popes what a dangerous ally they had encouraged in the Emperor Charles V.

Duke Francesco was now a sick man, grey-haired and unable to walk without a stick. For a few more years he lived in the impoverished city of Milan, kowtowing to Charles V and moving out of his own castle in 1533 so that the Emperor could reside there. In 1534 he married Christina of Denmark, an eleven-year-old niece of the Emperor, but survived her by less than a year. It seems that he treated her extremely well, and that she was genuinely concerned for him. But the last Sforza Duke of Milan died childless on 24 October 1535, and was buried in the cathedral of Milan.

THE SFORZAS IN MODERN TIMES

The Sforza dynasty has continued to the present day, and after a period of relative obscurity has produced men of exceptional interest into the twentieth century.

The Dukes of Milan came to an end with Francesco II, but his uncle Sforza Secondo, who had the title Conte di Borgonovo, was at that time in the Sforza stronghold at Pontremoli on the route south from Milan to the port of La Spezia. When the duchy was taken, he prudently retreated to the Republic of Lucca. There he was made consul of the village of Montignoso, a fortress which controlled the important Roman north–south artery Via Aurelia, where the family still owns property. It is in fact worth recalling that Francesco Sforza once fought for Lucca, saving the city from Florence and being offered the lordship by its grateful citizens. Now Count Sforza Secondo established a dignified but reduced situation, and that branch of the family continued to feature in the history of Lucca in the succeeding centuries. The direct line continued from his son Giacometto. Members of the family married into the nobility of Lucca, while some achieved importance in their own right. Captain Pier-Domenico Sforza (1764–1802) was a member of the Grand Council of the Republic of Lucca, and was nominated a Gentleman of Vienna by Maria Theresa of Austria.

It was his great-grandson Giovanni (1846–1922) who emerged from this provincial obscurity to become a national figure, and create the modern importance of the Sforza family. He became famous as historian and archivist, writing many important volumes of Italian history and contributing to an understanding of the political history of modern Italy at the crucial moment of unification. He had a particular interest in the history of Pontremoli and the ancient area between Liguria and Tuscany called the Lunigiana, both associated with the history of the Sforza. His large library was donated to the Provincial Library of La Spezia, while in Luni there is a 'Giovanni Sforza Museum' devoted to the history of the area. Giovanni Sforza had four sons: Alessandro, Carlo, Ascanio, and Giovanni, of whom the most interest-

Illumination of Massimiliano Sforza in his garden.

ing and important was Carlo (1872–1952) for his role in the resistance to Mussolini's dictatorship and his fundamental importance in the foundation of the modern Italian Republic in 1948.

Carlo entered a diplomatic career and soon achieved success with an appointment to the Ministry of Foreign Affairs in 1910. He served in China, Serbia, and

Turkey and became Minister in the Giolitti government of 1919–21; in 1922 he became Italian Ambassador in Paris, but resigned in protest at the Fascist regime and spent the next twenty years in France, Belgium, and the United States. He wrote many books on Italian history and politics in this time and during the Second World War he was a professor of European History at Columbia University. He returned to Italy in 1944, served immediately as a minister in the post-Mussolini coalition, and became a close collaborator of Alcide de Gasperi, one of the fathers of the Italian Republic. From 1947 to 1951 he was again Minister of Foreign Affairs in De Gasperi's cabinet.

He was a reserved man, noted for his rather British sense of understatement, but at the same time vivacious in conversation and gifted with a fine sense of humour which survives in family anecdotes. Once, in his home in the Roman suburb of Parioli, he mistakenly entered a bathroom then equipped with a swing door not knowing that his niece was inside. She was sitting on the lavatory, and he was stark naked, but his comment reveals much about the man's extreme self-confidence and lack of self-consciousness — or arrogance — for he is supposed to have said: 'Don't worry, you don't embarrass me in the slightest'. His nephew Giovanni, the present Count Sforza of this line, recounts that he worked as private secretary for his uncle as a young man just after the war. Carlo Sforza was at that time Minister of Foreign Affairs. One day, while Carlo was in bed with flu, Alcide de Gasperi, founder and first Prime Minister of the Italian Republic, came to visit him. Giovanni remained in the bedroom during their conversation about vital political matters of the day, and when De Gasperi left was visibly shaken. His uncle observed, to his surprise, that De Gasperi had been nervous of him too, and taught him the lesson that whenever he felt nervous or intimidated by someone he must always remember that the other person also has his problems and shyness. A piece of advice which his nephew has often found useful. On another occasion, Carlo was heard to complain about his tailor when rice from a risotto he was eating at a formal lunch continually fell onto his suit.

Carlo's son Sforza achieved political success as Secretary-General of the Council of Europe, but died without an heir. The present head of the family is Count Giovanni Sforza, son of Alessandro, who divides his time between a business life in Milan and his property at Montignoso. His son Alessandro and daughter Muzia both currently live in London, where the former works in the advertising business and the latter is a student of architecture.

It is interesting to see how this branch of the family maintains its historical connection both in maintaining residence in Montignoso and Milan, and in perpetuating the family names. Thus it is fitting that Muzia, the last in direct line of this ancient and important dynasty, should bear the name of its founder Muzio Attendolo.

5

THE MALATESTA

Like many of the feudal families considered here, the Malatesta spawned legends which trace their lineage to Roman times. More reliable stories trace their history to a certain wealthy and powerful Giovanni who lived in Ravenna in the eighth century. But the surname Malatesta was given to Rodolfo, who in the tenth century was admired for his capacity to hold his own (*tener testa*) against both popes and emperors. Extant documentary evidence begins in the twelfth century with diplomas concerning the ownership of lands and castles near Rimini, including the castle of Verucchio from which the first significant member of the dynasty took his name. This evidence was thought to provide a respectable lineage by Sigismondo Malatesta, Lord of Rimini in the second half of the fifteenth century.

From 1295 to 1528 the Malatesta were Lords of Rimini, with lands which extended along the Adriatic coast in varying degrees according to temporary strength and prestige. They were in constant conflict throughout this period with their rivals and neighbours, the Montefeltro of Urbino. But even before the Lordship of Rimini the family had achieved literary immortality by means of a dramatic murder which led to one of the most celebrated passages in Dante's *Divine Comedy*. Since the Malatesta family were consistently Guelph in their political affiliation and Malatesta da Verucchio became powerful as the leader of the Guelphs of Romagna, family members are systematically disparaged by the partisan Ghibelline Dante — who was exiled from Florence by the Guelph party on charges of conspiring against the pope and Charles of Anjou. Similarly, their Guelph enemies the Montefeltro of Urbino are always presented in the best possible light by Dante.

Paolo and Francesca receive the most detailed treatment. Malatesta's eldest son Giovanni the Lame (Gian Ciotto) had married Francesca, daughter of the Lord of Ravenna, Guido da Polenta. The marriage was never successful, since Giovanni seems to have been unattractive both in features and in personality and Francesca had been forced into it for obvious motives of political convenience. It was while

Opposite *Tempio Malatestiano: right elevation*

103

Sarcophagus of Margherita Malatesta, wife of Francesco I Gonzaga, in the ducal palace at Mantova.

Giovanni was absent from Rimini as *podestà* of Pesaro that the relationship between his wife and his handsome brother Paolo seems to have begun. The story is told in some detail in one of the most famous passages of *Hell*, and it is likely that Dante himself met Paolo while he served as captain of the city of Florence in 1282. When their love affair was discovered, Paolo and Francesca were both put to death by Giovanni.

When Dante encounters Francesca in the second circle of Hell, the circle of the lustful in Canto V, he listens sympathetically to her version of the story. Clearly her great love for Paolo, which she claims 'has not yet abandoned me' and which led them to the same death, makes her attractive to him. He replies to her that 'your torments make me weep with sadness and pity' and desires to know how this great love came about. She explains how her reading together with Paolo one day the story of Launcelot and Guinevere had led her to fall in love with Paolo. At the point of the story where Launcelot kisses Guinevere they were overcome with lust: Francesca relates the 'he who shall never be parted from me kissed me on the mouth, trembling'. The scene is reminiscent of Dante's own love poetry, and his love for Beatrice recounted in *The New Life*. It has been suggested that it represents his personal denunciation of the ethos of courtly love poetry — although the passage is marked by a powerful sense of nostalgia, as if the poet wishes he had been so fortunate in his love when he swoons at the end of the scene.

Notwithstanding an attempt by the Malatesta family to maintain secrecy over this affair, and the consequent double murder, the story quickly spread through Romagna. Although Dante places the fated couple in Hell, he treats the episode as a statement of the frailty of human nature — drawn by love — and expresses pity for them. Ironically, many years later, it was under the protection of Francesca's nephew the Lord of Ravenna that Dante spent his last years in that city and died there.

In the Romantic period of English literature the story of Paolo and Francesca was taken up by Leigh Hunt (1784–1859), best known today as the sponsor of Keats, in his poem *The Story of Rimini*, which shows the couple in pathetic rather than tragic light. Later the now forgotten poet and playwright Stephen Phillips (1866–1915), once compared to Sophocles, Dante, and Shakespeare, and author of a book of poems which sold five editions in a single year, wrote a verse drama called *Paolo and Francesca*. It was performed in London in 1902, enjoyed an extraordinary vogue and was thought to have marked a new birth of poetic drama.

MALATESTA DA VERUCCHIO
(*c.*1212–1312)

Paolo and Giovanni were the younger sons of Malatesta da Verucchio by his second wife, Concordia, daughter of the Imperial Vicar of Romagna, who brought four castles as her dowry. Their elder brother was known as Malatestino dell'Occhio (*c.*1251–1317) after the reference in Dante's *Hell* to the 'traitor who saw even with one eye'. It is interesting to note that his 'treachery' consisted in attacking Urbino and Count Guido da Montefeltro. Elsewhere Dante refers to Malatesta da Verucchio as the 'Mastin Vecchio' or Old Mastiff with reference to the cruel use he made of his fangs; Malatestino was also known as the 'Mastin Nuovo'. However, the main line descended through Pandolfo I, Malatesta's only son by his third wife Margherita dei Paltrinieri.

Malatesta da Verucchio was as a young man courageous, courteous, and friendly in nature. Through his personality and the political alliances deriving from his father-in-law he managed to make himself temporary Lord of Rimini in the 1250s. After the death of the Emperor Frederick II, the power of the Guelphs like Malatesta declined, while the Ghibellines rose and Taddeo da Montefeltro became *podestà* of Rimini. With the arrival of Charles of Anjou, supported by the papacy, the Guelphs rose again in power and Pope Urban IV awarded prebends to Malatesta's sons in gratitude for his support of Charles. During those quiet years Malatesta was gathering new feuds and castles until his position in the area became unassailable. His third marriage, to Margherita, though less rich in dowry and name than Concordia, was useful in strengthening his ties to the Guelph leaders.

In 1274 a struggle broke out between the Guelphs of Romagna led by Malatesta and the Ghibellines led by Guido da Montefeltro. The following year at the Battle of San Proclo the Guelphs — Bologna, Rimini, Ravenna with help from Modena, Reggio, and Ferrara — took terrifying losses against the Ghibellines — Urbino, Forli, Faenza, together with the Ghibelline exiles from Bologna. Guido da Montefeltro gained the reputation of the greatest soldier of the day. Yet the result of that battle did not break Malatesta's power, since he was consistently aided in moral support and finances by the Church. Together with Guido da Polenta, Francesca's father, Malatesta travelled to Rome and placed Romagna in the hands of Pope Nicholas III (1277–80). In the meantime he consolidated his power in Rimini, becoming once again *podestà*. An attempt to end the quarrel was made by marrying Malatesta's grandson Malatestino, son of the unlucky Giovanni, to Guido da Montefeltro's daughter Agnese. But it was with the advent of Pope Nicholas IV (1288–94) that a solution was finally achieved. The diplomatic work leading to this resolution was carried out by Stefano Colonna of the Roman dynasty, and in 1295 Malatesta da Verucchio became absolute Lord of Rimini by popular acclaim over the rival Parcitadi family, friends of Guido da Montefeltro. This dominion was to last for three centuries.

Malatesta da Verucchio was a figure of heroic and almost mythical qualities, who steered his course through nearly a century of dramatic tussles with the Montefeltro, founded the family power in Rimini and rode to Arezzo at the head of his army at the age of ninety-four. The only surviving image, on a contemporary seal, is too vague to give us an impression of his face. But he must have been strong, and of exceptional physical resistance. At the age of ninety-nine he was still actively concerned with his territories and legacy, as witnessed by a document in favour of Pandolfo written then. Such a heroic and powerful man was also generous with those loyal to him, and his friends and servants. As a man who outlived most of his children, he was especially affectionate towards his grandchildren. Above all, in a touch of tenderness not expected of such a man, he seems to have remembered with extraordinary love his last wife Margherita, with whom he had lived for forty-five years. It was the son born from her, Pandolfo, who succeeded him and continued the principal line of the Malatesta. He was buried in the church of San Franceso in Rimini, which from that moment became the family mausoleum and in which frescoes of the Malatesta family can still be seen.

PANDOLFO I
(1266–1326)

Malatesta's two sons Malatestino and Pandolfo were assured a peaceful succession, prepared by almost a century of careful long-term planning. But the battles did not cease, and Malatestino fell in action five years after his father's death, leaving Pandolfo I as the Lord of Rimini.

The most important event of his short rule was the pact between the papal Rector of the Marches against Federico da Montefeltro, the son and successor of Count Guido. The army was to be led by Pandolfo and Malatestino's son Ferrantino. In the spring of 1321 Federico had led a series of furious raids against Rimini and several papal towns nearby, reinforced by militia from friendly towns and members of the minor branches of the Malatesta family who for decades conspired against the rulers of Rimini. That year, they arrived as far as Umbria, causing bloodshed and plundering in Spoleto and Assisi. Federico was declared heretic by Pope John XXII (1216–34), so that the campaign was perceived as a 'crusade' against enemies of the Church. The revenge was quick and violent, in true Malatesta fashion. The papal army besieged and took Urbino, ransacked and plundered the city and then murdered Federico and his son.

With this success the lands of the Malatesta increased to include Fano and Pesaro, while Rimini itself began to take on the air of a regional capital. The Lord of Rimini now controlled the bureaucratic machine which included a treasury and a chancery. All attempts at insurrection were suppressed with bloody determination: one such rival appeared in the person of Pandolfo's nephew Uberto Malatesta of Ghiaggiolo, son of the Paolo who was murdered with Francesca. When Pandolfo heard of the threat, he invited Uberto to dinner. As soon as the guest entered the hall where the dinner was to be eaten, he was seized and murdered. With typical Malatesta ferocity, the body was bundled into a sack and thrown away as if it were rubbish.

Pandolfo arranged for himself and his sons Malatesta and Galeotto to be created 'Knights of Christ' by Pope John XXII. When he then arranged for Galeotto to marry Elise de la Villette, daughter of the papal legate to the Marches, he realized his ambition of being considered amongst the great nobles of Italy. Lords from the whole of Italy and from France attended the wedding in 1323, and Pandolfo could see his political and diplomatic triumph over the Montefeltro consummated in this event. He possessed the sense of timing and persistence, and above all the ability to know when to seek or accept compromise, of his father Malatesta da Verucchio. He consolidated Malatesta power in Rimini by his policy of extending their territory as far to the south and north as possible. He was buried beside his father in the church of San Francesco.

MALATESTA 'GUASTAFAMIGLIA'
(c.1299–1364)

Pandolfo was succeeded by his nephew Ferrantino, son of Malatesta dell'Occhio, but this line was soon beaten in a violent power struggle which ended with Ferrantino and his sons being imprisoned and replaced by his more adventurous and violent cousins, Pandolfo's sons Malatesta and Galeotto. It was from the latter that the main Malatesta line was to descend.

The nickname of the notorious mercenary Malatesta, 'Guastafamiglia' ('family-breaker'), goes a long way towards describing one of the most unscrupulous and evil characters in the dynasty's long history. His real name was the unmanageable Malatesta II Malatesta. His first military experience was in the crusade against Federico da Montefeltro in 1322, when he was already *podestà* of Pesaro; the following year he is thought to have participated in the murder of Uberto arranged by his father. From the moment of the death of his father he led Galeotto in the violent task of eliminating his cousins so that they could rule the Malatesta territories. Until that time the Malatesta had been plagued by internal rivalries and the competition of cadet branches of the family: it was in this sense that Malatesta II 'broke' the family, reserving power and the direct lineage for himself and his brother Galeotto. Malatesta II became Lord of Rimini, and Galeotto Lord of Fano, leaving Pesaro to 'Guastafamiglia's' sons Pandolfo and Ungaro.

Until that time the Malatesta had been faithful Guelphs, as we have seen in their constant battles with the Montefeltro. Now, when Louis I of Hungary entered Italy, they performed a remarkable power-seeking shift of loyalties, joining the Emperor

Sigismondo, by Piero della Francesco.

against the pope and obtaining imperial sanction for their rule. In a sense this shift of loyalties was facilitated by the fact that the popes were distant in Avignon. The Malatesta then extended their territory southward to Ancona, Ascoli, and Senigallia. From that moment they are no longer merely the Lords of Rimini, and neither Guelph or Ghibelline in loyalty: the two brothers were simply 'the Malatesta', with no need for further explanation or definition, creating the name and power which Galeotto's grandson Sigismondo was to honour.

But Pope Innocent VI (1352–62) did not accept their changed loyalty so readily, and sent the terrible warrior-cardinal Egidio Albornoz against them. For centuries the Romagna had produced warriors and rebels, and it seemed time to put an end to this phenomenon once and for all. Albornoz was an excellent strategist and ferocious soldier, exhorting the people of the towns to rise against the tyrants and oppressors of their land, turning town against town, fighting savagely when these techniques failed. At first defeated and in the case of Galeotto ignominiously captured, the Malatesta then negotiated with Albornoz and finally became official Vicars of Rimini, Pesaro, Fermo, and Fossombrone. Thus the two brothers who had opposed the pope in the years 1357–9 subjugated Romagna in his name. In a campaign of extreme subtlety and soldierly merit they took Bologna, thwarting Bernabò Visconti's desire to take control of that city, in a celebrated battle at the gates of Bologna in 1361. 'Guastafamiglia' completely destroyed the forces of the Milanese army. Bernabò Visconti is said to have dressed in mourning for his dead soldiers.

At the end of his life 'Guastafamiglia' seems to have been overwhelmed by a deep sense of remorse. The ruthless warrior, who had given away his lordships to his sons and to his brother, confessed his sins in public, distributed food to the poor, and freed the men in his prisons in a general amnesty. But in spite of this Christian conclusion to his life, Malatesta II Malatesta was without doubt the most ferocious and unscrupulous member of the dynasty, as the few incidents recounted here suffice to illustrate.

DESCENDANTS OF MALATESTA 'GUASTAFAMIGLIA'

Pandolfo II (1325–73) and Ungaro (1327–72), the two sons of Malatesta II, succeeded him as joint Lords of Pesaro two decades before his death. Pandolfo gained an excellent reputation fighting with Gian Galeazzo Visconti's army, so much so that he was nearly stabbed to death with a sword by Visconti's jealous and irascible brother Bernabò — since his success was making Gian Galeazzo stronger. On another occasion he achieved a brilliant strategic victory in defence of Florence, and gained the honour of a sonnet written by Petrarch. Later he aspired to gain the ascendancy over Florence, but was thwarted in his ambitions and retired to his own Pesaro. His brother Ungaro, who was really another Galeotto but earned his nickname after fighting for Louis I of Hungary, also achieved fame as a *condottiere*. He defeated Bernabò Visconti, and became captain-general of the papal armies in his uncle Galeotto's place.

Pandolfo II's only son Malatesta 'dei Sonetti' (1370–1429) inherited Pesaro at the age of three, but his great-uncle Galeotto took the city for himself rather than act as regent. On the death of Galeotto in 1385 he was able to recover the city and rule over it for the remainder of his life while combating throughout Italy. For ten years he also held Todi, in Umbria, and he served as *condottiere* for the Republic of Venice. He rebuilt the city walls of Pesaro according to the designs of Brunelleschi and was to a certain extent a patron of the arts and cultivated man. His nickname, 'the sonneteer', derives from the fact that he wrote rather conventional love poetry.

His son Carlo II (*c*.1390–1438) was yet another *condottiere*, who learned the arts of war fighting with his uncle against Braccio da Montone. Yet his career was marked by one enormous failure, in which he and ten thousand men were captured in 1427 against the *condottiere* Carmagnola, under the orders of Gianfrancesco Gonzaga. Niccolò Piccinino and Francesco Sforza were also on the losing side, but it seems that Carlo II's ineptitude was the real cause of the defeat. When he died, Pesaro was taken by his brothers Pandolfo IV and Galeotto, who attempted to maintain independence from their cousins of the main Malatesta line. Unable to resist the persistent assaults of such adversaries as Francesco Sforza, Federico da Montefeltro, and the forces of Pope Eugenius IV (1431–47), this Galeotto sold the feud of Pesaro to Alessandro Sforza rather than give it to his cousins. Thus ended the direct line of Malatesta II Malatesta, 'Guastafamiglia', none of whom matched their ancestor in either military or diplomatic skill.

GALEOTTO
(c.1305–85)

The main Malatesta line continued through 'Guastafamiglia's' brother Galeotto, companion-in-arms in the campaigns of 'Guastafamiglia' and himself one of the great warriors of his time. As early as 1322, when he was about seventeen, the chronicles mention his participation in a bullfight staged by the Roman Senate inside the Colosseum. In the battles for expansion of Malatesta control over the towns of the Adriatic, Galeotto was notable for a famous victory over Fermo in 1348.

Then followed an uncharacteristic action for a Malatesta. No document tells us the reason, but in the following year Galeotto went on pilgrimage to the Holy Land and remained there for two years. The year of his departure was the year of the worst episode of the Black Death in Italian history, when as many as two-thirds of the population of cities such as Siena and Florence died and the rapid artistic development of the small city states was truncated by the simple absence of artists. That may have been the cause of Galeotto's decision, but it is pleasant to think that he may have felt some pull of his conscience after a career of at least twenty-five years of almost constant massacre, battle, and plunder. However, he returned from Jerusalem to his old ways, and in the next few years was again present at every important battle along the Adriatic coast from Lanciano in the Abruzzi to Cesena. From 1360 he fought for the city of Bologna against Bernabo Visconti: four years later he was fighting for Florence in their war with Pisa; in 1372 he was appointed captain-general of the papal forces by Pope Gregory XI (1370–8), and the next year won a resounding victory against his old enemy Bernabò Visconti.

This was the moment of the height of power of the English *condottiere* John Hawk-wood, who was supposed to fight for the papal army against Florence but on receiving an offer of a higher salary promptly switched sides. Immediately Siena and Pisa offered him more money too, so that Galeotto suddenly found himself with his strongest ally on the other side. In those years he managed to maintain Rimini, of which he was the only lord, but other Malatesta cities such as Faenza and Cesena saw horrible massacres of their citizens — in the latter case a three-day orgy of murder, rape, and plunder that ravaged the city and left five thousand dead. This was carried out by Cardinal Robert of Savoy, the anti-pope Clement VII, notorious for his savagery.

Yet all was not warfare in Galeotto's life, and in patronage and art he built the basis upon which his grandson Sigismondo was to achieve lasting fame as a Renaissance prince. He attempted to provide an educated and cultivated environment for his sons, employing a well-known humanist called Giacomo Allegretti to teach them Latin and French and to inculcate them in the humanist values of poetry and rhetoric. Leonardo Bruni (c.1370–1444), one of the earliest Florentine humanists, who insisted on the civil function of humanities and preached eloquence as the summit of study, served as secretary to his son Carlo and at that time wrote his famous work *On Study and Literature* addressed to Anna Montefeltro, wife of Galeotto's youngest son Galeotto Novello. Another early humanist Francesco Filelfo (1398–1481), who had spent six years in Constantinople and wrote poetry in Greek, Latin, and Italian, was secretary to Pandolfo. Filelfo might be described a *condottiere* of letters, who worked for whoever paid best — including Filippo Maria Visconti and Francesco Sforza — and at the end of his life was invited to teach Greek in Florence by Lorenzo de' Medici. A man who loved the good things of life and realized that his learning could earn them, he was a formative influence on Pandolfo and probably set the classical frame of mind which he was to pass on to his son Sigismondo. It was also in this court that the Malatesta could produce a girl like his daughter Margherita, who would not have felt too shocked when she transferred to the intellectual court of her husband Francesco Gonzaga.

In his late seventies, like his grandfather Malatesta da Verucchio, Galeotto went out to battle to recover the lost cities. He recovered Cervi and Cesenatico from Guido da Polenta, then in 1383 fought a dramatic and victorious series of violent battles and recovered other Malatesta feuds and castles. Two years later he died in Cesena at the age of eighty. His body was taken to Rimini in a carriage covered with a velvet baldachin escorted by soldiers mounted on horses covered in black cloth. Thus died a soldier who had spent perhaps sixty-five years in the saddle or in battle, save the brief respite of two years in the Holy Land.

CARLO
(1368–1429)

Galeotto had arranged his legacy so that Malatesta power was neatly divided between his four sons: Carlo was Lord of Rimini, while his brothers Pandolfo III, Andrea, and Galeotto Novello were Lords of Fano, Cesena, and Cervia respectively.

This led many people to believe that it would be easy to provoke disagreement between the brothers and strip the Malatesta of their lands. But they reckoned without Carlo — and to a lesser extent Pandolfo — who was already an experienced soldier and strategist in spite of his seventeen years. In a series of determined moves accompanied by Pandolfo he not only conserved Malatesta power but managed to extend it. Through his own marriage to Elisabetta Gonzaga, and that of his youngest brother Galeotto Novello to Anna Montefeltro, he also made important alliances with neighbouring states.

Supreme commander of the forces of Venice, Padova, Mantova, and Florence against Gian Galeazzo Visconti when he was thirty, Carlo won glory in several victories, fighting side by side with his brother Pandolfo. He was the prime mover behind the truce of 1398 between Milan and the League of Venice, thus playing a vital role in the entire struggle for power in northern Italy between Venice, Florence, and Milan. Although their power base was relatively small, the Malatesta were sustained by the Church in Rome and made themselves indispensable as the weight which could shift the balance between larger states like Mantova and Ferrara. Even while fighting personally for the Visconti as a young *condottiere*, Carlo had managed to maintain friendly relations with Florence as Lord of Rimini. It was this intermediary role which he exploited with such success, together with his now proven ability as a military commander.

After the sudden and unexpected death of Gian Galeazzo Visconti in 1402, which left Italy shocked and unable to believe such a fortuitous death had really occurred, Carlo returned to Rimini. Meanwhile Pandolfo became a member of the council appointed along with Gian Galeazzo's wife Caterina Visconti to supervise the young heirs to the Visconti lands, together with the *condottieri* Facino Cane and Alberico

Tempio Malatestiano: façade.

da Barbiano. Until that time the brothers had always operated together, but then began the period in which Pandolfo sought to create his own state in northern Italy. They were turbulent times in which any able and courageous man could carve out for himself a territory while the greater powers dithered. For a time Carlo himself was called upon to be Governor of Milan, and came close to making that city a Malatesta fief.

Around 1412 many people believed that Carlo and Pandolfo Malatesta were so powerful that they could virtually impose their wishes on both papacy and Empire. Carlo retired to Rimini, where he became virtually the last defender of the official Roman pope Gregory XII (1406-14) while the anti-pope John XXIII was in Bologna. Gregory was later to abdicate the papal throne at the Council of Constance, where he was represented by Carlo Malatesta. He died in the town of Recanati in the Marches — best known today as the birthplace of Leopardi — where his tomb is in the cathedral. He was succeeded by the Colonna pope, Martin V (1417-31), whose pontificate ended the Great Schism. The presence of the pope at Rimini was sufficient to draw writers and artists to the city in droves. It was that time that Leonardi Bruni was in Rimini as secretary to Carlo, and spoke of the Malatesta lord as an unusual example of a man who could be 'invincible in battle and the same time mild in peace and law-abiding'. At that time Rimini was an important centre of book production, including copies of works of history made for Carlo, new Latin poems in his honour, an edition of Giovanni Boccaccio's work *De montinus* and a history of the Malatesta family. Although the painters who came from Rome and other centres were not of great renown, many of the works which can be seen in Rimini and Fano are of excellent quality.

But the rapid and tenacious rise to power of Filippo Maria Visconti, with the consequent weakening of Malatesta power, soon brought this brief apogee to an end. The new Visconti duke assumed Braccio da Montone as leader of his army, and the *condottiere* soon inflicted the ignominious defeat near Assisi which led to Carlo's captivity in Visconti hands in 1416. This was also the period of the resolution of the Great Schism, which diminished the importance of the Malatesta lands in the political equilibrium. Although he then rebuilt the port of Rimini, which allowed better communications between Malatesta feuds at Pesaro, Fano, and Senigallia, and also imports of grain from Apulia and Dalmatia both for the Marches and for Tuscany, his political power was in decline from the moment of his captivity. In continuing power struggles and battles the Malatesta territories were sacked and gradually diminished. He died in 1429 without leaving a male heir, so the lordship of Rimini passed to his brother Pandolfo II's bastard son Sigismondo Pandolfo, who had been born in Brescia.

PANDOLFO III
(1370-1427)

At the age of eighteen Pandolfo was already in command of a band of brigands operating throughout Tuscany with eight hundred horsemen. For fourteen years he accepted contracts as *condottiere*: for Venice against Padova, and for Florence and Bologna against the Visconti in defending Mantova — a particularly delicate task, since both his sister and brother Carlo had married into the Gonzaga family. Before the war between the Visconti and Gonzaga was resolved by the truce of 1398, Pandolfo had suffered serious defeats and losses at the hand of Alberico da Barbiano.

Following the paternal example, he celebrated this pause — and perhaps recovered self-esteem — by visiting the Holy Land. On his return he was welcomed at Fano as a returning hero, and lauded with festivities and dances. It was then that he began his successful military career as a captain of the Visconti armies, an apparently paradoxical position given the eminence of his brother Carlo as papal vicar and enemy of the Visconti.

But this apparent change of side was simply a mask for his real intentions, for, while declaring loyalty to the Visconti, he raided throughout Tuscany and Romagna and slowly added to his own small possessions in Fano. In 1404, employing his skill in duplicity, he achieved the greatest coup of his life and took possession of Brescia — far from the Malatesta feuds in Romagna. This was performed by cheating Facino Cane, who aided him in convincing Brescia to cede to them in the name of the Visconti. Once inside the city, Pandolfo revealed his true intention, produced a letter from the duchess declaring the city to be his in payment of debts for his services, and promptly sent Facino Cane away. He eradicated opposition in the surrounding area and governed Brescia with a firm hand. In the next few years he fought and plotted continuously, adding Bergamo to his territory notwithstanding the objections of the new Visconti duke, Giovanni Maria.

Pandolfo's ambition was unlimited. He became captain-general to the army which defended Venice from the invasion of King Sigismond of Hungary, obtaining a palace on the Grand Canal in gratitude for his services. For shorter periods he managed to gain sway over Cremona and Piacenza. Yet holding Brescia and Bergamo against the Visconti, Fano against innumerable enemies, and fighting for the Venetians, left him no time to establish a permanent base or undispersed state. Even his control of Brescia and Bergamo had only been possible in a temporary power vacuum. When the next Visconti duke, Filippo Maria, decided to make war against the Malatesta with all his forces, there was little to be done. In 1424 Brescia and Bergamo were lost, and the Visconti continued to advance into Romagna. The Malatesta risked losing everything, and it was only with the support of Pope Martin V — Oddone Colonna, who remembered Malatesta services to the Church — that he managed to save Fano, the town from which his adventures had begun.

Pandolfo III died in Fano on 3 October 1427, and was buried in the church of San Francesco where part of his severely classical tomb can still be seen. The *Corte Malatestiana*, two fifteenth-century buildings containing a collection of paintings, also date from Pandolfo's lordship.

Sigismondo kneeling before St Sigismondo, by Piero della Francesca.

SIGISMONDO PANDOLFO
(1417–86)

Pandolfo III's son was the celebrated Sigismondo Malatesta. He was universally recognized as one of the great princes of the Renaissance, although in fact the Malatesta name had seen more glory at the time of his uncle Carlo.

Even in such a family of precocious warriors, Sigismondo excelled by going victoriously into battle in 1430 against papal troops who came to claim his uncle Carlo's debts. At seventeen he took Bologna. From that moment he seems to have spent most of his life with weapons in his hand, fighting like so many other *condottieri* for and against the Church, as captain-general for Venice, for Florence and Sforza against Naples, and for Siena. Described by a contemporary as more beast than man, his fighting ability was unequalled by any *condottiere*. He was the perfect type of the warrior prince idealized by Machiavelli.

In the fresco portrait in his 'Temple' at Rimini, Sigismondo appears with deep impenetrable, slightly almond-shaped eyes, and a commanding mouth. He was then thirty-four, at the prime of his life, and the portrait is enough to convince us that his strong personality made him the natural leader. He was tall and strong, an excellent horseman, and appears to have embodied just about every virtue and every vice imagineable. As a *condottiere* he was noted for his courage, and his cruelty towards enemies. A man of violent passions who had virtually ruled his own life since being orphaned at the age of ten, Sigismondo married three times for reasons so overtly political that he was suspected of murdering his first two wives — Ginevra d'Este and Polissena Sforza — for his own advantage. Only the third, Isotta degli Atti, seems to have received genuine love and affection as testified by his project for their double tomb.

Sigismondo was renowned as one of the cruellest and lustful men of his time. His enemy, Pope Pius II, called him the 'prince of all wickedness'. In one of the many poems he composed as part of his variegated activity as a Renaissance man he begins:

> I confess my sins to you Father,
> And first of all your ten commandments,
> Which I have often debased and corrupted
> With my enormous and wicked vices...

This illustrates with eerie beauty a life of unlimited ambition and lust, disloyalty, and power. Tradition has it that he tortured and then poisoned Ginevra d'Este, marrying the powerful and dangerous Francesco Sforza's daughter Polissena for obvious political and military advantage. But soon he betrayed Sforza, cheated him out of a large sum of money and nurtured for him a hatred only second to that for Federico da Montefeltro — his mortal enemy. Then Polissena too died in mysterious circumstances, possibly strangled by Sigismondo. In 1461 he was declared a heretic by Pope Pius II (1458–64), excommunicated and sentenced to be burned at the stake for a series of crimes which omits none known to man, including robbery, adultery, incest, sodomy, rape, parricide, uxoricide, sacrilege, murder, and less vile crimes such as counterfeiting money. An effigy of his body was burnt in Rome, and a crusade set out to destroy him. The war lasted for two years, but Sigismondo fought valiantly and desperately, and managed to save Rimini for himself. He ended his life stripped of all power and most of his money, a man of extraordinary gifts who could have had everything, but by over-reaching and allowing his violent passions to rule him finished by losing nearly everything his father and uncle had created. It was only by the desperate stratagem of signing a papal treaty that he maintained Rimini at all: that city was to be left to him until his death, but would revert to the Church if he died without a legitimate heir.

Yet this strange character was also a man of artistic sensitivity. His many-faceted personality enabled him to correspond with the learned men of his age, write poetry and patronize writers to create Latin verse in honour of his passionate love for his long-time mistress and third wife Isotta degli Atti. His love for her was such that he adopted the initials SI — rather like an adolescent might carve on a tree — for his stem, and decorated the columns and statues of his 'Temple' with them. He was also accepted as friend by exceptional men like Leon Battista Alberti (1404–72).

Isotta degli Atti, by Matteo de'Pasti.

It was in fact through Alberti that Sigismondo created the main achievement of his life: the rebuilding of the church of St Francis in Rimini, usually known as the 'Tempio Malatestiano'. Although the building was and is nominally a church, Sigismondo's concept was closer to the Roman ideal of a temple which would function as a monument to himself and Isotta — and to their love. In fact, the unfinished façade with its four Corinthian columns separating three arches is reminiscent of a classical triumphal arch, of which one of the best examples — the arch of Augustus — can be seen in Rimini itself. The rebuilding began under another architect in 1446, but the façade was designed about four years later by Leon Battista Alberti, whom Sigismondo probably met when in service to Florence. It is celebrated as the first time a classical solution was applied to the west façade of a church.

Alberti was one of the leading scholars of the fifteenth century, writing plays, Latin poems, and treatises on subjects varying from moral philosophy, grammar,

Sigismondo, relief in Tempio Malatestiano.

and marriage to hydraulics. From his study of ancient buildings in Rome he deduced what he thought were the rules of classical art, and in a series of treatises on painting, sculpture, and architecture he put forward a scientific theory concerning perspective and proportion. His observations on the classical orders of architecture and ornament were of fundamental importance for late fifteenth-century architecture and the incomplete 'Temple' provides one of the first examples of his theories put into practice. Later buildings included the church of Santa Maria Novella in Florence and Sant'Andrea in Mantova. At the time he accepted the commission Rimini was a thriving port city with a newly completed castle near the cathedral, new defence walls and a population of about 15,000. It was an elegant and well-run city, relatively clean and with many fine buildings.

In his *Ten Books on Architecture* Alberti insisted upon two elements of architecture: beauty and ornament. Beauty consisted of harmonious, that is to say classical, proportions; ornament consisted of elements 'added on' to improve external appearances, including columns, capitals, and pilasters. We can see this put into practice in the 'Temple', where the severe proportions are perfectly finished by the sparse decoration. The columns on the façade are not structural, but merely ornament. In this case, he was not designing from scratch but refurbishing a thirteenth-century Gothic church; thus he could not choose the proportions of the basic structure, but skilfully adapted his design to the existing building. His beautifully modulated use of columns and arches masks the obvious difficulty of altering the basic structure. Faultless marble was brought from Venice for the chapel walls.

The elegant and reposing result of his reconstruction in Rimini is a church which appears at first sight to be a temple standing on its plinth, with the façade borrowed from a triumphal arch. The secondary arches on the façade were intended to hold the sarcophagi of Sigismondo and his wife, while other family members were to be remembered in the niches on the side of the 'Tempio'. The unusual aspect of the commission is that the architect designed the building by correspondence, sending corrections and details when they were needed and maintaining overall control of the work. The local architect Matteo de' Pasti is in fact credited with the interior, and seems to have been a second architect on site. The unfinished façade was to have had a further storey repeating the central arch, with a huge dome surmounting the whole building which can be seen in a medallion made by Matteo de' Pasti. Inside, where a single aisleless space surprises the visitor, the classical decoration was never completed. But even as it stands, the 'Temple' is an impressive monument both to the taste of its patron and to the skill of Alberti. The exterior was to be the model for many classical churches in the later Renaissance and stands as one of the great originals of the history of architecture.

Inside is the monumental tomb of Sigismondo and Isotta with frescoes which are badly decayed but which must have once been splendid. In one by Piero della Francesca (*c.*1420–92) we see Sigismondo kneeling before his patron saint St Sigismondo, an Aryan king who was converted by St Avitus of Vienne and became King of Burgundy for a year before his death by drowning, set between two classical pilasters with the barely discernible Malatesta castle of Rimini behind him. Something of his character and priorities may be suggested by the superbly painted hunting dogs at rest. The head of Sigismondo here is probably copied from the more famous oil-painting in a private collection in Florence. The mathematical and classical perfection of Piero's painting again reflects the taste of Sigismondo and his contemporaries. It is a fitting monument to this the greatest member of the Malatesta family, who unfortunately died in 1466 before the building was completed.

THE LAST MALATESTA

The Malatesta dynasty began a slow decline with the loss of territory by Sigismondo. Both his brother Malatesta Novello (1418–65) and his bastard son Roberto (c.1442–1534) continued the family tradition of *condottieri*. Roberto, who was legitimized by Pope Nicholas V in an attempt to maintain Rimini for the family, was an excellent soldier and won several famous victories. As part of a policy of creating new alliances he married Elisabetta, daughter of Federico da Montefeltro. But Pope Paul II (1464–71) feared this courageous and ambitious *condottiere* and sought to bring him into the papal pay. The pope suspected that Sigismondo's widow Isotta would come to an agreement with Venice, and on the whole he preferred a Malatesta ruler to losing Rimini altogether. In 1468 Roberto entered Rimini in disguise and took the city from his stepmother in the name of the Church.

In a new and complicated turn of events, the pope realized he had been tricked and attempted to intervene when he realized Rimini was lost; ironically it was Federico da Montefeltro who aided Roberto — fearing papal encroachment on his own state. Roberto took the city in firm control in true Malatesta fashion, murdering his two brothers Sallustio and Valerio and probably poisoning Isotta. He pursued a victorious military career, becoming captain-general of the Venetian army and holding Rimini through his personal prowess and diplomatic ability. He died in Rome, possibly poisoned, after winning a battle against Alfonso, Duke of Calabria and son of King Ferdinand I of Naples, in 1482. For this victory he appears in the fresco representing the Pharaoh being drowned in the Red Sea on the wall of the Sistine Chapel. He was very much his father's son, as can be seen in the fine bas-relief erected by Sixtus IV — for whom the Sistine Chapel is named — in St Peter's in Rome, and now in the Louvre.

His bastard son Pandolfo V (1475–1539) and his grandson Sigismondo (1499–1543) brought the dynasty to an ignominious end, fighting almost perpetually in the desperate enterprise of holding Rimini, alternatively taking and losing the city. In 1500 Pandolfo fled from the city as Cesare Borgia advanced against him, and on another occasion sold Rimini to Venice. After the Sack of Rome in 1527 he managed to take it once again, but was kicked out by the people the following year after committing atrocious crimes and cruelty against them. He too died in Rome, where he was buried in the church of Santa Maria di Trastevere. With Pandolfo the dynasty of Rimini ended: his son Sigismondo fought like his father and grandfather for Venice, but died in poverty and obscurity in Reggio. His own son, another Sigis-

Malatesta Novello, by Pisanello.

mondo, also enjoyed the protection of the Este family: he lived as a gentleman of the court of the last Duke of Ferrara, Alfonso II, and then with Duke Cesare at Modena when the Este were forced to leave Ferrara. He died an old man in the first decades of the seventeenth century, and was the last of the principal line of Malatesta descending from Pandolfo III.

THE MALATESTA IN LITERATURE

Having been immortalized in the *Divine Comedy* in the thirteenth century, the Malatesta had an unexpected revival of poetic interest centuries after their demise in the works of the American poet Ezra Pound (1885–1972). He chose Sigismondo Pandolfo to be a major figure representing the entire Renaissance in his epic poem *The Cantos*. In his attempt to compress the civilization of the centuries not taken account of by Homer, Virgil, and Dante, Pound set up a series of subject rhymes. Thus the Malatesta cantos (VIII–XI) represent the rebirth of Italy in the last half of the fifteenth century, which 'rhymes' with the birth of the American nation in the 1770s. Jefferson rhymes with Malatesta; Monticello with the Malatesta 'Temple'. It is fascinating to watch this imaginative enterprise take shape as the modern poet's mind takes pertinent details from historical documents and brings Sigismondo alive in the twentieth century in quite a new way. Clearly Pound felt some kind of empathetic relationship with Sigismondo, for the effect is occasionally spectacular — although it also often falls into banality.

Pound works from letters and documents written or dictated by Sigismondo, achieving an authentic voice which seems to echo from the fifteenth century. When the *condottiere* assumes a new command the terrible conditions of life in battle and the paramount importance of income are evoked:

> Venice has taken me on again
> At 7,000 a month, *fiorini di Camera*
> For 2,000 horse and four hundred footmen,

> And it rains here by the gallon,
> We have had to dig a new ditch.
> In three or four days
> I shall try to set up the bombards. (Canto VIII)

The rapid and often confusing changes of employer are amusingly expressed:

> Who stood with the Venetians in November,
> With the Milanese in December,
> Sold Milan in November, stole Milan in December
> Or something of that sort,
> Commanded the Milanese in the spring,
> The Venetians at midsummer,
> The Milanese in the autumn,
> And was Naples' ally in October,
> He, Sigismondo ... (Canto VIII)

Cantos IX and XI provide a marvellous narration of Sigismondo's campaigns, introducing his friends, enemies, and wives. A final quotation from the closing lines of Canto IX will illustrate the poet's fine powers of description when he refers again to the Temple:

> ...in the style 'Past ruin'd Latium'
> The filigree hiding the gothic,
>   with a touch of rhetoric in the whole
> And the old sarcophagi,
>   such as lie, smothered in grass, by San Vitale.

They can still be seen exactly as Pound describes them in Ravenna.

This poetry demonstrates a remarkable instance of bringing the past to life by significant detail. That the Malatesta merit such attention is beyond all doubt, and Pound's *Cantos* stand as the last monument to them together with the unfinished 'Temple'. The lands the Malatesta fought for and held are now part of the almost continuous strip of holiday beach from Ravenna to Pescara. Rimini itself is a modern city of hotels and restaurants in which the Roman triumphal arch stands incongruously. More than any of the other Italian dynasties, it is difficult to evoke the Malatesta in the few physical signs of their passage which remain.

6

THE GONZAGA

The Gonzaga family originally came from the town of the same name twenty-five kilometres due south of Mantova on the right bank of the River Po. Known as the Corradi of Gonzaga, they appear in the twelfth century as powerful local landlords who received grants of land from the monastery of San Benedetto di Polirone, north of Gonzaga. The land reclamation of which these grants were a part contributed to the future wealth of the whole region, and the plains south of Mantova are still the most fertile of Italy. The monastery has long since ceased to exist, but the magnificent façade of the church of San Benedetto evokes the splendour it must once have possessed. The church was redesigned in the sixteenth century by Giulio Romano, a pupil of Raphael, who built a classical façade onto the Gothic structure in the manner of Alberti's façade on San Francesco in Rimini.

The importance of the Gonzaga increased gradually through the thirteenth century. But dynastic rule of Mantova was established by Luigi Gonzaga (c.1268–1360), who in 1328 seized the city and was acclaimed captain-general. Mantova then consisted of four islands situated in four lakes. Still today it is surrounded on three sides by water, and in winter mist appears mysterious like an island-mirage — rather like Venice approached from Mestre or the airport. By exploiting the power vacuum in Italy at the time, and creating new wealth by selling weapons to the many small states in a perpetual state of war, Luigi managed in few years to make himself a vital member of the League against King John of Bohemia in 1332. In this way his name was linked with well-established powers such as the Este and the Visconti who also participated. Between him and his eleven sons it had been possible to create a solid hold over the city, making vital marriage alliances with the above families. He was succeeded as captain-general by his son Guido (c.1290–1369) and grandson Ludovico (c.1325–82), but although they achieved some prominence beyond Mantova it was with Ludovico's son and heir Francesco I, born of his marriage to Alda d'Este, that the Gonzaga began to play the major role in Italian politics that they maintained for three centuries.

Opposite *Federico Gonzaga, by Titian.*

Mantova: the Gonzaga fighting their rivals for control of the city.

FRANCESCO I
(1366–1407)

Francesco succeeded his father at the age of sixteen. The previous year he had been married to Agnese Visconti, daughter of Bernabò and one year younger than him, thereby confirming the new alliance with Milan. Immediately after the succession he made a formal visit to Venice, the other major neighbouring power. These diplomatic manoeuvres, together with the consolidated Gonzaga power, facilitated the transition. He was immediately recognized by the Emperor as Imperial Vicar of Mantova, and also accepted by the city council. But formal designation as captain-general only came when he reached the age of twenty-one.

His marriage was destined to be brief because three years later Bernabò was murdered by his nephew Gian Galeazzo. Francesco deemed it wise to remove the presence of a link with Bernabò which could create difficulties in his relations with the Visconti, especially since Agnese was a declared enemy of her cousin, the new ruler of Milan. She invited her brothers to Mantova, and plotted with them against Gian Galeazzo. Francesco found it impossible to prevent their activities, and considered it useless to send the brothers Carlo and Ludovico away from Mantova because Agnese would in any case maintain contact with them. So he arranged a patently false trial in which his wife was accused of conspiring against him, and also of committing adultery. Agnese was naturally found guilty, and was beheaded in 1391 together with her presumed lover.

Following this execution Francesco travelled through Italy, visiting Florence, Pisa, Bologna, Ferrara, and, above all, Rimini, where his sister Elisabetta was married to the *condottiere* Carlo Malatesta. As the result of this visit Francesco married Carlo's sister Margherita, just two years after Agnese's death. Although his new wife lived only for six more years, she produced an heir in the Gian Francesco who was to become the first Marquis of Mantova.

Ironically, the execution of Agnese did not prevent Gian Galeazzo Visconti from turning against Mantova a few years later. In 1400 Francesco was forced by the imminent threat to sign an alliance against Milan, together with Venice, Florence, Bologna, Padova, and Ferrara. Visconti, now Duke of Milan, had extended his power over much of northern Italy and part of Tuscany, and there seemed no limit to his ambition. Certainly it included the extension of the Duchy of Milan along the valley of the Po towards Bologna, and this meant absorbing Mantova. Francesco's diplomatic endeavours trod a perilous knife-edge between independence from the Visconti and making alliances against them on the one hand, and fighting for or with the Visconti when greater enemies threatened their delicate balancing act within the Po valley. Thus when the new Emperor Rupert of Bavaria attacked the Duchy of Milan in 1401, Francesco Gonzaga fought alongside his brother-in-law Carlo Malatesta, and *condottieri* such as Facino Cane and Alberico da Barbiano. The situation improved from his point of view the following year when Gian Galeazzo Visconti died before his grandiose ambitions could be completed. After that Francesco fought only once more, for Venice against the Carrara of Padova. He died in 1407 at the age of forty-two, having been named Count of Gonzaga in 1394 by Pope Boniface IX but never obtaining the imperial title of Marquis that he so much desired.

His legacy was more practical. He made the first physical changes which identified the city of Mantova with the Gonzaga. He employed Bartolino da Novara, who had designed the citadel of the Este at Ferrara, to build a huge new castle with a massive tower at each corner. This magnificent structure is still today the most impressive monument to Gonzaga power. He also rebuilt the bridge of San Giorgio which leads across the lakes surrounding the city to the castle. The cathedral was rebuilt at that time, although the improvements disappeared when it was later completely transformed by Giulio Romano into a late Renaissance building. Count Francesco reorganized the administration of the city, and provided for the poor and needy by providing a foundation whose administrators were to search the streets of Mantova once a month, taking notes. The city grew richer, and a large Jewish community soon developed under his tolerant rule. In 1390 a bank was established, providing loans on the guarantees of deposited valuables — rather like a pawnshop. Inside the castle Francesco founded the Gonzaga library, which at the time of his death contained over four hundred volumes including French books which he brought back from a visit in 1389.

Eleonora Gonzaga, by Titian.

GIAN FRANCESCO, FIRST MARQUIS
(1395–1444)

Francesco's eldest legitimate son, born of Margherita Malatesta, succeeded to his father at the age of twelve. He was officially recognized as Lord of Mantova, while in fact the city was governed by his uncle Carlo Malatesta, nominally regent. The regency in turn was guaranteed by Venice, whose troops presided over the city. This was the time when the Malatesta sought to extend their power beyond the Marches and Romagna, and Carlo's brother Pandolfo III ruled Brescia and Bergamo. The Malatesta ascendancy over this Gonzaga was to last his whole life, since two years after his father's death he married Paolo Malatesta, daughter of Malatesta Malatesta the ruler of Pesaro, a highly cultivated lady who exercised a long-term influence on her husband.

Like the small states of Rimini and Montefeltro, Mantova flourished because of its unique strategic position on the borders of the greater powers of Milan and Venice, with Bavaria to the north. Gian Francesco exploited this small advantage to the full. His military career set the seal on a family which survived and prospered perhaps more than any other by putting itself at the service of the most powerful — even if that meant rapid changes that led to accusations of treachery. At one time he even fought in the army of the anti-pope John XXIII while his mentor Carlo Malatesta fought for the enemy in the person of Pope Gregory XII. Like many of his contemporaries, war provided important extra income through the often generous *condotte* stipulated when soldiers of renown provided an army for the greater powers. Thus Gian Francesco fought for Filippo Maria Visconti, then in the anti-Visconti league between Venice and Florence; later he fought for Venice while his son Ludovico was part of the Visconti army they were opposing.

The ruthlessness and overriding ambition of Gian Francesco led him to purchase the title of Marquis from the Holy Roman Emperor Sigismond I for 12,000 florins in 1433, succeeding where his father had failed. Sigismond travelled to Mantova and personally conferred the title in a grandiose ceremony which made the Gonzaga hereditary lords of the city. In order to seal the importance of this political and social progress, Gian Francesco's son Ludovico was engaged to the Emperor's niece, Barbara of Brandenburg. While the family had disdained to use the title of Count of Gonzaga, they were now happy to brandish the more impressive title of Marquis of Mantova.

Gian Francesco strengthened the city's fortifications, drained the neighbouring marshes, and built a system of dykes. On the reclaimed land he encouraged the development of agriculture and gave a new impulse to the economy of the area through this and the cloth industry he also promoted. He introduced the production of tapestries for the first time in Italy, importing experts from Flanders to teach local artisans. He was recognized as a wise prince and patron of artists. Alberti dedicated his *Treatise on Painting* to him and other artists who worked at Mantova under his rule. But his most remarkable achievement lay in his patronage of the humanists, and consequent founding of the famous school of Mantova, the *Casa Giocosa*, or house of play.

This was the private school or *gymnasium palatinum* of the Gonzaga court, which the humanist and teacher Vittorino da Feltre (1378–1446) moulded into one of the finest schools in Europe in a period of over twenty years. Vittorino had himself studied at Padova, where he was taught and influenced by two of the foremost scholars of the time: Vergerio — Petrus Paulus Vergerius — who invented the new humanist approach to education in his treatise *The Education of the Gentleman (c.*1404) based upon Roman ideas of education, emphasizing liberal arts and individuality; and Gasparino da Barzizza, a leading Latin scholar who used the educational works of Quintilian and Cicero as the basis of his teaching. Following his studies, Vittorino first ran a school in Padova and then taught at the university until in 1423 he accepted the position of court tutor at Mantova. The choice of tutor is itself indicative of the open-mindedness of Gian Francesco Gonzaga, but Vittorino went beyond his expectations in creating a distinguished school and setting educational precedents which were to influence schools throughout Europe.

Initially his task was to educate the three sons of Marquis Gian Francesco and his wife Paola Malatesta, including the future Marquis Ludovico. But the 'school' soon expanded as more children were born and prominent local families were also invited to send their children. Eventually other humanists such as Guarino da Verona, who, as we have seen, taught the Este children in Ferrara under Niccolò and Leonello, and Francesco Filelfo, who was secretary to Pandolfo II Malatesta and served the Visconti and Sforza, also sent their children there. Federico da Montefeltro studied at Vittorino's school as a young boy. It was housed in a separate building which had once been a kind of pleasure kiosk called the *Casa Gioiosa*, or house of joy, whose name Vittorino transformed to *Giocosa*.

The school was based upon ideas which have since become familiar in English public schools: a rigorous curriculum of classical studies together with a spartan emphasis on physical exercises and games. Vittorino himself was ascetic by temperament and insisted on physical activities being carried out regardless of temperature or weather conditions. They were intended as part of the cultivation of moral and religious values. But the real emphasis of his method was on classical letters, and Vittorino himself was responsible for the teaching of Latin for the first five years, using texts by Ovid, Virgil, Cicero, Sallust, and Livy. At the same time the pupils learned Greek, which was taught by other scholars who were brought in from as far afield as Constantinople. Homer, Demosthenes, and Plato were the core of the Greek curriculum. Beyond these classical studies, logic, rhetoric, and some mathematics and natural philosophy were taught. A library was developed which contained copies of most of the important works of antiquity, and was often in the vanguard of classical studies even though it was 'merely' a school library.

In fact, the *Casa Giocosa* was widely regarded as superior to many of the universities of the time, and was at one time designated a *studium generale* or university. But Vittorino seems not to have cared for this status, and preferred to concentrate on the perfection of his teaching methods. These were based largely upon oral drills and memorizing passages of Latin and Greek texts, but also involved class discussion and the use of notebooks by pupils. Above all, Vittorino seems to have been a remarkable teacher who in twenty-three years' continuous service laid the foundations for the greatness of the Gonzaga family in the succeeding century. He was accepted as an intimate member of the court by Gian Francesco, and contributed to the atmosphere and learning of the court far beyond his function as teacher to the Gonzaga children. Ludovico and his schoolmates — including Federico da Montefeltro, on whom the effects of this exemplary schooling were profound and permanent — were extremely fortunate in having a teacher who fully understood the importance of formal education. The schoolmaster was seen by Vittorino and other humanists as vital to the humanist project.

The general consensus nowadays is that Gian Francesco Gonzaga overreached himself, for his last years were spent in relative political and financial decline. That he had been a great Renaissance prince is not in doubt; but it is clear that he owed much to the Malatesta, first to Carlo's diplomatic expertise and second

Opposite *Elisabetta Gonzaga, by Raphael.*

128

to the intelligence of his wife Paola. Having been granted lands by the Venetians for his past actions in their service, he dreamed of conspiring against them in order to obtain Verona and Vicenza. But without Carlo's counsel he seems to have gone ahead more on the basis of a naïve belief that his prestige as Marquis would make success inevitable than on any solid grounds. The result was that he lost much of the land and power previously conquered. He died a disappointed man in 1444.

MARQUIS LUDOVICO I
(1414–78)

The influence of the *Casa Giocosa* may best be seen in the character and life of Gian Francesco's son Ludovico, who was one of the least cruel of Renaissance princes and a notable patron of the arts. It is said that even when he had become Marquis he would never sit down in the presence of Vittorino da Feltre.

Ludovico was forced by necessity to pursue the career of *condottiere*, and like his father spent his life in a delicate balancing act between Milan and Venice. Financially he was far more successful. In 1446 he accepted a contract from the Visconti in Milan, but in the following year passed to Venice in the hope of obtaining lands in the western part of the Republic. He was extremely well paid by Venice, so that when he passed back into the service of the new Duke Francesco Sforza a few years later, Venice began to attack his own possessions near Mantova in revenge. Finally, in 1466, he again turned to Venice and won a *condotta* of princely dimensions which guaranteed him 36,000 florins a year in peace, and 80,000 florins a year in times of war; shortly afterwards, he took on another, secret *condotta* with King Ferdinand of Naples for a sum only slightly inferior. Throughout, he also maintained cordial relations with the minor powers, and kept up correspondence with such men as Cosimo de' Medici, and Leonello and Borso d'Este. He was fortunate to be able to follow the career of *condottiere* in a period of relative peace, and was never pushed to demonstrate what he might have been capable of in battle. Thus through genuine military operations and what can only be described as financial opportunism, Ludovico managed to steer a middle course through the political and military confusion of those difficult years and to enrich himself and his city.

While Ludovico was often absent from Mantova for long periods during his military campaigns, the administration of the city — and education of their children — was overseen by his wife Barbara. She encouraged the cloth industry, ensured that expenditure was kept within bounds, and showed a constant and sincere charitable interest in the people of Mantova. Her presence, and the visits of her uncle the Margrave Albert of Brandenburg and father the Elector John of Brandenburg, gave international lustre to the court. It was through her offices that in 1459 Pope Pius II (1458–64) called a General Council at Mantova to proclaim a crusade against the Turks. This was a prestigious event for the Gonzaga, since apart from the honour derived from the pope's four-month residence in Mantova other participants included such figures as Francesco Sforza, Duke Sigismond of Austria, Cardinal Rodrigo Borgia, Barbara's father, and ambassadors from France, Brittany, Venice, Savoy, and Poland. In Mantegna's portrait of Barbara one can see the combination of seriousness, gentle concern, and sympathy as she looks on her husband. She seems to have been the ideal wife for such a proud, ambitious but often absent man who needed her strong support. Yet her policy of dividing power amongst her children led ultimately to the disintegration of Gonzaga wealth and power into a myriad of branches which made their decline as a single ruling dynasty inevitable.

But for the moment such a decline appeared impossible. The immense earnings from Ludovico's military career and considerable income from the rich agricultural holdings around the city were entirely devoted to improving the splendour of his family name and of his city. When money was short, taxes were increased or invented, including an interesting 'tax' on workdays which provided free labour to Mantova by arranging that each village should give a certain number of days a year in proportion to its population. The streets and main squares of Mantova were paved and many new palaces and churches built, some, as we shall see, designed by famous architects brought in from Tuscany. A covered market was built and the hospital of San Leonardo founded. Churches and monasteries were built in neighbouring villages and towns as well as in Mantova. Another sign of growing prosperity was the foundation of the first Gonzaga mint, producing fine gold coins with the image of the Marquis.

Ludovico retained the interest in letters which he absorbed at the *Casa Giocosa*. Throughout his life he collected manuscripts of the poet Virgil, who had been born in Mantova, and added copies of other classical authors to the library. He admired recent Italian poets, especially Dante and Petrarch, and had copies of the *Divine Comedy* and Boccaccio's *Filocolo* richly illuminated. He also collected works of natural history. He encouraged printing in Mantova, patronizing the press which as early as 1473 published its first book, Boccaccio's *Decamerone*.

His taste and patronage of the visual arts was of even greater importance. He invited the greatest living architect, Leon Battista Alberti (1404–72), to Mantova — perhaps inspired by his mother's knowledge of Sigismondo Malatesta's 'Temple' in Rimini. Alberti designed the chapel of the Incoronata in the cathedral of Mantova, and the two severely classical churches of S. Sebastiano and S. Andrea, whose façades are based upon temple fronts. The designs were executed by Luca Fancelli (*c.*1430–95), who also built and expanded the Gonzaga villas at Cavriana, Revere and Gonzaga itself. Although Fancelli was Tuscan he spent most of his working life in collaboration with Alberti or completing Alberti's projects. As an insight into the flexibility of Renaissance architects it is also interesting to note that he worked both on the cathedral of Milan and that of Florence. S. Andrea is an important and interesting Renaissance church, the interior of which is surprisingly large due to the absence of aisles. The single barrel-vaulted space is reminiscent of the Malatesta 'Temple'.

Amongst other artists patronized by Ludovico, Antonio Pisanello (1395-1455) went to Mantova to decorate one of the halls in the castle with frescoes, fragments of which were recently rediscovered. The sculptor Donatello (1386–1466) spent two years in the city in 1450-1 and made two bronze busts of his patron. It seems that Donatello also acted as an agent for Ludovico, purchasing pieces of antique sculpture that came on the market.

His, and his successors', patronage of Andrea Mantegna (c. 1431–1506) ranks as one of the most fruitful and important in the history of Italian painting. From 1460 Mantegna was official court painter to the Gonzaga. His paintings flatter and laud their power, but at the same time an undeniable intellectual strength and passion lift them beyond mere sycophancy. He was required to illustrate the classical tastes of the Gonzaga court, and did so in series of paintings like those of the life and deeds of Hercules, now lost, and the nine panels of the Triumph of Caesar which can been seen in the Royal Collection at Hampton Court.

The most interesting work Mantegna did was the frescoes for the 'Camera degli Sposi' in Ludovico's own nuptial chamber in a corner tower of the castle of S. George within the ducal palace. He spent nine years painting this room about eight metres square, and the lunettes and vault above it contain a series of frescoes of the Gonzaga family. In the section showing Ludovico with his family and court, above a fireplace, the use of a low viewpoint increases the physical stature of the family members so that they seem to rise almost supernaturally over the viewer. Mantegna has used this trick of perspective to create a kind of stage above the onlooker on which the family members stand or sit as tangible beings. Their eyes gaze around the group, covering every possible direction as if staking out their rights over the entire world. Arrogance is unmistakable on the faces of individuals, yet the overall sensation is of a benign and sophisticated group of men and women, each of whom bears a distinctive personality. Ludovico himself listens with particular attention to a courtier or secretary who has just brought him a letter, as if demonstrating his interest in and concern for his subjects. The portraits appear to be an extension of the space in the room, as if the frescoes themselves open up the room; this illusion is sustained by the remarkable ceiling, where beneath an open sky human figures standing on a balcony gaze down into the room. The painting is open and optimistic, reflecting the present power and future prospects of the dynasty.

Mantegna's character must have caused considerable displeasure to his patron. Although he was well paid by Ludovico, he constantly complained about the smallest of matters — about his tailor, or a neighbour who had stolen fruit from his orchard. His patron always replied with courtesy and understanding, promising to provide a greater income as soon as possible, even in times of financial restraint. His letters reflect a constant lack of money, and he seems to have been driven by a desire to become a nobleman himself. He built a new and expensive house in Mantova as soon as he could afford it, and spent years in obtaining a Palatinate countship. His ambitions were satisfied by a grateful family who arranged for Mantegna to be buried in the cathedral of Mantova.

Mantegna was one of the major painters of the Renaissance and there can be no doubt that his work at the Gonzaga court is to the glory of the dynasty. For all Ludovico's failings, it must be said that Mantegna was fortunate to have found such a long-suffering and generous patron.

MARQUIS FEDERICO
(1442–84)

Although Federico succeeded his father on the latter's death in 1478, much of the real power associated with the title had been distributed amongst his brothers at the instigation of Barbara of Brandenburg. From Gian Francesco (1443–96), who became Prince of Bozzolo, descended the cadet branches of the Gonzaga of Bozzolo and Sabbioneta; from Rodolfo (1451–95), who became Prince of Castiglione and married Anna Malatesta, sister to Roberto Malatesta of Rimini, descended the Gonzaga of Castiglione. The Gonzaga property of Gazzuolo was given to Ludovico, who had taken holy orders and later became Bishop of Mantova.

Federico himself became a widower when his wife Margaret of Bavaria — sister of the Duke of Bavaria — died in the following year, leaving him with five small children who were brought up by their grandmother until she herself died two years later. But her influence over the Gonzaga family history had already been extended into the future by her choice of Isabella d'Este, daughter of her friend Leonora d'Este, as future spouse for her grandson Francesco.

Federico had already fought with the Milanese army of Galeazzo Maria Sforza before his father's death, and now continued to follow the tightrope policy established by Ludovico. As a result of his *condotta* with Milan he spent much of his short rule distant from Mantova. It was the period when Girolamo Riario, nephew to Pope Sixtus IV (1471–84) was attempting to create a state for himself beyond the papal states, as we have seen in the story of the Este and Malatesta dynasties. Federico naturally allied himself with Milan and Florence against Venice, Sixtus IV, and Riario, since their success would destroy the balance of power that favoured Mantova and would threaten Gonzaga power. Apart from that, the allies were led by the old Gonzaga friend Federico da Montefeltro — who died during this campaign. After two years of skirmishes, battles, and negotiations, the threatened war dissolved in a peace treaty that all parties were pleased to sign. But Federico had been kept away from Mantova for most of this period.

Federico's short rule and the constant wars that plagued it allowed him little time to imprint his personality on the city. He planned to enlarge the castle in Mantova, and wrote to Federico da Montefeltro asking for the plans of the castle at Urbino. He continued his father's patronage of Mantegna, and commissioned him to decorate a new villa he was building. He also bought new manuscripts and books for the library and maintained contact with the scholars and humanists he had known since he was a child. He seems to have been an intelligent, understanding, and sensitive man who would have made an excellent ruler if he had not died in 1484 at the age of forty-two.

Mantova: ducal palace.

MARQUIS FRANCESCO I (1466–1519) AND
ISABELLA D'ESTE (1474–1539)

When Francesco succeeded his father his first task was to assert his right to rule over his ambitious uncles Gian Francesco and Rodolfo. This he did by renewing his father's *condotta* with the Duke of Milan, thus obtaining Milanese protection while he established full control. Some years later, however, he transferred his allegiance to Venice, obtaining military glory at the battle of Fornovo against Charles VIII of France. But he was then shelved by the Venetians for suspect loyalty, and spent the remainder of his military career fighting for Lodovico il Moro and King Louis XII — always against the Venetians, who once humiliated him by taking him prisoner. His last *condotta* was ironically again for Venice, but under the orders of the warrior Pope Julius II. Thus he repeated the career pattern of his wily grandfather Lodovico, and like him earned the major part of his income from military *condotte* — both in time of peace and in war.

Marquis Francesco was a brave and perhaps impetuous soldier. He was known as an excellent horseman and swordsman whose favourite pastimes were jousting and tournaments. He showed little interest in literature, and enjoyed obscene stories as much as the Bible. He spent much of his adult life away from his court, either at war or engaged in diplomatic discussion. For instance, in the single year 1491 he went to Milan for a joust, to Bologna for his brother's wedding, then to Urbino for a visit, and later to Milan again. He maintained an excellent diplomatic service, Baldassare Castiglione being one of his finest ambassadors, the result of which was to enable him to forestall problems and maintain his position — for example on the arrival of Charles VIII of France in Italy. He also exploited to the full his direct relationship with the rulers of Milan, Ferrara, and Urbino. In all this activity his real devotion was to the Gonzaga dynasty and his own intimate family. Although he began as one of the great *condottieri*, his military career declined after his capture by the Venetians. In later years he was a changed man, humiliated by his period of imprisonment, deluded in his ambition, and severely weakened by syphilis.

In fact the wisest move he made, both politically and personally, was to marry Isabella d'Este in February 1490. As can be seen in the portrait by Leonardo da Vinci, she was a beautiful woman with golden hair and sparkling black eyes. She possessed exquisitely good artistic taste and an excellent background in literature, having been taught by Battista Guarino, the son of Vittorino da Feltre's friend and peer Guarino da Verona, and was naturally inclined towards study and meditation. But although she knew Virgil and Cicero, she also played the lute and enjoyed dancing. Her great joy in life and personal vitality were matched by a strong sense of duty and dedication to her family — over'which she exercised a profound influence behind the scenes, well beyond her husband's rule, for a total of nearly half a century. Isabella d'Este was without question one of the most exceptional figures of the Italian Renaissance, and the Gonzaga court at Mantova was a suitable setting for her talent.

The wedding was celebrated at Ferrara in February 1490 following a year of detailed preparations. After the ceremony she rode through the city in a chariot draped with gold cloth, and was feasted at a huge banquet inside the castle, in a hall draped with Arras tapestries brought from Naples by her mother. Guests ate on a gold dinner service specially made for the occasion in Venice. The next day she set off for Mantova on a gilded barge attended by four galleys and fifty other boats, together with the Duke and Duchess of Ferrara, her brothers Alfonso, Ferrante, and Ippolito, and a hundred courtiers. The reception was even more dramatic, with pageants and music at churches and squares on the way into the city. While bride and groom, with relatives, and ambassadors from France and all the Italian powers, feasted inside, another banquet was provided for the people outside — as many as seventeen thousand, or more than half the population — and wine flowed from the city fountains. The celebrations lasted for days, with tournaments, plays, processions, and banquets each day.

In his declining years Francesco lived in a single wing of the castle, and then in a country villa near Mantova with hounds, falcons, and buffoons as his company. Meanwhile, Isabella decorated a suite of rooms with frescoes and alabaster which she called her 'paradise', and filled it with her collection of paintings and sculpture. From this privileged position she corresponded with family members, painters, and writers including Ariosto, Trissino, Pietro Bembo, Castiglione, Sebastiano del Piombo, Cristoforo Romano, Niccolò da Correggio, and Leonardo da Vinci. Another, and more unusual, correspondent was the Knight of St John Brother Sabba da Castiglione, a relative of Baldassare, who spent much of his time during a three-year sojourn in Greece seeking out antique sculptures for Isabella. She also patronized Mantegna, Giulio Romano, Giovanni Bellini, Antonio Correggio, Leonardo, and Titian — who painted a celebrated portrait of her during a visit to Mantova in 1529 — and tried in vain to commission works by Gentile Bellini, Perugino, Michelangelo, and Raphael. She made a *studiolo* in the castle, where her collection of Greek and Latin texts, French and Spanish romances, illuminated manuscripts, and new printed books was kept carefully under lock and key. She bought the whole series of books then being printed in Venice by Aldo Manuzio, bound in fine dark green and gold morocco. Her interest extended to using the best papers, and her bindings were closed with silver clasps, some of which were specially imported from Flanders.

It was with Isabella and Francesco that Mantova reached its acme as a centre of culture and a model for the whole peninsula. The administration of the city was not improved, and few new buildings were erected during their combined rule.

Ducal palace: the court of Ludovico Gonzaga, by Mantegna.

But Mantova, thanks to the patronage and taste of Marquis Ludovico, was already one of the finest cities in Italy so that Francesco was fortunate enough to rule in a splendour which he had inherited. From a modern perspective he was an extremely lucky man, whose weaknesses and failures are compensated for by the presence of his extraordinary wife.

Shortly before he died in 1519, Marquis Francesco made an official will which assured the succession to his eldest son Federico, and left an annual income of 8,000 ducats to his younger sons Ercole and Ferrante. Although Isabella tried to obtain a design for his tomb from both Raphael and Michelangelo, neither was ever built — and Raphael's design has been lost.

FEDERICO II, FIRST DUKE OF MANTOVA
(1500–40)

The new Marquis was nineteen years old, and was to rule under the regency of his mother and Francesco's brothers Cardinal Sigismondo and Giovanni until he was twenty-two. But it was Isabella who continued to exercise effective control of policies in the following years. She was widely respected and her influence was vitally important in the early years of Federico's rule. The two major projects she conceived were to make Federico captain-general of the Church, and to restore her nephew Duke Francesco Maria Sforza to power in Milan. That she succeeded in both is a measure of her diplomatic skill and influence. She provided a haven for the exiled Duke and Duchess of Urbino, the latter being her sister-in-law Elisabetta. She also arranged the futures of her other sons Ercole and Ferrante, who were to become vitally important in the history of both Italy and the family, and later acted as regents for Federico's successor Francesco II.

Ercole (1505–65) was destined for the Church. He became a bishop at fifteen and would have become a cardinal soon afterwards had there not been a new rule forbidding such a position to anyone under thirty. He was sent to study with the famous humanist and scholar Pietro Pomponazzi (1462–1525) at the University of Bologna. He became an excellent scholar of Latin and Greek, and took lessons in Arabic. With his mother's flouting of rules and the immense Gonzaga wealth behind him, he became a cardinal in 1527, a few days before the Sack of Rome. Ferrante (1507–57), on the other hand, was destined for a brilliant career as a soldier. At seventeen he was sent with the Mantovan ambassador Baldassare Castiglione to the court of Charles V in Spain, where he soon became an intimate of the Emperor. There he learned the arts of politics and diplomacy as well as those of war. He returned to Italy in 1527 to participate in the Sack of Rome with the Spanish army, fortuitously meeting Isabella who was in the city attempting to purchase a cardinal's hat for Ercole. She took refuge in the secure haven of Palazzo Colonna. Ferrante later fought for Charles in Flanders and Germany, against Suleiman the Magnificent in Hungary, and in the destruction of Tunis. From 1546 to 1555 he was Governor of Milan for Charles V, rebuilding much of the city and imposing its modern shape through the construction of the Spanish bastions which still form an important part of the city's toponymy.

Federico became the commander of the papal army under Pope Leo X in 1521 and almost immediately prepared for war against Milan together with Prospero Colonna. Once Milan had fallen, the army would move against France. Yet the Gonzaga, and especially Isabella, did not wish to appear publicly as enemies of the Emperor, so it was specified in Federico's *condotta* that he would not be required to combat against Charles V. He fought courageously under Colonna at Milan, and then at Piacenza and Pavia. The following year, after the death of Leo X, he became a paid captain of Charles V with a hundred lances at his command, fighting in the next few years against the remaining French outposts in Italy. But his position as commander of the papal army was renewed by Popes Hadrian VI and Clement VII, the latter at one time suggesting Federico as suitable candidate to rule the Duchy of Milan. With consummate and presumably inherited skill he managed to remain neutral when Clement VII began to express his hostility towards Charles V. Like his mother Isabella and brother Ferrante, however, his fundamental loyalty was to the Emperor.

The apogee of Federico's life and rule occurred in 1530 when the Emperor Charles V travelled in pomp and state from Bologna, where he had just been solemnly invested with the golden crown of the Holy Roman Emperor by Pope Clement VII (1523–34), to Mantova. He entered the city of the Gonzaga in state, and was greeted by fifty noble youths dressed in white who carried a white satin canopy on silver staves which protected the Emperor as he rode through a series of triumphal arches. He was greeted at the ducal palace by Isabella d'Este, and remained as guest of the Gonzaga for four weeks, hunting, banqueting, and visiting the family palaces and art collections. It was during this visit that he became enchanted by the paintings of Titian, who was later to be his favourite and court painter. During this visit he raised the marquisate of Mantova into a duchy and proclaimed Federico Duke of Mantova. The next morning, the new duke was betrothed to Charles's cousin Giulia of Aragon, although the marriage was in fact never to be celebrated.

Federico inherited an interest in the arts from his mother. In the early months of his rule Titian (*c.*1487–1576) paid a visit to Mantova and admired the frescoes of Mantegna in the 'Camera degli Sposi'. Later, Castiglione persuaded Giulio Romano (*c.*1492–1546), who was Raphael's chief assistant until the master's death in 1520, to come to Mantova. He built the Palazzo del Te, then just outside the city walls, and decorated it with extraordinary frescoes. One room is entirely covered — both walls and ceiling — with a series called 'The Fall of the Giants', in which the onlooker has the sensation of participating in the destruction of the giants by Jove and his thunderbolts.

DUKE FRANCESCO II (1533–50)
AND THE LATER GONZAGA

Mantova could no longer claim to be an independent power. Between the oppressive forces of the Habsburg Empire and the Kings of France there was no space for the balancing act which the Gonzaga had practised so assiduously between Milan and Venice, and even between pope and Emperor. When Federico's son Francesco was acclaimed Duke of Mantova, his regents Ferrante and Cardinal Ercole followed the wise policy of siding openly with the Emperor. In that way imperial investiture of the new duke followed without difficulty in 1543, when Francesco was still only ten.

With Francesco the decline began. Events continued to spiral around them: Charles V's son Philip was invested as Duke of Milan; the Farnese pope Paul III attempted to create a new state for his son Pier Luigi; Charles himself was attacking Muslim pirates in the south; and French and Imperial troops fought in Piemonte. But in Mantova nothing of more than local significance happened. The ten-year-old duke was betrothed to Catherine of Habsburg, daughter of King Ferdinand of the Romans, and Cardinal Ercole ruled the city after the death of Isabella d'Este in 1539. While Ferrante maintained the Gonzaga military reputation throughout Europe, Mantova itself was an island of peace and virtual exclusion from contemporary politics. The Gonzaga were both short of money, and incapable of political initiative.

The dynasty, already weakened by the policies of Barbara of Brandenburg, continued to disintegrate in the absence of a single powerful leader who might have coagulated family power. During a brief visit to Mantova in 1545, Ferrante Gonzaga had created a separate entity of his own subsidiary lordship at the town of Guastalla, where his descendants were to become the Gonzaga Dukes of Guastalla. Federico's younger brother Lodovico (1539-95) left Mantova to claim the lands and title of his maternal grandmother Anna di Alençon, Marchesa of Monferrat. In 1566 he married Enrica de Clèves of the ducal family of Nevers and Rethel. His son Carlo Gonzaga, born in 1580, would return to Italy in the seventeenth century to reclaim the Gonzaga inheritance from Duke Vincenzo II.

The primogenital line ended tragically with Duke Francesco II. In 1549, when he was sixteen, his regents decided that it was time for his marriage to Catherine and then to begin the gradual process of transferring power to him. She was greeted at Trento by her spouse, and then in grand style by Cardinal Ercole and Don Ferrante at Verona. She arrived to a triumphal reception in Mantova, and it must have seemed to her that she was destined for a magnificent marriage in this romantic setting. On 22 October 1549 Francesco and Catherine were married; but the happiness was destined to be brief. On 21 February 1550 Duke Francesco died without having conceived an heir, after falling into the lake at Mantova.

Francesco was succeeded by his twelve-year-old hunchback brother Guglielmo (1538-87), who was created duke and began to rule under the continuing regency of Ercole and Ferrante. But while Don Ferrante was primarily concerned with his new position as Governor of Milan, and Cardinal Ercole with the affairs of the Church — including several vain attempts to have himself elected pope — Mantova declined even further in importance. Guglielmo was notorious for his avarice and bigotry. He was devoted to hoarding the wealth which derived from his immense property in Mantova and Monferrat and ruling over his subjects as an absolute monarch. He was unpopular with the people, and even members of his own family at one time conspired to murder him. He was a man of average intelligence, obsessed by his deformity, and with neither the soldierly ability nor the artistic taste of his predecessors.

Guglielmo's son Vincenzo I (1562–1612), who married Grand Duke Francesco de' Medici's daughter Eleonora, was quite the opposite in character. He was violent, impulsive, and depraved as few others in the history of the dynasty. But he was at the same time courageous and noble in spirit, not hesitating to set off in 1595, 1597, and again in 1601 against the Turks in Hungary. Unlike his father, he was also generous in patronage and loved music — to the extent that he took his court musician and opera pioneer Claudio Monteverdi (1567–1643), and five other musicians, with him on his campaigns. He was a good administrator of the city

Ducal palace: detail from Mantegna's frescoes.

of Mantova, repairing bridges, founding a shipyard and improving locks and water-ways. He was as much a Renaissance man as some of his ancestors, and the last major figure in the history of the dynasty.

Duke Vincenzo's son Francesco became duke in June 1612 and died of smallpox in December of the same year. He was followed in rapid succession by his brothers Duke Ferdinand (1589–1626) and Duke Vincenzo II (1594–1627), with whom the principal line of the Gonzaga ended. These dukes dissipated what remained of dynastic prestige and wealth. Vincenzo II in his few months of rule managed to sell the Gonzaga collection of about 2,000 paintings, mainly assembled by Isabella d'Este, to King Charles I of England, who was one of the seventeenth century's greatest collectors. They were later redispersed when the late king's collection was auctioned by the Commonwealth. The castle and its many rooms decorated under the guidance of Isabella d'Este were sacked by German soldiers of the Emperor Ferdinand III in 1630, and the remaining paintings by Mantegna and Perugino were sold to Cardinal Richelieu. Both the castle and the city were besieged and ransacked once again by Napoleon's army in 1797.

In a sad and desperate attempt to continue the dynasty Vincenzo II designated Carlo Gonzaga-Nevers his successor, while the latter's supporters arranged for his son Carlo Duke of Rethel to marry Maria — daughter of Duke Francesco II and niece to Vincenzo. But nothing could now prevent the decline of the family. It took three years of war, diplomacy, and a plague which decimated the population of the duchy before Carlo Gonzaga-Nevers was recognized as Duke of Mantova. He ruled until 1637, when he was succeeded by his eight-year old nephew Carlo (1629–65), son of Carlo and Maria, who ruled as Duke Carlo II until his death at thirty-six. The last of the Gonzaga rulers, Carlo II's son Duke Ferdinando Carlo (1652–1708), was forced into exile in 1707 and died in Padova the following year. The cadet branches of the dynasty, the Gonzaga of Castiglione, the Gonzaga of Guastalla, and Gonzaga of Sabbioneta were all extinguished by the end of the eighteenth century.

7

THE MEDICI

The conscious architect of the Medici dynasty was Giovanni di Bicci de' Medici, who lived from 1360 to 1429. From his two sons, Cosimo and Lorenzo, derive the two main lines of the Medici which survived into the eighteenth century, having at two points in the sixteenth century been rejoined by marriages between first cousins.

Legend takes the family back to a certain Averardo, a knight of Charlemagne, or to unidentified apothecaries, and already in the early fourteenth century members of the family held high civic office in Florence. But early prominence and wealth were lost in the tumultuous years of that century and during the Black Death of 1348, which decimated both the population and the wealth of Florence. It is for that reason that to all intents and purposes it was Giovanni di Bicci, whose real name was Giovanni di Averardo III, who established the dynasty that was to dominate Florence and much of Tuscany for three hundred years. The celebrated Medici of fifteenth-century Florence descended from his son Cosimo, while the later Grand Dukes of Tuscany were in direct descent from Lorenzo.

GIOVANNI DI BICCI DE' MEDICI

To a certain extent Giovanni di Bicci de' Medici was a self-made man. Although he started work in the bank owned by his cousin, and worked as a merchant in the traditional Florentine trade of refining and dyeing wool, he later transformed the bank out of all recognition to become one of the wealthiest bankers in Italy. This was achieved as the city enjoyed a rapid economic expansion during the recovery from the Black Death of 1348; the conquest of a port at Pisa in 1406 and the purchase of Leghorn in 1421 facilitated trade and stimulated the economy.

Opposite *Detail from Botticelli's 'Adoration of the Magi' showing Lorenzo the Magnificent with Poliziano and Pico della Mirandola.*

But his greatest coup derived from his long friendship with Baldassare Cossa, who, according to rumours, had bought his cardinal's hat with money supplied by Giovanni. When Cossa became Pope John XXIII (1410–15), after the Council of Pisa in 1409 failed to settle the dispute between the popes at Avignon and at Rome, it was natural that the Medici should become the papal bankers. Giovanni supported Pope John in the war against King Ladislas of Naples in which we have seen Guidantonio da Montefeltro and Muzio Attendolo Sforza engaged. While the Medici bank had branches in Rome, Venice, Genova, Naples, and Gaeta in addition to Florence, over half the profits came from Rome during this period. When John XXIII was deposed and imprisoned in Heidelberg, Giovanni remained loyal and was instrumental in securing his release; he was buried in the Baptistery in Florence. Then when Oddone Colonna was made pope in 1417 as Martin V he spent the first three years of his pontificate in the Florentine monastery of Santa Maria Novella. The Medici continued to do business for the pope, although not with the virtual monopoly they had enjoyed under John XXIII.

When Giovanni di Bicci died in 1429 he was able to state to his sons without exaggeration that 'I leave you with a larger business than any other merchant in the Tuscan land'. He had used his wealth to finance loans, provide gifts, and assist the people of Florence in paying their taxes. He was an honest and understanding man who became popular without pushing himself forward, who avoided public office when possible but was quick to use his money to political advantage. Above all, he had created a new power to contend with in a city which had for generations been dominated by the Albizzi family. Thus, although he was unwilling to play a role in Florentine politics beyond his three two-month stints as one of the *Priori*, or nine members of the Signoria or government of the city, and another two-month period as *gonfaloniere*, or standard-bearer, he employed his immense fortune towards creating a powerful political base for the future of the Medici family and bank.

Giovanni was a reserved man in his private life, and passed on to his sons Cosimo and Lorenzo the precepts which they were to follow. His advice was simple and practical, and underlies his essentially commercial vision of the world which enabled him — unlike his descendants — to steer a course through the hazardous political situations of his life. According to his counsel, they were never to go against the will of the people, but to strive for peace so that the prosperity of the city would increase; they should never speak as if they were giving advice but discuss matters calmly and reasonably. Above all, they should be cautious in frequenting the corridors of power, and rather wait until they were summoned there. In the event of being summoned, they should act with humility and obedience, and not allow pride to consume them.

COSIMO THE ELDER
(1389–1464)

Giovanni's elder son Cosimo followed this excellent counsel. He was quietly dressed,

Giovanni di Bicci, by Bronzino.

modest in speech, and never conspicuous in the social life of Florence. By nature he was inclined to a scholarly life. He had an excellent classical education, learning Latin, German, and French; from an early age he cultivated the humanists in Florence and began to assemble a formidable collection of manuscripts. He also had a strong sense of duty. Until the death of his father he had played a vital but modest role in the family bank, and even later seems never to have developed the aura of a great banker. But although he was always ready to lend an ear, and was much liked by the ordinary people of the city, he was just as sharp as his father when it came to hard business. He did in fact make the Medici bank even richer and more powerful than before.

But the path to power was not all smooth. As he took full control of the family bank and sought friends, consolidating his popularity with the Florentine people, he became more of a threat to the Albizzi. Rumours against him were spread about the city, and one night his door was even smeared with blood. Following his father's advice, and perhaps his own personal inclination, he retired to the villa which the Medici family had owned for over a century at Cafaggiolo, in the Mugello valley on the way to Pistoia. This villa was always to be a favourite refuge of the Medici: it was later rebuilt and enlarged by Michelozzo Michelozzi (1396–1472),who was also a collaborator of Donatello and Ghiberti. By staying out of the city, Cosimo hoped to avoid conflict, but this simple physical removal of his person was not enough to satisfy his enemies. He was duped into returning to Florence, seized and imprisoned, and only narrowly avoided beheading. But through careful use of his money and influence, with important clients like the Marquis Niccolò III d'Este and the Republic of Venice supporting him, he was able to avoid the death penalty. As a less severe punishment, the entire family was banished from Florence.

Cosimo went to Padova and Lorenzo to Venice, where they were greeted with honour and treated as if they were ruling princes. Meanwhile, Rinaldo degli Albizzi failed in his attempt to bring the Signoria under his control, and less than a year after his banishment Cosimo returned to Florence in triumph on the invitation of the new government. He then became the *de facto* lord of a Republic which never officially recognized his rule. Pope Pius II wrote that Cosimo was 'the arbiter of peace and war and the moderator of the laws, not so much a private citizen as the lord of the country. The policy of the republic is discussed in his house: he it is who gives commands to the magistrates'. His son Piero and grandson Lorenzo were to perpetuate this disguised form of dictatorial rule until Lorenzo's son Piero the Fatuous was exiled from Florence in 1494. Cosimo was then looked back upon as the 'father of his country' (*pater patriae*).

Before the Black Death of 1348 Florence had a population of about 100,000, but during Cosimo's time it was between 40,000 and 50,000. This made it the third city in Italy after Milan and Venice. While Venice had recently increased its power by conquering Verona, Vicenza, Belluno, and Padova, Cosimo's foreign policy was largely devoted to forestalling the encroaching power of Filippo Maria Visconti of Milan; it was as part of this strategy that he financed Francesco Sforza, whom he met and liked personally. Sforza was in constant financial need, and as we have seen it was with Medici loans and the diplomatic support of Cosimo that he managed to succeed in his ambition of becoming Duke of Milan in 1450. With Milan as an ally, Cosimo reasoned, and Venice unlikely to extend its territory so far south-west, Florence would be safe to concentrate on extending its role as a banking and trading city. He played a vital political and diplomatic role in the Peace of Lodi in 1454, and when Florence and Milan joined Venice and the pope in a league against the menace of the Turks a few months later his policy was seen to have been wise.

At the same time the bank flourished, with Cosimo working often through the night and supervising the selection and operations of staff with a dedication reminiscent of modern tycoons. The branch at Milan became far more important under the Sforza, and there were now branches throughout Europe, including London, Cologne, Geneva, Lyons, Avignon, Bruges, and Antwerp. These branches also operated as export and import companies, so that Cosimo de' Medici in fact presided over the largest commercial empire in Europe and was one of the richest men in Italy. Yet he continued to follow the advice of his father. He was modest in dress and in habits, happier on his farm in the country than in the great palaces of the city, a distant and watchful man. In the portrait by Jacopo Pontormo (1494–1556) in the Uffizi Gallery he seems reluctant to have his picture painted, like somebody turning away from a camera.

In his thirty years of indirect rule — in which initiative always appeared to come from others but was inspired by him — Cosimo laid the foundations for the Renaissance glory of Florence. In the words of one contemporary he was 'king in everything but name'. His classical learning and long-term friendship with such important humanist scholars as Leonardo Bruni and Poggio Bracciolini prepared him well for the function of patron.

In a series of important moves, Cosimo laid the basis for future humanist studies and made Florence a centre of European intellectual life. First, in 1437, he bought what was perhaps the largest private library then in existence, which had been created by his friend Niccolò Niccolì and consisted of over eight hundred volumes. He added his own library and set copyists to work in order to improve the collection still further. This task was supervised by the bookseller Vespasiano da Bisticci, who was at the same time buying and copying books for Federico da Montefeltro's library. To house this collection Cosimo commissioned Michelozzi to design a library in the monastery of San Marco, and in 1444 opened the first public library in Europe, which all Florentine citizens were free to use. Inspired by the need to study Plato, he then adopted the gifted son of his doctor, Marsilio Ficino (1433–99) and encouraged him in his study of Greek — and especially Plato. From 1462 to 1482 Ficino was engaged in the translation from Greek to Latin of all thirty-six of Plato's dialogues, and established what was to become known as the Platonic Academy of Florence with such gifted disciples as Pico della Mirandola (1463–94). This was the most important of the many academies which began to appear in the thirteenth century, and was to have enormous impact on European learning.

This lead in scholarship was paralleled by lavish promotion of the visual arts. The list of artists Cosimo employed and attracted to Florence reads like a roll-call

Cosimo the Elder, by Pontormo.

of great painters and sculptors. While the Florentine Renaissance is often said to have begun with the commission for reliefs of the bronze doors of the Baptistery, announced in 1401, the full thrust came in the 1430s with Donatello, Alberti, Masaccio, and Brunelleschi — all of whom were patronized by Cosimo. It is in fact likely that Giovanni di Bicci was involved in the original commission for the bronze doors of the Baptistery, which was won by Lorenzo Ghiberti (1375–1455). The first set of doors was completed in 1424, and Ghiberti set to work on the second set commissioned the following year, which he finished only in 1452. During this long period his workshop served as a training ground for Florentine artists including Donatello, Paolo Uccello, and Masolino.

The architect Filippo Brunelleschi (1377–1446) travelled to Rome with Donatello measuring classical ruins and sketching their forms and ornaments. He devised an architecture which used classical forms such as pediments and columns and which has survived into the twentieth century. For Cosimo he built the abbey of the Canons-Regular in Fiesole, overlooking the city, which became one of the banker's favourite retreats. He was later commissioned to design the family palace for Cosimo, who judged it too elaborate and gave the job to Michelozzi. He completed the church of San Lorenzo and built the Medici chapel inside it. His friend Donatello (1386–1466), whom Giorgio Vasari referred to in his *Lives of the Artists* as 'friend and servant' of the Medici, was a particular favourite of Cosimo — who commissioned many works from him and later arranged for the ageing artist to receive a pension. The famous marble statue of St George for the guild church of Orsanmichele was commissioned by Cosimo, and the astonishingly beautiful bronze David, which was the first free-standing bronze since classical times, was destined to be shown in the courtyard of Palazzo Medici.

Masaccio (1401–28), a nickname meaning 'Clumsy Thomas', was regarded by Florentine painters as one of the founders of modern painting. He is said to have learned from Brunelleschi the tricks of perspective, which set off the grandeur of his figures to such effect — for instance in 'The Holy Trinity' in Santa Maria Novella. Although he received no direct commission, Vasari tells us that Masaccio enjoyed the support and favour of Cosimo, and that he returned from Rome where he was working when he heard that Cosimo had come back to Florence from exile. Masaccio died before he was twenty-eight and his only known pupil was Fra Filippo Lippi (c.1406–69); Vasari reports that it was often said that Masaccio's soul had entered into his master's body. Lippi was also a close friend of Cosimo, and among other commissions painted a Nativity for Palazzo Medici. He was said to be so lustful that Cosimo once locked him inside the palace for a few days so that he would not waste his time running after women. One of Lippi's pupils was Sandro Botticelli (c.1445–1510), whom Cosimo probably met as a young man in the master's workshop, and who included a portrait of Cosimo in a panel of the *Adoration of the Magi* he painted for Santa Maria Novella, now in the Uffizi Gallery.

Cosimo was also close to Fra Angelico (1387–1455), who worked for him in the monastery of San Marco, painting over fifty frescoes in the cells as aids to contemplation, and also altarpieces for the same monastery. Paolo Uccello (1397–1475) was a close friend of Donatello, and knew Cosimo well. Between 1454 and 1457 he painted three battle scenes for Palazzo Medici, one of which, 'The Battle of San Romano', is one of the finest pictures in the National Gallery in London. It may also have been on Cosimo's instructions that he painted the fine equestrian portrait of the *condottiere* John Hawkwood inside the cathedral of Florence.

In the visual arts the problem raised by Plato concerning how beauty can be adequately apprehended led to the search for an ideal form which later received expression in the works of Botticelli and Michelangelo. The belief of these artists that perfect form can be found in the human nude, and that nudity could be beautiful — unlike the mere nakedness of medieval paintings — was derived from and supported by the speculations of the Platonic Academy. Botticelli's *Venus* and Michelangelo's *David* represent the superior nature of man, and celebrate man as a being capable of ordering his own affairs and his vision of the cosmos. It is unlikely that these superb works of art would have been made without the theoretical background of discussions in the Academy.

Thus Florence took on the aspect we know today during Cosimo's rule. In 1436 Brunelleschi's great double dome on the cathedral was consecrated and provided the city with its focal point and symbol. He designed it amidst controversy, after studying the domes of classical Rome — like the Pantheon and the collapsed dome of the Basilica of Maxentius. The next year Cosimo financed the rebuilding of the monastery of San Marco, which later included the Medici library. Later he commissioned Michelozzi to build the Palazzo Medici, now known as Palazzo Riccardi, an immense but sober building which set the style for many other Florentine families. In addition, he completed Brunelleschi's church of San Lorenzo, which houses the Medici chapel, and built other villas outside the city.

The fortunate combination of the relative period of peace in Italian politics from 1454 to 1494, the continuous Medici rule over Florence from 1434 to 1494, and the expanding economy meant that many great families were able to use money and energy, that might otherwise have been spent in war, to build new palaces and villas. Two good examples are Alberti's richly textured Palazzo Rucellai, which is architecturally of greater interest than the deliberately simple Palazzo Medici, and Palazzo Pitti, whose enormous size still shocks and certainly made the Medici palace modest by comparison.

Without the increase in family fortunes due to Cosimo's business acumen and the school of humanists and artists patronized and stimulated by him, his grandson Lorenzo might not have achieved such fame. While Lorenzo is usually known by the title 'Magnificent' this was no more than a courtesy title accorded to many other princes of the Renaissance. He was in fact addressed as *magnifico signore*. The reverence shown by all Florentine writers to Cosimo, and the attribution of the epithet *Pater Patriae*, point rather to him as the greatest of all the Medici.

PIERO THE GOUTY
(1416–69)

Straddled between these two giants, the five years of the rule of Piero the Gouty may be regarded as an interlude. He had been prevented from playing an active role in business or political life since youth by a hereditary gout, which caused arthritic pains in his limbs and rendered him virtually an invalid. Even his father expected him not to live long, and rested his hopes in his younger brother Giovanni. But Giovanni died a year before Cosimo, leaving Piero as his sole heir.

The gout, which caused painful paroxysms in his joints and in his case probably of the internal organs, was accompanied by the goitre which is visible in portraits in the swelling of the thyroid gland and sleepy-looking eyes. He also suffered from arthritic pains in his limbs, but with extraordinary courage managed to keep up appearances of strength, and rule with kindness and courtesy. He was a determined man, perhaps forced to be so by his crippling illness, and dealt ably with a major conspiracy against him. He was also an excellent diplomat, maintaining the Medici reputation gained by his father. Although less brilliant than his father, Piero worked hard at both bank business and diplomacy and was successful in both. He married Lucrezia Tornabuoni, of the well-known Florentine family remembered today in one of the city's principal streets, who gave birth to two sons, Lorenzo and Giuliano, and three daughters, Maria, Bianca, and Nannina, who each married into a prominent Florentine family — the Rossi, Pazzi, and Rucellai families respectively. In the last few months of his life he was bedridden, yet still exercised control over both the Medici family business and the affairs of Florence.

Although Piero had fine taste and enjoyed the company of artists as much as his father, his motives seem tarnished in comparison with the genuine and long friendships Cosimo maintained with the men he patronized. He began to see the precise value of paintings and sculptures in terms of prestige, a well-known example being the inscription on the tabernacle commissioned by him in the church of the Annunziata. There, blatantly and in contradiction with what we normally think of the Medici, it states clearly that 'the marble alone cost 4,000 florins'. Lorenzo's later computation of the money spent in three generations of Medici patronage suggests a similar concern.

With few exceptions, in fact, Piero continued with the painters his father had known — and whom, in many cases, his own son Lorenzo would patronize. He continued to favour Donatello, fulfilling the sculptor's last wish in burying him inside the Medici chapel in San Lorenzo beside Cosimo. He also commissioned works from Uccello and Botticelli, who was invited by Piero to live in Palazzo Medici. Other painters who worked for Piero included Benozzo Gozzoli (c.1421–97), a pupil of Fra Angelico who decorated the walls of the chapel inside the family palace with frescoes, the most successful of which is a representation of the Medici family as the Magi. A charming story, which tells us much about the attitudes of painters, concerns some seraphs which Gozzoli added to these frescoes. When Piero complained to him, the painter replied 'I'll do as you command; two little clouds will take them away'. Antonio Pollaiuolo (*c.*1432–98), also worked in Palazzo Medici, painting mythological scenes from the life of Hercules which are now in the Uffizi Gallery.

The last artistic tribute to Piero was the magnificent marble and porphyry tomb for him and his brother Giovanni designed by Donatello's pupil — and later Leonardo's master — Andrea del Verocchio (1435–88) in the old sacristy of San Lorenzo.

LORENZO THE MAGNIFICENT
(1449–92)

Cosimo's son Lorenzo was both precocious and, presumably, aware that great responsibility would soon be thrust upon him. Although he was only twenty when he succeeded his father he had already achieved success as a diplomat on several occasions. There was little doubt that this bright and intelligent boy would grow to great things, and an education at the hands of the best teachers in Florence — including Cristoforo Landino, the translator of Aristotle, and his grandfather's protégé Marsilio Ficino — enabled him to shine during a visit to the court of Ercole I d'Este when he was sixteen, and to carry out diplomatic missions to the Doge in Venice, to the wedding of Ippolita Sforza in Milan, and the Spanish King Ferrante in Naples. The letters written to him by Piero during these journeys show no sign of being addressed to a boy of sixteen, except perhaps in their insistence that he should amuse himself. Instructions that he should spare no expense set Lorenzo on the road to the magnificence for which he became celebrated.

In 1469 he was married to Clarice Orsini, of the Roman family we have seen in constant opposition to the Colonna. Lorenzo himself was not attracted by Clarice, and in a sense the real celebration was a public tournament held in the most popular of Florentine squares, Piazza Santa Croce, a few months before, when he honoured Lucrezia Donati — whom he loved but could not marry since political wisdom dictated his choice. The wedding was celebrated by proxy in Rome, as was often the custom, and feasted in grand style for three days in Florence. Piero de' Medici distanced himself from an event that must have seemed to him grandiose and exhibitionistic, so that Lorenzo himself arranged the wedding and festivities.

The bride rode to Palazzo Medici on 4 June with her future brother-in-law Giuliano to a feast which took place in the courtyard and gardens of the palace. She wore a white-and-gold brocade dress, and rode a white horse which was the gift of King Ferrante. Her arrival was greeted by music from the orchestra in the courtyard, and then the first of five wedding banquets began. Nearby towns and villages had provided 150 calves and 2,000 pairs of capons, with geese and other poultry. There were sugar plums, sweetmeats, almonds, and many other sweets, all accompanied by casks of wine, both local and imported. It was said that a hundred barrels of wine were drunk for each of the three days of the celebrations. But it must have

Lorenzo the Magnificent, by Bronzino.

been a strange feast: the host was absent, the bridegroom was reluctant, and the mother entertained her friends and guests separately on a balcony overlooking the courtyard.

As might be expected, the marriage was not happy. Lorenzo sought his mental stimulus and amusement elsewhere, while Clarice remained aloof from the brilliant intellectual and festive atmosphere of Florentine life. She was a Roman from an ancient and powerful family, and never fully accepted Florence. The open and joyous atmosphere of Palazzo Medici, where artists mingled freely and Lorenzo's friends were always welcome and often ready with practical jokes, was quite different to the austere life of the Roman aristocracy — whose life was devoted to Church and war. In Lorenzo's letters to his wife there is little sign of real affection; but Clarice was a dutiful wife and was fully occupied by giving birth to ten children — seven of whom survived. When she died suddenly in 1488, Lorenzo was away taking the waters for his gout and did not attend her funeral. Only then does it seem that he grieved with some sincerity. Yet even when she was alive the marriage did nothing to calm his zest for feasts and tournaments, pageants, parades, carnivals, football games, and dances.

Lorenzo's foreign policy was facilitated by the fact that his entire period of rule occurred after the Peace of Lodi. He continued his grandfather's policy of maintaining Florentine independence through good relations with the Sforza in Milan and with the Republic of Venice. The most serious problem from a personal point of view derived from the more difficult relations with the Church, and led to the attempted assassination of 1478 — when his brother Giuliano was murdered. The trouble started when the friendly Venetian Pope Paul II died in 1471 and was succeeded by Pope Sixtus IV, Francesco della Rovere, who was second to none when it came to nepotism. He made six of his nephews cardinals and distributed Church properties and titles as if they were personal fiefs. The future Pope Julius II was his nephew. As we have seen, the desire to create a state for his nephew Girolamo Riario had serious repercussions in the Marches and Romagna. When the new pope made a request for a loan from the Medici bank to buy the city of Imola for Girolamo, Lorenzo had refused and the commission passed to the rival bank of the Pazzi family. After what the pope considered further affronts to his family, Girolamo conspired with Francesco de' Pazzi and other men who held grudges against the Medici to murder Lorenzo and his brother Giuliano. Thus, they reasoned, it would be possible to take open control of Florence — and presumably of the wealth of the Medici bank.

The attempt was to have been made during a banquet given for a visiting papal nephew, Cardinal Raffaele Riario, but changed circumstances forced a last-minute change in the plan. The brothers were to be stabbed during Mass in the cathedral, when it was assumed they would be off guard. The attempt was to be made on the morning of 26 April 1478. But the bungling continued, and two priests were chosen to replace a professional soldier who backed down when he heard the assassination was to be in a church. Giuliano, whose bad luck left him to the only experienced murderers, was killed instantly; Lorenzo was able to pull himself free of his amateurish assailants, draw his sword and escape from them. He received a flesh wound in his neck from one of the priest's daggers. Other conspirators, unaware of the failure to kill Lorenzo, attempted to storm the town hall and take control of the city. But they were thwarted by Medici supporters, and the dead bodies of the conspirators — including the Archbishop of Pisa and Francesco de' Pazzi — were suspended from the town hall for all to see. Lorenzo de' Medici appeared before the crowd that had now gathered, to reassure them he was alive; but his presence was not enough to prevent riots which lasted for several days. Later, the two priests were found, castrated, and hanged. The result of the conspiracy was, ironically, to provide a popular demonstration of support for Lorenzo, and strengthen his position in the city. The extent of Medici, and Florentine, influence at that time is illustrated by the fact that one of the conspirators was arrested in Constantinople, where he was handed over to Medici agents. He was brought back to Florence and executed.

Pope Sixtus was now a bitter enemy of Lorenzo, and found willing allies in Alfonso of Calabria, son of the King of Naples, and the Tuscan cities of Siena and Lucca. But through a combination of luck and good diplomacy Lorenzo managed to thwart the papal ambitions and restore peace to Florence. For the last fourteen years of his rule he was able to live to all intents and purposes as a kind of enlightened despot, but with neither an official role nor the encumbrances it would have brought. Lorenzo's only real failing seems to have been his neglect of the Medici bank, which eventually led to a decline of family wealth. He had no special talent for banking, and seems to have left the running of the bank to his agents. Unpaid loans, extravagant expenses, and a general decline in the importance of Florentine banks led him nearly to bankruptcy. Eventually he too was affected by the inherited gout, and died in 1492 at the relatively early age of forty-three.

But if he was inferior to his grandfather Cosimo in business acumen and dedication to work, he would certainly have been equal in patronage of the arts if he had had more money. He once calculated that between 1434 and 1471 the Medici family spent the astonishing total of 663,755 gold florins, commenting that he was content that the money had been well spent and that he was pleased. When he could not patronize directly, he helped the painters he liked to find commissions elsewhere. The artists he employed were often guests in Palazzo Medici, and there was nothing he liked better than their company at table with his literary companions, Ficino, Pico della Mirandola, the poet Angelo Ambrogini, known as Poliziano (1454–94), and Vespasiano da Bisticci. His favourite artist was Antonio Pollaiuolo, who had worked in the family palace when Lorenzo was a small boy. He also employed Filippo Lippi's son Filippino (1458–1504), Botticelli, and Domenico Ghirlandaio (1449–94), Michelangelo's first master, on the frescoes for his villa at Spedaletto.

In 1489 he took into his house as a permanent guest a young boy of fourteen who in later years was to surpass all the artists patronized by the Medici, and who even then was producing work which impressed his patrons and tutors. For the remaining three years of Lorenzo's life, Michelangelo studied in the school of sculpture which had been founded in the Medici gardens to compensate for the lack of sculptors Lorenzo felt existed at that time. The 'school' was presided over by Bertoldo di Giovanni (d.1491), and Andrea da Verocchio also worked there until he left Florence for Venice. In this period Michelangelo not only lived as part of this stimulating household, but studied with and befriended two Medici boys who were to be important in his future: Lorenzo's son Giovanni, who was to become Pope Leo X, and his dead brother Giuliano's natural son Giulio, who was to become Pope Clement VII. It was in that household where poetry was held in such honour, with two of the period's leading poets present in the persons of Poliziano and Lorenzo himself, that Michelangelo began to write sonnets and madrigals.

Lorenzo was one of the most important and versatile of Italian poets. He wrote formal religious poetry and love songs. The delicate opening quatrain of his 'Canzona di Bacco' are often quoted for their emphasis on the transience of youth: 'How fair is youth,/ That flies away!/ Then be happy, you who may:/ Of tomorrow who can say?' But more interesting are the vivid evocations of country life, full of pertinent detail that only a genuine lover of the country could use. In these poems it is possible to note an accent of sincerity in choice of subject matter and mode of thought which tally perfectly with the complex personality of this man. For instance, in the sonnet 'Cerchi chi vuol le pompe e gli alti onori':

Villa Medici at Cafaggiolo, by G. Utens.

Search who will pomp and other honours,
Squares, temples, and splendid buildings,
Delights and treasure, to accompany
A thousand hard thoughts, a thousand sorrows.

A green meadow full of lovely flowers,
A brook that moistens the grass beside it,
A bird which moans for love
Refresh our ardour much better.

The shady woods, stones, and high mountains,
Black caves and fugitive beasts,
Some graceful timid nymph:

Here I keep watch with vague and ready thoughts
With light flickering as if it were alive,
Here something or other takes them away.

Although Lorenzo ruled Florence and lived at the centre of Italian political life, he was happiest at one of the Medici villas in the countryside near Florence: at Fiesole, Careggi, the villa at Cafaggiolo where Cosimo had retired from Florentine life before taking power, or at the villa rebuilt by Giuliano da Sangallo at Poggio a Caiano. He died while in Careggi. In any other man it would be hard to reconcile his love of the countryside and the thoughts in these poems with the art-loving, exhibitionistic, and dynasty-conscious aspects of his public personality.

This fact explains the perennial interest in Lorenzo de' Medici, the Magnificent. He was larger than life in almost every aspect, a prince to be set beside Isabella

155

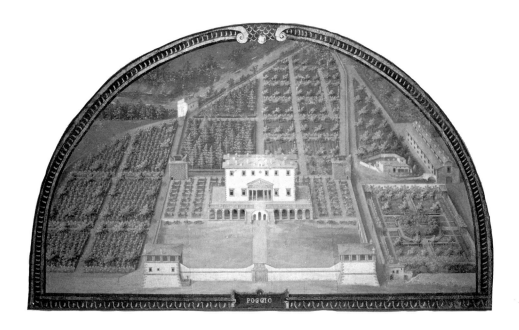

Villa Medici at Poggio a Caiano, by G. Utens.

d'Este and Federico da Montefeltro. A man who loved Florentine football, hunting, obscene stories, practical jokes, who fed his own horse and enjoyed the physical aspects of farming, and at the same time sang well, played the lyre, wrote excellent poetry, made architectural drawings, and read Plato, was clearly both universal and paradoxical. It was perhaps Machiavelli who best expressed the paradox, or impossibility, of measuring such a man by ordinary standards. He asserted that the light and voluptuous side of Lorenzo and his seriousness were 'joined in an almost impossible conjunction'.

THE MEDICI IN EXILE
(1494–1531)

Lorenzo was believed to have stated that he had three sons, one good, one wise, and one a fool. It is unfortunate for the Medici dynasty that it was the fool — Giuliano (1479–1516) — in whose person the future of the family rested, since his eldest brother Piero (1472–1503) died young and the wise one, Giovanni (1475–1521) became pope as Leo X (1513–21).

Piero, known as 'the Fatuous', succeeded Lorenzo in 1492, but lacked the political and diplomatic skill of his forebears. His power was from the beginning threatened by his conspiring Medici cousins on one hand, and the preaching of Savonarola on the other. His surrender of several Florentine strongholds to the invading French king Charles VIII exasperated a nervous populace, which accused him of betraying their city. Two years after beginning his rule he was forced to flee from Florence, and Palazzo Medici was sacked. He died by drowning, still in exile, after the Battle of Garigliano in 1503. But after a difficult period, in which Florence became — like many other of the cities ruled by these dynasties — a pawn in the struggle between Charles V and the French kings, with the added component of Savonarola, the Medici returned to power with Piero's younger brother Giuliano in 1512. Giuliano was followed by Piero's son Lorenzo (1492–1519), after whose death the legitimate line of direct male descent from Cosimo ended.

While direct Medici rule was endangered, indirect control was exercised from Rome by two popes who — with the brief interval of Adrian VI's pontificate (1522–3) — ruled the papacy for twenty years. Leo X (1513–21), Lorenzo the Magnificent's son Giovanni, is famous for his statement: 'God has given us the papacy. Let us enjoy it.' He maintained a huge personal household and indulged in constant banquets and feasts, full of surprises such as nightingales flying out of pies which were being served. He loved practical jokes as much as his father had, but was serious in his religious duties and his desire to improve Rome. Above all he was devoted to the Medici family and its prestige. Leo X followed his predeces-

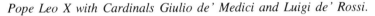

Pope Leo X with Cardinals Giulio de' Medici and Luigi de' Rossi.

157

sor in patronizing Raphael (1483–1520), who completed his work in Julius II's private apartment during the first Medici pontificate, including the 'School of Athens'. In Raphael's magnificent portrait of Leo X, now in the Uffizi — with its rich textures, the soft hands, illuminated manuscript, and chubby confident expression — the character of this pleasure-loving pope is perfectly captured.

His cousin Giulio, natural son of the murdered Giuliano, succeeded Adrian VI as Clement VII (1523–34). He was quite different in character to Leo X, preferring scholarly discussions of philosophy and theology to the grand entertainments of the former. But he too was a generous patron, commissioning works from Raphael, Leonardo, Giulio Romano, and Benvenuto Cellini. His tortuous foreign policy, switching his loyalty from Spain to France with the slightest change in political wind, brought disaster to the Church in the form of the Sack of Rome. He escaped with his life only by fleeing from the Vatican palace to the impregnable fortress of Castel Sant'Angelo beside the Tiber, running through the fortified corridor which can still be seen above the streets. He surrendered and eventually managed to travel north to Orvieto. Two years later he arranged, by skilful wheeler-dealing, to salvage his own and his family's future by coming to terms with Charles V. In exchange for the return of the Medici to Florence he would crown Charles as the Holy Roman Emperor. His last service to the family was in arranging the wedding of Caterina to the son of King Francis I of France, who was later to rule as Henry II.

Leo X entrusted the lordship of Florence to his cousin Cardinal Giulio, and when the latter became pope as Clement VII he passed the role to his bastard son Alessandro (1511–37). In 1522 Alessandro was created Duke of Penna by Charles V. In 1527, after the Sack of Rome, the Medici were again forced to flee their city during a violent uprising, and it was only after a siege by the army of Charles lasting eleven months that Alessandro was able to return with imperial support in 1531. In the following year he was made the first hereditary Duke of Florence.

It was during this turbulent period of Florentine history that Michelangelo returned from Rome. During the papacy of his childhood companion Leo X, he had been working on his massive project for the unfinished tomb of Pope Julius II, of which his Moses is the best-known extant part. As the result of this immense task and consequent disputes with Julius's heirs Michelangelo never worked for Pope Leo in Rome. His intractable personality, and the history of problems with the tomb of Julius II must have advised against close co-operation at that time. In those years, however, Michelangelo also worked on the unfinished designs for the façade of San Lorenzo, and in 1520 — under the patronage of Clement VII — began to work on the Medici chapel to be built beside the church. The chapel is conceived as a sculptural space, where the huge tombs of Piero the Fatuous's brother Giuliano and son Lorenzo seem to grow out of opposite walls of the chapel. But Michelangelo, as so often, never finished the chapel: many of the statues intended to fill the niches were never made. The tombs of Lorenzo the Magnificent and his brother Giuliano, which were to stand on the other two walls, were also never made.

In 1524, for the new Medici Pope Clement VII, he began work on the Laurenziana Library in the same church, including the extraordinary double staircase which

The Medici Chapel, with the tomb of Giuliano.

seems to flow out of the library like lava. At the end of the decade he designed new defences for the troubled city, with diagonal and curved bastions and walls, which were so avant-garde that they were in fact rejected. His last work in Florence was in fact supervising the building of the new fortifications.

GIOVANNI DELLE BANDE NERE
(1498–1526)

The brief and violent life of Giovanni, named for his leadership of a famous band of men on the frontier between *condottieri* and brigands, gained him the fame of being the last 'captain of fortune' in the great *condottiere* tradition. He was of the direct line of Cosimo's brother Lorenzo, the son of Giovanni de' Medici and the Sforza virago Caterina, and nephew of Lodovico 'Il Moro' Sforza. He was born in Forlì.

His unconventional and primitive character was not dominated by the attempts of his tutor Jacopo Salviati, husband to Lorenzo the Magnificent's daughter Lucrezia. At the age of thirteen he was banished from Florence for killing a boy of his own age, and his tutor complained of him in Rome constantly associating with prostitutes and undesirable characters. His relative Pope Leo X employed him in the papal army, a task to which he took like a duck to water. In a series of rapid, and violent actions he won an excellent military reputation. He then founded his own band of soldiers, under strict discipline and wearing the same simple tunics, but led by their leader himself to rape and pillage when occasion presented itself. He adapted a new form of guerrilla warfare, using light horses, little armour, and attacks designed to take the enemy by surprise. The rest of his life was spent in battle, or in the associated pastimes of hunting and womanizing.

Giovanni died of gangrene following a falconet wound, characteristically throwing off his bandages when he realized there was nothing to be done to save his life. Although he was virtually an outlaw, his own son Cosimo was to become the first Duke of Tuscany and continue the Medici dynasty.

GRAND DUKES OF TUSCANY
(1532–1737)

As we have seen, the Medici were restored to Florence by Charles V, and thereafter Duke Alessandro ruled their lands as a satellite state to Spain. In 1536 he consolidated his position — and Spanish dominance — by marrying the Emperor's natural daughter Margherita of Austria. A year later Alessandro was murdered by a distant cousin, and soon afterwards Margherita married Duke Ottavio Farnese.

Duke Alessandro's sister Caterina de' Medici (1519–89) is known in France as the 'Black Queen'. She is portrayed as a kind of Lady Macbeth who embodied all the evils thought to appertain to Italians, who were in turn associated in the popular imagination with Machiavelli — whose *Prince* she studied assiduously all her life. She was credited with instigating the St Bartholomew's massacre, when on 14 August 1472 as many as 50,000 Huguenots were massacred in Paris and the provinces. For over fifty years she exercised influence over the kings of France. Her 'flying squadron' of seductive and beautiful women was used ruthlessly to reward loyalty and to spy on suspects. Her three sons, Francis II, Charles IX, and Henry III, were kings of France in the most notoriously corrupt period of French history.

With Alessandro's death the legitimate line of Cosimo de' Medici ended, and the ducal title passed to the son of Giovanni delle Bande Nere, who ruled as Duke Cosimo I (1519–74). Cosimo married Leonor, daughter of the Spanish viceroy of Naples Pedro de Toledo, thus bringing the family yet closer to Spain. Beginning as the elected head of the Florentine Republic, he gradually increased both his own power and the territory he ruled. In 1569 Pope Pius IV (1566–72) conferred on him the title of Grand Duke of Tuscany, and for the remainder of his life he ruled despotically over Florence and Siena.

Duke Cosimo was never fully accepted by his fellow European sovereigns. As if in a kind of revenge for this fact he sought to establish himself as an equal by artistic patronage, and with characteristic Medici ambition carried out an extraordinary building programme. Giorgio Vasari built the Uffizi for him as administrative offices, hence the building's name. After his death the eastern loggia was closed to make a gallery for sculpture, then paintings were added and extensions were made through the centuries until it became the present art gallery. One of his more pharaonic projects was the enclosed corridor linking the Uffizi to the ducal residence in Palazzo Pitti, passing over the Ponte Vecchio across the Arno. After a great flood in 1557 he built the Ponte alle Carraia and Ponte Santa Trinità over the Arno. He recognized the importance of possessing a navy, and created a base on the island of Elba — which was to have Leghorn added to it by his son Francesco. He founded the Academy of Drawing, opened the Laurentian Library, created a botanic garden, and generated a kind of second renaissance by his lavish patronage. Benvenuto Cellini (1500–71) was commissioned to make the bronze *Perseus* which stood outside the town hall with Michelangelo's *David*. Vasari also decorated rooms in the town hall for Duke Cosimo, and Jacopo Pontormo painted frescoes in one of his villas.

With Grand Duke Francesco (1541–87) the decline of the Medici family began. Dynastic squabbles and a series of brutal crimes marred the fine reputation of the family: the Duke's brother Piero murdered his own wife, and his sister Isabella was murdered by her husband; Francesco himself was thought to have been poisoned when he died in 1587. As if it were tired of Florence, the Medici taste and love for art was transferred to Paris in the person of his daughter Maria (1573–1642), who married King Henry IV of France. Her arrival in France was painted in the beautiful 'Reception of Marie de' Medici at Marseilles' by Rubens, now in the Louvre with the rest of what is known as the 'Medici Cycle'.

Francesco's brother Ferdinand I (1549–1609) was a cardinal when he succeeded as Grand Duke, but renounced his position twelve years later in order to marry. His rule was a temporary revival of prosperity and splendour. He was a cultivated man who had built the Villa Medici which overlooks the Spanish Steps as his Roman residence, and brought new art patronage to Florence. He is particularly noteworthy for his patronage of music, for the 'Camerata de' Bardi' which he sponsored are generally accredited with the invention of opera. It was under his rule that Jacopo Peri's 'Euridice' was performed in the apartment of Antonio de' Medici on 6 October 1600.

From the death of Duke Francesco the Medici dynasty went into an irreversible decline, as three successive dukes (Cosimo II, Ferdinando II, and Cosimo III) squandered the dynastic name without restoring its fortunes. Cosimo II is interesting in having been the man who appointed Galileo to his post at the University of Pisa, while his son Ferdinando II is equally notorious as the man who did nothing to protect his own teacher and protégé Galileo from the punishment of the Inquisition.

The last Grand Duke, Gian Gastone, ruled from 1723 to his death in 1737. His sister Anna Maria Lodovica, the last of the Medici, died in 1743. But in spite of the grandeur of Duke Cosimo I and the temporary revival of Medici glory under Duke Ferdinand I, the most significant branch of the Medici dynasty and that which achieved the greatest renown, descended from Cosimo the Elder. It was *that* Cosimo and his grandson Lorenzo who stamped Florence with the Medici name and taste, and made it the centre of the Italian Renaissance.

8

THE FARNESE

T oday the Farnese name is above all associated with Pope Paul III, and the Dukes of Parma and Piacenza. It evokes gardens, palaces, and villas of the sixteenth and seventeenth centuries from Rome to Varese. But the origin of the dynasty was medieval and feudal. They first appeared in the border region of Tuscany and Lazio, between Lake Bolsena and the sea, at the end of the first millennium. Their name is said to derive from the feud of 'Castrum Farneti', and they possessed many other minor feuds in the area. But they came to prominence in the nearby city of Orvieto. Pietro Farnese was consul of Orvieto in 984 and in succeeding centuries family members were consuls, captains of the militia and bishops of the city. The famous Gothic-style cathedral of Orvieto was consecrated in 1302 by Bishop Guido Farnese. Other family members were captains of the militia of neighbouring cities like Viterbo, Siena, Arezzo, and later Florence.

It was in the fifteenth century that they began to emerge from this local importance with the *condottiere* Ranuccio III Farnese. His policy of marrying his sons into the great feudal families of Rome provided a foothold in that city which the dynasty was quick to exploit.

RANUCCIO III (*c.*1380–1449) AND
PIER LUIGI I (*c.*1430–1488)

Ranuccio learned the profession of arms from his father Pietro, a captain in the army of Bologna with fifty lances and then captain-general of the army of Siena. He succeeded his father in commanding the Sienese, and then became captain-general of the papal army at Orvieto. This direct service for the Church at a moment when it was recovering prestige after the end of the Great Schism marked the begin-

Opposite *Galatea, from Raphael's frescoes in the Farnesina.*

163

ning of an important shift of ambitions towards Rome. His favour with the Colonna pope Martin V was probably won by more than a decade of service against the traditional enemies of the Colonna, the Orsini family, but he also opposed the Colonna on occasions and later made an alliance with the Orsini. He continued to be favoured by Martin V's successor Eugenius IV. Ranuccio received honours and titles from the Church at this time, and may even have been a banker to the Holy See for a short period.

By force of arms and political skill, he managed to create a small 'state' out of the original Farnese feuds. But in terms of historical importance his great achievement lay in arranging the marriage of his sons with two of the four families which in the Middle Ages had contended Rome: Pier Luigi was married to Giovanella Caetani, daughter of the Lord of Sermoneta and descendant of the family of Pope Boniface VIII; Gabriele Francesco married Isabella Orsini.

Pier Luigi I (c.1430–c.1488) succeeded his father as captain-general of Orvieto, and devoted his life to military exploits in the service of the Church. But he seems to have conceived the role of his family in a new light, perhaps at the instigation of his Roman aristocratic wife. During his life the Farnese began to emerge from relative provincial obscurity, and to build for posterity. It seems that the construction of the first great Palazzo Farnese — with its fine architraved porch and small courtyard — was begun by Pier Luigi I beside the cathedral of Viterbo. He also founded a monastery on an island in Lake Bolsena, and created there a family tomb for the worthy burial of his father.

He is remembered today as the father of Giulia and Alessandro, who between them took the Farnese family to their apogee after more than five centuries of a subsidiary role in Italian history.

ALESSANDRO: POPE PAUL III
(1468–1549)

The energy which fuelled his ambition to power can be clearly discerned in Titian's portrait of Paul III. His eyes show a man proud of what he has accomplished through his nepotism, penetrating the onlooker but revealing little of the subject. The mouth suggests wiliness, and it would be easy to imagine those hard hands with their long fingers — so different from the chubby fingers of Leo X, or of Velasquez's portrait of Pope Innocent X — used in argument.

His early education may have initiated the ambition, for after studying with the humanist teacher Pomponio Leto in Rome he spent some years at the school of Lorenzo de' Medici in Florence. In view of his later classical taste, which as we will see was passed on to his grandson Cardinal Alessandro, the Roman period is of great interest. Pomponio Lcto (1428–97), who was also known in the Latinized form of Julius Pomponius Laetus, was a brilliant, much admired but erratic classi-

Pope Paul III with his grandsons, by Titian.

cist who wrote on a wide variety of subjects and published many early printed books. Around 1464 he founded a school which became known as the *Accademia Pomponiana*. In the search for authenticity, members of his academy used pagan names and observed pagan rites and festivals, to such an extent that they were accused of paganism. Following these charges the school was closed down by Pope Paul II four years after it was opened. Some people spoke of it as a semi-secret society working against the Church, as Freemasons were spoken of in later centuries. Leto himself was imprisoned, but after three years he again opened the school — which continued to function even after his death. It is intriguing to reflect that a future pope studied in that strange environment, especially when the circumstances of the accusations and details of what the members of the academy actually did have never been clarified. Could it be due to this period that Paul III, throughout his life, rarely took an important decision without consulting his astrologer? The refinement and lesson in taste that he received in Lorenzo's house was therefore based upon a solid classical education by one of the century's leading scholars.

The formal education Alessandro received from Pomponio Leto was certainly of high quality. He always impressed visitors and ambassadors by his ability to express himself elegantly both in Latin and in Italian. It is easy to imagine how his taste for art and splendour could be increased by residence in such a household. In some ways he was a man of the fifteenth century forced to adapt himself to the dramatically changed circumstances. In his youth he seems to have been a wild young man, once being imprisoned in Castel Sant'Angelo on the orders of his Caetani mother — and managing to escape. He also fathered a son and a daughter by unknown women, yet was not prevented by this fact from becoming a cardinal. If anything, it may have helped, since his patron in this matter was Pope Alexander VI, Rodrigo Borgia, who was certainly no moralist. In fact it was probably as the result of Alexander's love for the beautiful Giulia Farnese that her brother was elevated to the purple. But his friendship with the two Medici popes must also have been in his favour.

His first step towards the pontificate was to buy the position of Apostolic Secretary from Pope Innocent VIII in 1491. When Rodrigo Borgia succeeded Innocent the following year Alessandro was made Treasurer-General of the Church, and in 1493 Cardinal-Deacon while still only twenty-five. This lower rank of cardinal, as an unordained member of the Church beneath the ranks of Cardinal-Bishop and Cardinal-Priest, allowed him to continue to indulge in fashionable life — and later even legitimize his own children. Using the continuing influence of his sister on Pope Alexander, he soon gained promotion as Cardinal-Legate; in 1499 he even became Bishop of Montefiascone and of Corneto, in the Farnese territory of northern Lazio, although he was still not ordained as a priest.

When Alexander died in 1503, he was succeeded — after the one-month pontificate of Pius III — by Giuliano della Rovere, who had been his strongest adversary. It says much for the diplomatic skill he must already have acquired that Alessandro, who was known to everybody as a Borgia man, managed to enter into the graces of the new pope, Julius II, and continued to prosper. In the same year his son Pier Luigi was born, of an unknown woman who was his mistress for a decade, and two years later Julius II paid him the courtesy of legitimizing the birth. Another son, Ranuccio, who died when he was twenty, was born of the same woman; there was also a daughter Costanza who married a Count of the Sforza of Santa Fiora — descended from Bosio, illegitimate son of Muzio Attendolo. Julius also appointed him papal legate of Ancona, and thus of the vital Marches. Finally he was appointed Bishop of Parma in 1509, a move which appears prophetic with hindsight and may have led to his ambitions concerning that city. It was while Bishop of Parma that he became ordained, perhaps intuiting that such a step was essential to further advancement.

Yet it also seems that there was an authentic conversion: that the wayward, unordained power-seeker found genuine inspiration in the doctrines of the Church. For it is striking that this conversion occurred just as the Protestant Reformation began, and that as Pope Paul III he was later to become the instigator of the Counter-Reformation by initiating the Council of Trent. For although he continued to live as a fifteenth-century prince-prelate his urge to reform and his dedication to the Church seem authentic enough. Be that as it may, from about 1520 his star was constantly rising and his power within the Church increasing. With the support of the Medici pope Clement VII, who had recommended him before dying, Alessandro became Pope Paul III in 1534 at the age of sixty-seven.

As pope his natural inclination for magnificence made him popular with his subjects. Even the grandness of his policy of nominating cardinals marked him out as unusual: he simply named whoever he thought was worthy without bothering to consult them, and did not insist that once raised to the purple they should necessarily side with him in every discussion. This was in contrast to the normal highly politicized procedure of balancing possible gains and favours in making appointments. His policy for the Church had four main points: to establish peace between France and Spain, to destroy the Protestants, to resist the Turks, and carry out the great reform many people deemed necessary. But one of his dominating concerns was to make princes of his son and nephews, and increase the historical importance of the Farnese. More than perhaps any member of the Italian dynasties, Paul III perceived his own family as an incipient dynasty.

Like many of his contemporaries he maintained an ambiguous attitude towards France and Spain. Dynastic needs meant that he generally favoured Charles V, since the Emperor's agreement was essential towards his policy of establishing a Farnese state for his son Pier Luigi; to this end he also arranged the marriage of his grandson Ottavio to Charles's natural daughter Margherita. France's attempts to make alliances both with the Protestants and with the Turks automatically placed it beyond the pale. Yet later he attempted to move towards France: just as he had made a diplomatic marriage of Ottavio, the young man's sister was given in marriage to the royal Duke of Vendôme. In this way his family was related to the two greatest powers of the time. It is a curious fact that already as a cardinal he had used his sons Pier Luigi and Ranuccio, until the latter's death, in his diplomatic game: while one fought for the Empire, the other was aligned with France. But the unfortunate result of this shift of alliances was the murder of Pier Luigi at the instigation of Ferrante Gonzaga, the Imperial Governor of Milan.

His policy for reform was forced upon him by circumstances he could not avoid; no doubt he would have been content to pass his life in the pleasures of the papacy like Leo X, but the consequences of the Reformation were impossible to ignore. Although the idea of reform had been in the air for some time, it was Paul III who made the important step of summoning the Council of Trent for the first session in 1545. Over the next twenty years the policies, dogmas, and principles of the Roman Catholic Church were established, and with few changes have continued to be in practice until today. In the first session effort was concentrated on the problems of clerical discipline and the remedy of abuses within the Church.

Another aspect of the process of reform was the pope's support for the new religious orders founded specifically for this purpose, including the Capuchins, the Theatines, and the Jesuits. The Capuchins were founded in about 1520 with the precise scope of restoring the original strict observance of the rule of St Francis, and were recognized in 1542; the Theatines were an order of clerks regular founded in 1524 by Giovanni Pietro Carafa, then Bishop of Chieti, to foster the old values of austerity and charity; the Jesuits were founded in 1534 to propagate the new doctrines of the Church, but were formally approved by Paul III six years later. It was in fact his grandson Cardinal Alessandro who financed the building of the Church of *Il Gesù* in Rome, not only the first Jesuit church but also the model for all Baroque churches. The same Carafa who founded the Theatines was made

La Farnesina: a perspective by Peruzzi.

cardinal by Paul III, and later became Pope Paul IV — one of the most zealous of all popes. It was he who convinced the Farnese pope, whose character would appear to suggest an opposer of such an idea, to refound the papal Inquisition. He did so with the bull *Licet ab initio* issued in 1542, thus paving the way for many celebrated trials and the notorious Index of Prohibited Books.

One of the first actions of Paul III as pope was to create cardinals of two of his grandsons. Then Pier Luigi was given fiefs of the Church and made commander of the papal army, while his son Ottavio was made Duke of Camerino in the Marches; later Pier Luigi's third son Orazio Farnese was made Prefect of Rome. The building projects Pope Paul had already conceived in the past were increased in size and style to match his new dignity. His nepotism at least matched and probably exceeded that of his predecessors, Sixtus IV della Rovere, Alexander VI Borgia, Julius II della Rovere, and Leo X de' Medici, each of whom was prepared to go to war in order to create new states for his sons and nephews. But in an age of endemic uncertainty, violence, and conspiracy it was essential to create a loyal entourage, and no loyalty was greater than filial loyalty. Hence the enrichment of members of the family and close friends was as much a political necessity as a matter of mere nepotism until more stable times rendered such insurance superfluous.

His patronage of the arts was exclusively aimed at glorifying the Farnese name. Already as Cardinal Alessandro he had begun construction of Palazzo Farnese, the finest and most extravagant of all Renaissance buildings in Rome. It was the age of grand designs, when St Peter's became the focus of a series of town plans which were to stamp the modern identity of the city that remained untouched until the urban developments of Mussolini. The first key to these plans was the Piazza di Ponte, just across the Tiber from Castel Sant'Angelo, from which a series of streets radiated out to draw pilgrims in to St Peter's from whichever gate they entered the city. A short street led to Via Giulia, designed by Bramante for Pope Julius II as part of a magnificent new approach to St Peter's — but left unfinished as the result of lack of funds. It was on Via Giulia, then an unbuilt street away from the traditional centre of Rome, that Alessandro Farnese decided to build his palace. When it was finished Via Giulia became the most fashionable street in Rome, and is still today one of the most unspoilt and attractive.

The original design was by Antonio da Sangallo the Younger (c.1483–1546), who had previously served as Bramante's assistant on the new St Peter's then in construction. He worked on the palace from 1513 until his death. It is a massive block of stone with a façade some seventy metres long and thirty metres high, divided into three horizontal parts by heavy cornices. The top storey was added by Michelangelo, who crowned the whole with a massive cornice which required the increased height of this storey so that it would not crush the building aesthetically. This audacious cornice, and the grandeur it conveys to the palace, is its most noticeable external aspect. Had the project been completed it would have been even more impressive, since Michelangelo planned a bridge across the Tiber which would connect the palace to the Villa Farnesina in Trastevere. The first arch of this ambitious viaduct remains, with its drooping ivy, the first thing that a visitor to Via Giulia notices. It was also Paul III who commissioned Michelangelo's fresco of *The Last Judgement* for the Sistine Chapel. As with so many of his works, the palace was incomplete when Michelangelo died in 1564; it was eventually completed after Pope Paul's death by Giacomo della Porta in 1589.

The magnificence is continued inside by the columned vestibule and porticoed courtyard, which opens onto a garden that runs downwards to Via Giulia. The state staircase leading to the first floor was made broad enough for Cardinal Alessandro — under whose patronage the palace was completed — to ride up to the *piano nobile* on horseback. The state rooms are in proportion to the exterior: the Salon d'Hercule, in which a famous Greek statue once stood, extends for two complete storeys, while galleries lead on both sides around the central courtyard to the Carracci gallery overlooking the garden. This gallery is so called after the painter Annibale Carracci (1560–1609), who decorated the barrel vault of this splendid room some twenty by eight metres with an illusionistic system of mythological scenes which rivals the Sistine Chapel ceiling in importance. The ceiling was seven years in painting, and its voluptuousness and colour are still striking. The gallery and frescoes were once completed by the collection of classical sculpture formed by Paul III's grandson Cardinal Alessandro, one of the greatest collectors of his day. The collection later became the nucleus of the National Museum of Naples, one of Italy's most underrated museums.

Beyond the monuments to the glory of his family, Pope Paul was also a notable patron of learning and public buildings. He sponsored the growth of the University of Rome — where his own teacher Pomponio Leo had also taught — and the Vatican Library; he encouraged the development of the printed book; such authors as Copernicus, whose ideas were later to cause so much controversy with the Church, dedicated their works to him. He renovated the fortifications of Rome, and especially the same Castel Sant'Angelo in which he had once been imprisoned — as defence against the Turks or a new 'Sack of Rome'. He improved Rome by restoring churches and roads, and pushed forward the building of the new basilica of St Peter's. The grand staircase leading up to the Capitol, together with the beautiful oval piazza and the palaces which now house the Town Hall of Rome and the Capitoline Museum, were designed by Michelangelo on the orders of Paul III. Only a man born in the fifteenth century would have conceived such a grandiose project for the sole purpose of the visit of an Emperor, Charles V, who, ironically, never actually came. He also commissioned numerous frescoes in the Vatican palace, including the 'Cappella Paolina' named for him.

It was, above all, Paul III who continued the building of St Peter's. In 1539 he ordered Antonio da Sangallo to build a new model for the basilica, which had originally been designed by Bramante. When Sangallo died seven years later, his model barely completed, the pope managed to persuade Michelangelo to carry on the commission. The pope had once written to Michelangelo: 'For thirty years I have longed to employ you, and now that I am pope shall I deny myself this wish?' Now he issued an order. But to obtain the artist's agreement Michelangelo was given a free hand to change whatever he wished, and this decision totally revolutionized the design for the basilica and, with few changes, created the building we see today. Michelangelo simplified the design, changed the plan, and above all designed the immense dome. Except for the extended nave, the Basilica of St Peter is today substantially the work of Paul III and Michelangelo, who after Paul's death wrote that the pope 'never showed me anything but kindness'.

Paul III was one of the great popes, a talented and intelligent man who managed to have his way in enriching his family and founding a duchy, and at the same time remaining popular with his subjects while his son and grandsons were hated. He was a man with clear visions of the importance of the Church, himself, and his family, and although belonging in a certain sense to the century of Lorenzo the Magnificent he made important steps towards putting the Church on the right road for the future. He was one of the main authors of reform. His support of the new religious orders and interest in missions towards the Americas, India, and Asia suggested how the Church could compensate for the loss of much of northern Europe and forge a new identity. He was a genuinely popular pope. When he died at the age of eighty-three the whole of Rome went to kiss his feet.

The qualities of pathos and nobility, the common touch and grandiose ambition, can be seen in the superb monument to Paul III inside St Peter's. It was sculpted by Guglielmo della Porta under the direction of Michelangelo, then in his seventies. The monument was never completed in its allegorical design, but it is ironic that the figure of Justice which does exist was a naked woman based upon the pope's sister Giulia — to whom he owed his papal tiara. Her naked breasts were covered on the orders of a later pope.

PIER LUIGI II
(1503–47)

Since Peter Luigi II died before his father, it is natural that his life was completely conditioned by the presence of such a powerful man to whom he owed everything. Little is known of his early life. From the moment of his marriage to Girolama Orsini at the age of sixteen he was destined to fulfil the family destiny as conceived by his father. First of the Farnese dukes, he yet remains in a sense only half-known since his mother was never identified.

His military career began with the armies of Charles V, but was short and without particular success at first. The only interesting fact is that he fought in Tuscany and Umbria under Don Ferrante Gonzaga, who was later to decide his destiny. Already at the age of twenty-six he was virtually a retired *condottiere*, and spent the following six years out of the limelight on the Farnese estates in northern Lazio. Then his career took on fresh impetus when his father became pope in 1534. He immediately became captain-general of the papal army, and carried out reforms designed to strengthen it into a strong and permanent militia which could then be used to further Farnese ambitions by forging a new state within the state. In 1537 he was named *Gonfaloniere*, or standard-bearer. This was the highest military honour possible within the Church, and the triumphal tour of the papal state which Pier Luigi embarked upon immediately afterwards was designed to impress upon onlookers the fact that he was destined for even greater office. The following year he became Duke of Castro, a town within traditional Farnese territory but which then assumed a new importance and even minted its own coins. The territory was increased by the simple method of 'buying' for next to nothing neighbouring properties and feuds from the Church.

With Paul III's strongly pro-Spanish policy in those years Pier Luigi rose in the favours of Charles V, who created him Marquis of Novara. He led successes of the imperial forces against the revolt of the Colonna south of Rome, in the suppression of another rebellion at Perugia in 1540, and many other minor actions. At the same time he entered further into the graces of the Spanish Emperor when his son Ottavio married Margherita of Austria, Charles's natural daughter. At one point there was talk of investing Ottavio with either Siena or Milan, but the obstacles were prohibitive since Spanish interest in Milan and Medici power in Tuscany were too strong. Then, in 1545, Pier Luigi was nominated Duke of Parma and Pia-

Pier Luigi II, by Titian.

cenza, although Charles V did not at first recognize the new title.

Pier Luigi's tenure as Duke was primarily concerned with Piacenza. The Duchy of Parma and Piacenza was a single duchy containing two distinct parts, neither of which was allowed to overwhelm the other part. Equal and separate in fact, but joined in law.

His rule as Lord of Piacenza was brief, but enough to disturb the powers around him. The city stands in a position of strategic importance on the River Po, which was then vital for river transport, and only fifty kilometres from Milan. He immediately started refortifying the city, building a new castle and creating a military élite loyal to him by distributing noble titles to his soldiers. The old Visconti castle was to become the Farnese residence. Furthermore, in a burst of expansionist energy sustained by his father, he took castles and towns from such families as the Sforza and Gonzaga. But in doing so he became a threat to Ferrante Gonzaga, who was then Governor of Milan for Charles V. It was thus his over-ambition which caused his downfall. When he financed a rebellion against the Doria family in Genova, who were loyal to Spain, Gonzaga was forced to move against him. On 10 September 1547 he was assassinated inside his residence in the old Visconti castle by a task force commanded by Count Giovanni Anuissola, a member of a local feudal family whose power was threatened, but instigated by Gonzaga. The Duke was taken by surprise in his dining-room. His body was shown from a window and then dropped into the moat beneath. He was succeeded by his wife, who later removed his body to Parma; but his journey was not finished there, since it is said that it was later taken to the family tomb on the island in Lake Bolsena.

Yet he had not been a bad ruler. Pier Luigi Farnese was a man of strong character and determination. In that brief span of time he had introduced important new administrative reforms which, together with the fortifications, would indeed have made Piacenza a more important city. He began a census of the population and property of his new duchy, established a supreme council of justice and seemed intent on creating an efficiently operated state. The city, too, was to have become a well-planned, healthy, and elegant capital in accordance with the new ideas of the late sixteenth century which were transforming Rome. With his own drive and ambition, together with the support of his father and neutrality on the behalf of Ferrante Gonzaga, he might have created an excellent addition to the diminishing band of independent states in the Italian peninsula.

CARDINAL ALESSANDRO
(1520–89)

Pier Luigi's eldest son became cardinal on the election of his grandfather to the Holy See in 1534. From that moment he was literally submerged in a sea of bishoprics, honours, and titles. He travelled as papal legate to Avignon and to Germany, and played an important role in the elections of successive popes. He was also present at the first session of the Council of Trent. When his father was assassinated, Cardinal Alessandro was forced to go into temporary exile in Florence. But with consummate diplomatic skill he managed to sustain his brother Ottavio's

Rome: courtyard of Palazzo Farnese.

attempt to hold Parma, and thereby retain the duchy they had seemed destined to lose.

His temporal power extended over the traditional Farnese territory, where he was papal legate. He exercised political influence in that role, encouraging his Orsini relatives to extend their power and seeking to contrast the power of Grand Duke Cosimo de' Medici. It was in this context that he completed the most interesting building associated with the Farnese, their villa at Caprarola in the heart of the ancestral territory near Viterbo. Begun in the 1520s by the same Antonio da Sangallo who designed Palazzo Farnese in Rome, it was completed by Giacomo Barozzi da Vignola (1507–73), who also designed *Il Gesù* in Rome. The villa has the unusual plan of a pentagon, with a circular courtyard inside. In fact the pentagon derives from a castle plan, and was based upon five bastions which from below give the villa the appearance of a castle.

The interior is characterized by a fine and richly decorated spiral staircase supported by thirty pairs of Doric columns leading to the *piano nobile*. The State Hall, the Hall of the 'Fasti Farnesiani', Hall of the Council of Trent, and especially the 'Sala degli Angeli' or Hall of Angels, are decorated by fine frescoes. It is a building of the farmhouse-villa type — probably descended from the Villa Medici at Poggio a Caiano by Giuliano da Sangallo — which later became well known in England after the model of Palladio. But the elegant circular courtyard is quite different to previous farmhouse-villas. Its rusticated ground floor and colonnaded gallery on the first floor are reminiscent of Charles V's magnificent circular palace at Granada. Today this Villa Farnese is part of the official summer residence of the Italian President.

In Rome Cardinal Alessandro completed Palazzo Farnese, and bought from the Sienese banking family the Chigi the so-called Farnesina across the Tiber — to which Michelangelo's bridge was to lead. This villa was one of the first with a central block and projecting wings, built by Bramante's friend Baldassare Peruzzi (1481–1536) and decorated by Raphael and other painters. The paintings include Raphael's famous frescoes of Cupid and Psyche. This villa was intended, like the later Villa Borghese, to be a summer refuge from the heat of Rome — although it is now considered in the centre of the city. It is today the official residence of the Italian Minister of Foreign Affairs. The cardinal's collection of classical sculptures which adorned Palazzo Farnese was one of the most celebrated of the time. He created on the Palatine the Farnese Gardens, one of the earliest botanic gardens in Europe — now recalled in the geometrical plan of the gardens which overlook the Forum, with avenues of cypresses and bays, and a fountain which is one of the coolest spots in a Roman summer. It was he who had the inspiration to move the bronze equestrian statue of the Emperor Marcus Aurelius from the Lateran palace to the square on the Capitol designed by Michelangelo.

Cardinal Alessandro aspired to a second Farnese pontificate, and it is interesting to speculate what a man of his taste and means might have made of the office. But his enemies were too strong: first and foremost the Medici and the Gonzaga. Furthermore, after the reforms sponsored by his own grandfather it would have been difficult to allow a second pope from the same family, and Alessandro had committed the traditional sins of Renaissance cardinals — including a love affair with a great beauty of the time. Yet for over half a century he was one of the key figures behind the scenes in the Church. He was buried in the Roman church of *Il Gesù*, built for the Jesuits under his patronage.

OTTAVIO
(1524–86)

When Pier Luigi I was assassinated, and Piacenza rebelled against the Farnese, Parma remained loyal and was far enough away from Milan not to interest Ferrante Gonzaga and Charles V. Thus while Paul III himself, weakened by the shock and almost certainly driven to his death by the tragic loss of his son, was ready to renounce the idea of a Farnese duchy and allow the two cities to revert to the papal state, his grandson Ottavio opposed this idea and took possession of Parma. It seems that the pope's anger at Ottavio's refusal to leave the city brought about his death. But shortly before this happened Cardinal Alessandro persuaded his father to give Parma to Ottavio. Pope Paul III died pronouncing the name 'Parma'.

That the Farnese retained Parma is entirely due to the tenacity and prompt action of Ottavio. Just as his brother was made cardinal immediately after his grandfather's election, so Ottavio was married when he was fourteen years old to Margherita of Austria, the natural daughter of Charles V, in an obviously dynastic marriage. Two years older than her husband, already the widow of Alessandro de' Medici as we have seen, she was never a happy wife and they usually lived quite separate lives. Yet her name is indissolubly linked with the Farnese, and, ironically, many of the most celebrated 'Farnese' buildings or connections derive from her. Their union in marriage was to last nearly half a century, and they both died in the same year.

Margherita was born in Oudenaarde in Flanders, today in Belgium, in 1522 when Charles — who was himself born in Gand — was Archduke of Austria. Her marriage brought with her name the possessions of lands and castles within the Kingdom of Naples that would later be associated with the Farnese, and also the inheritance of her late Medici husband — including Penna, in Abruzzo, which gave him his ducal title. Since both bride and groom were not yet adult, Pope Paul III stood as guarantor in the complex wedding contract. She was unwilling from the beginning, but even at sixteen was fully aware of the diplomatic importance of her person. In the fresco of the wedding by Taddeo Zuccari (1529–66) in Villa Farnese at Caprarola, where we may assume the artist wished to paint a favourable version, she regards her new husband disdainfully. The marriage was not consummated at once, and was characterized from the first by a coldness which all the efforts of Paul III and Pier Luigi Farnese did nothing to dispel.

She was a charming and intelligent woman, who loved hunting as much as jewels. Contemporaries speak of her masculine character, and later portraits show a severe woman reminiscent of Queen Victoria. She usually had her way, and desired above all a husband of suitable rank. To her the Farnese seemed parvenu and inferior in comparison to the Medici family and tradition. But the power and influence of Paul III were such that these matters could be overlooked. Within a few years she reconciled herself to her new position, perhaps aided by a genuine religious devotion, and was faithful both to the Farnese name and to her husband. From her marriage until 1550 she was mainly resident in Rome, visiting Tivoli, Elba and other places during the disease-ridden Roman summers. Ottavio was often absent on military or diplomatic business, but when he was in Rome she overcame her previous distaste for him and in 1545 gave birth to their heir Alessandro. Her residence there was popularly identified with her, and is still today known as Palazzo Madama. It is now the seat of the Italian Senate. That so many Farnese palaces were ideally suited to become formal government buildings is an interesting confirmation of their concept of prestige and grandeur.

As we have seen, in 1547 Ottavio took Parma against his grandfather's wishes. Three years later he was recognized as Duke of Parma by Pope Julius III, and Duchess Margherita moved to Parma with him. When Charles V abdicated in favour of his son Philip II in 1555, it was easy for Ottavio to negotiate an agreement with his brother-in-law which guaranteed the future succession of the Farnese duchy and the return of Piacenza to their rule. Thus Ottavio and Margherita ruled over Parma, Piacenza, and Novara, together with Penna, Castro, and other lands in the Kingdom of Naples. They were now virtually a Spanish protectorate, and this orientation was emphasized when Alessandro was sent to the court of Madrid for his education.

Parma became the Farnese capital. Duke Ottavio restored and reformed Parma as his father had done for Piacenza. A new and better organized army was formed, including artillery. He organized a Council of Justice and created new government officers to administer the duchy. With interesting far-sightedness he founded a Jesuit college which was to provide the men who would run the administration, and which later became the University of Parma. He also reorganized agriculture and established new industries; for instance Piacenza became a major centre of the production of velvet and silk. Banks were opened in many minor towns as well as in the two main cities. While Ottavio remained in Parma his wife set up home in Piacenza, maintaining their distant relationship in a regular correspondence which mainly concerns the affairs of state. In a kind of jealous retaliation she built the impressive but never-finished Palazzo Farnese in Piacenza, which neither of them was ever to use. Her choice of Piacenza represents her rebellion and independence from Duke Ottavio. It was in Piacenza — in the church of San Sisto — that she was buried according to her own express desire.

Then, in 1559, on the orders of the new King of Spain her half-brother Philip II, Margherita became Governess of Flanders and spent most of the next decade distant from Parma, although she was accompanied by soldiers from both Parma and Piacenza. Her reasons for accepting were probably two-fold: first, to obtain the final release of the citadel of Piacenza, still manned by imperial troops; and second, to secure future advancement for her son Alessandro. When, in fact, as Marguerite d'Autriche, Duchesse de Parme, she took up her new role in Brussels, the young Alessandro travelled to Spain with Philip II to complete his education and learn the arts of war and diplomacy. Amidst the many problems of governing a mixed bunch of provinces — which included Luxembourg, Hainaut, Artois, Zealand, Utrecht, and Flanders — in the name of an absent king, the local leaders were prepared to accept her as Habsburg ruler but not as a tyrant. The Duchess of Parma acquitted herself well, resolving at least in part such problems as reconciling the people to a Spanish military presence, and a series of religious problems which included an attempt to enforce the Catholic supremacy. It was during her governancy that there were violent protests and revolts against the introduction of the Inquisition. Her subjects demanded the suppression of that institution, and the end of public advertisements against heresy. Her letters to Philip II constantly emphasize the difficulties involved, and how they were increased by the lack of money.

But her rule was destined to end tragically. Faced with the impossibility of resolving the religious conflicts through diplomacy, and perhaps frustrated with the way in which his own sister refused to adopt his harsh methods, Philip II sent the repressive Duke of Alba, Francesco Alvarez da Toledo, to replace her in the vain hope of restoring peace. Alba succeeded in repressing the rebellion. But his violent victory was short-lived, while Margherita was long remembered for the positive and humane qualities of her rule. A letter which she wrote to the king before leaving demonstrates the stuff of her character. Having begged Philip to be generous and clement, she adds prophetically: 'Otherwise, my lord, using rigour it is impossible to avoid the good being overwhelmed by evil, and it is evident that a calamity and the destruction of this country will follow, with all the possible consequences.'

Thus she returned to Italy, but never to her husband. Her continued interest in the Farnese lands and power was sublimated in her concern for her son Alessandro, and *his* future. She became more interested in her lands in the south, those inherited from Alessandro de' Medici or held in her own feudal right. From 1569 she became Governor of the Abruzzi, where she resided in Cittaducale (now in Lazio) for three years. Then in 1572 she became Perpetual Governor of L'Aquila, where she took up residence in the building that is now the town hall. In her years there she seems to have taken care to improve the city, and amongst other things founded a model farm with new methods of farming which considerably influenced the local economy. It says much for the personality of this unusual woman that after a childhood spent as daughter of the Emperor, years at the great courts of Florence and Rome, with the title of one of the major duchies of Italy, and after her years as Governor in Brussels, she eventually found happiness in the small and relatively poor state of the Abruzzi.

If Margherita's greatest aspiration was most certainly Florence, the two places in which she found most happiness in her long life were Flanders and the Abruzzi. Ironically, she never enjoyed the city with which her name is identified, and never really lived there; neither did she live as a Farnese, while it was her presence which associated the Farnese name with buildings and palaces throughout Italy. Thus one of the most interesting characters in the history of the Farnese dynasty is barely a Farnese. The last years of her life were, symbolically, divided between Flanders and the Abruzzi, where she died in 1586 in the town of Ortona where she had been

Alessandro Farnese, by Mor.

building yet another 'Palazzo Farnese' — which has recently become the town library. Duke Ottavio died shortly afterwards in Parma.

DUKE ALESSANDRO
(1545–92)

As we have seen, Alessandro finished his education in Madrid. Although he bore the Italian title of Duke of Parma and Piacenza he was in fact more Spanish than Italian, or even Flemish, as can be seen in the very 'Spanish' portrait by Giovanni Roberto Salve.

Alessandro was a born soldier, excellent horseman and shot, who was said to have taken part in his first battle at fifteen — like many earlier *condottieri*. His personal courage was often praised. At twenty he was married to Maria di Braganza of Portugal, with obvious hopes on his mother's part of a future role on the contested Portuguese throne. But the marriage was no more successful than that of his mother, and never gained the glory she had hoped for. Instead Alessandro was to make his name in war, winning his battle spurs at the Battle of Lepanto in 1571.

Six years later he became Governor of the Spanish Netherlands, a position he held for twenty-one years through some of the most tumultuous times of Spanish colonial history and also the Wars of Religion. He arrived after the campaigns of the Duke of Alba to find only two of seventeen provinces under firm Spanish dominion. He initiated what appeared to be a futile campaign to reconquer the lost provinces from William of Orange. But he too was a brilliant military strategist: he won special glory for the siege of Antwerp in 1585, when he built a fortified bridge across the Scheldt to prevent supplies and reinforcements reaching the city by sea. When, after months of artillery bombardment, Antwerp was taken, he had succeeded in bringing the southern Netherlands back under Spanish control — and in leading the way to the formation of modern Belgium as a Catholic buffer to Protestant Holland. It was his most outstanding military achievement, while his major failure derived from his involvement in the Spanish Armada. It was in fact Alessandro Farnese who, on Philip II's orders, assembled the army and troop ships which were to invade England. He had previously formulated a different plan for an Armada, but to no avail, and a large part of the celebrated victory of Sir Francis Drake may in fact be attributed to Philip's arrogant refusal to consider Alessandro's plan. The destruction of that expedition signalled the end of his own military successes in the Netherlands.

Alessandro became Duke of Parma and Piacenza in 1586, on his father's death. But it was impossible for him to travel to Italy, since the Spanish League found itself threatened on a new flank by the recently converted protestant King Henry IV of France. This new problem virtually saved Holland from his attention, and led to that country's future independence. He saved Paris from Henry's attack in 1590, and spent the next two years on campaigns in France. He died at Arras, of battle wounds compounded by gout — and possibly his disappointment. His funeral was celebrated with great pomp in Brussels, but he was then buried in Parma.

Thus the most celebrated of the Dukes of Parma eventually reached the city whose name he bore. His tomb, in suitably classical fashion, bears the single word 'Alexander'.

THE LATER DUKES OF PARMA AND PIACENZA

After the splendours of the career of Duke Alessandro the last five Dukes of Farnese were fundamentally mediocre men. His son Duke Ranuccio I (1569–1622) had been regent in his father's place since Duke Ottavio's death in 1586. He was in fact the first Farnese born in Parma, and was brought up there virtually alone — a fact which contributed to his introvert and gloomy personality. Although he fought for a while under his father in the Netherlands, most of his life was passed as a politician and ruler in Parma, governing the city for thirty years. He was a good judge of men, and surrounded himself with wise and efficient administrators so that Parma lived a moment of true power and glory. He viciously repressed the nobles and brought all the feuds under his control, consequently increasing the wealth of the Farnese state. He restored and sponsored the University of Parma and encouraged learning.

Above all he gave Parma the urban aspect which still dominates the centre of the city today. He built the huge ducal palace known as the 'Pilotta' and the historically important wooden Theatre — rebuilt after its destruction in World War II — which testifies to the importance of drama and music during his rule. In many ways he was the true creator of the Duchy of Parma, since the previous — and intrinsically greater — members of the Farnese dynasty spent less time and energy on the duchy than he did. It is therefore ironic that this apogee was also the last significant moment in the history of the family.

Duke Ranuccio I was succeeded by his son Duke Odoardo I (1612–46), an arrogant and impulsive man whose rash decisions began the irreversible decline of family fortunes. With a decision his forebears would never have understood, in the Thirty Years War (1618–38) between the Bourbons and Habsburgs he joined the anti-Spanish league. A year before the war ended he was forced to renounce his allegiance to France, but soon engaged himself in another predicament when he challenged the powerful Barberini pope Urban VIII (1623–44) over the old Farnese fief of Castro, in Lazio, which Urban's nephews wished to take. In 1642 war broke out between them and Odoardo was excommunicated.

The dynasty reached its nadir with Duke Ranuccio II (1630–94), Odoardo's son. He became duke at sixteen, and never really took command: at first he ruled under the regency of his mother, then allowed the state to be ruled by his favourites — who clearly acted in their own interests. His inept handling of the Castro affair, which continued to smoulder, led him to a humiliating defeat in battle and led to his being abandoned by both France and Spain. When he died, the precariousness of the duchy was apparent to all. Neither of the two sons who succeeded him, Duke Francesco (1678–1727) and Duke Antonio (1679–1731), managed to halt the now rapid decline of Farnese wealth. Antonio never produced an heir, so the direct Farnese line ended with his death in 1731 after a brief rule of four years.

There was a brief appendix to the Farnese dynasty. Elisabetta Farnese, born in 1692 to Duke Francesco's younger brother Odoardo, had been married to Philip V of Spain in 1714 in a desperate diplomatic initiative to recover Farnese power. An intelligent and affectionate Queen of Spain, she was in effect the last of the Farnese dynasty, which died with her at Aranjuez in 1766. It was to her son Don Carlos that the Duchy of Parma and Piacenza passed by imperial edict on Duke Antonio's death. Don Carlos was to rule briefly over his new duchy, before his elevation in 1734 to the more prestigious title of King of Naples. In 1759 he became King Charles III of Spain.

Acton, Harold, *The Last Medici* (London, 1932).

Ady, Cecilia, *A History of Milan Under the Sforza* (London, 1907).

Ady, Julia, *Isabella d'Este, Marchioness of Mantua 1474-1539*, 2 vols. (London, 1915).

Antonetti, Pierre, *La Vie Quotidienne à Florence au Temps du Dante* (Paris, 1979).

Baron, Hans, *The Crisis of the Early Italian Renaissance* (Princeton, 1966).

Bellonci, Maria, *Segreti dei Gonzaga* (Milan, 1947).

Bonvesin da la Riva, *De magnalibus Mediolani* (Milan, 1974).

Boulting, William, *Women in Italy* (London, 1910).

Brinton, Selwyn, *The Gonzaga: Lords of Mantua* (London, 1927).

Burke, Peter, *The Italian Renaissance: Culture and Society in Italy* (Cambridge, 1987).

Castiglione, Baldassare, *Il Libro del Cortegiano* (Milan, 1972).

Chamberlain, E.R., *Everyday Life in Renaissance Times* (London, 1965).

——, *The World of the Italian Renaissance* (London, 1982).

Collison-Morley, L., *The Story of the Sforzas* (London, 1933).

Colonna, Prospero, *I Colonna: dalle Origini all'inizio del Secolo XIX* (Rome, 1927).

Commynes, Philippe de, *Memorie*, ed. Daviso di Charvensod (Turin, 1960).

Coniglio, Giuseppe, *I Gonzaga* (Milan, 1967).

Cronin, Vincent, *The Florentine Renaissance* (London, 1967).

——, *The Flowering of the Renaissance* (London, 1969).

Deiss, Joseph Jay, *Captains of Fortune: Profiles of Six Italian Condottieri* (London, 1966).

Dennistoun, James, *Memoirs of the Dukes of Urbino*, 3 vols. (London, 1909).

Ewart, K. Dorothea, *Cosimo de' Medici* (London, 1899).

Ferri-Mancini, Mons., *Manuale di Genealogia per la Storia del Medieovo e Moderno* (Osimo, 1883).

Franceschini, Gino, *I Montefeltro* (Milan, 1970).

Gage, John, *Life in Italy at the Time of the Medici* (London, 1968).

Gardner, Edmund, G., *Dukes and Poets in Ferrara* (London, 1904).

Hibbert, Christopher, *The Rise and Fall of the House of Medici* (London, 1979).

Hutton, Edward, *Sigismondo Pandolfo Malatesta, Lord of Rimini: A Study of a XV Century Italian Despot* (London, 1906).

Kristeller, Paul Oscar, *Renaissance Thought: The Classic, Scholastic and Humanist Strains* (New York, 1961).

Larner, John, *Culture and Society in Italy: 1290–1420* (London, 1971).

Lefevre, Renato, *'Madama' Margarita d'Austria* (Rome, 1986).

Litta, P., *Famiglie celebri italiane*, 4 vols. (Milan, 1835).

Machiavelli, Niccolò, *The Prince* (London, 1961).

Maguire, Y., *The Private Life of Lorenzo the Magnificent* (London, 1936).

Mallett, Michael, *Mercenaries and their Masters: Warfare in Renaissance Italy* (London, 1974).

Martines, Lauro, *Power and Imagination: City-States in Renaissance Italy* (New York, 1980).

Mesquita, D.M., Bueno de, *Giangaleazzo Visconti, Duke of Milan* (Cambridge, 1941).

Muir, Dorothy, *A History of Milan Under the Visconti* (London, 1924).

Murray, Peter, *The Architecture of the Italian Renaissance* (New York, 1965).

Noyes, Ella, *The Story of Ferrara* (London, 1904).

Plumb, J.H., *The Italian Renaissance* (New York, 1965).

Prescott, Orville, *Princes of the Renaissance* (New York, 1969).

Pullan, Brian, *A History of Early Renaissance Italy* (London, 1973).

Rendina, Claudio, *I Capitani di Ventura* (Rome, 1985).

Rocca, Emilio Nasalli, *I Farnese* (Milan, 1969).

Ross, Janet (Ed.), *Lives of the Early Medici*, as told in their correspondence (London, 1910).

Rowrdon, Maurice, *Lorenzo the Magnificent* (London, 1974).

Simon, Kate, *A Renaissance Tapestry: the Gonzaga of Mantua* (London, 1988).

Sizeranne, Robert de la, *Beatrice d'Este and her Court* (London, 1924).

Vasari, Giorgio, *Lives of the Artists* (London, 1965).

PLACES TO VISIT

This brief list does not constitute a complete guide to the places and buildings associated with the Italian dynasties; neither is it intended to replace a good guidebook for each of the towns and regions. When such a complex monument as, say, the cathedral of Milan or the Uffizi Gallery in Florence is mentioned, it is solely because there is some aspect of particular historical relevance to people or incidents recorded in this book. No attempt is made to compete with more detailed guides. In some cases, such as Palestrina for the Colonna family, a site is suggested for its power to evoke the influence of the family although there are no surviving examples of their building.

THE VISCONTI

Milan: Castello Sforzesco

Originally known as the Castello di Porta Giovia, this huge structure was originally built by the Visconti and started around 1370, presumably by Bernabò. Like so many other Visconti buildings, however, it was later rebuilt and enlarged by the Sforza, from 1450 onwards; the present tower and main façade was completely rebuilt in our own century.

Inside, the Castle Museum contains the magnificent contemporary equestrian statue of Bernabò Visconti.

Milan: cathedral

The immense cathedral of Milan, now the largest of all Gothic cathedrals, was started at the orders of Gian Galeazzo Visconti in 1386, although the only surviving original part is the present apse. The façade was completed only in the nineteenth century, and the spires and other external decorations were finished in the twentieth century. Just outside it, to the left on leaving, is the eighteenth-century Palazzo Reale, which stands on the site of the original palace built by Azzone, and walking through the courtyard of this palace leads to the surviving bell tower and apse of San Gottardo, also built by Azzone Visconti and where Giovanni Maria Visconti was assassinated in 1412.

Pavia: Visconti Castle

This castle was built between 1360 and 1365 by Galeazzo II, and completed by Giangaleazzo. This is the castle where Giangaleazzo waited in well-protected seclusion for seven years and plotted the murder of his uncle Bernabò in Milan. It is well-preserved and has an extremely attractive courtyard. It houses an interesting archaeological museum and a museum of sculpture.

Pavia: The University

Founded by Giangaleazzo as a *studium* in 1361, and frequented by the humanists and poets attached to his court, this is today one of the most ancient and attractive of Italian universities, retaining in its courtyards and alleys something of its Renaissance atmosphere.

Other Visconti castles

Among the most interesting of the many Visconti or so-called Visconti castles near Milan, the following are worth a short excursion for their position, state of preservation, and indications of medieval fortifications: the Rocca di Augera, Cusago, Pandino, S. Angelo Lodigiano, Belgoioso, Somma Lombardo, Abbiategrasso, the fine castle at Brignano Gera d'Adda near Bergano which was auctioned with its contents in May 1988, and the gloomy ruins of the castle at Trezzo d'Adda where Bernabò Visconti died a prisoner of his nephew Gian Galeazzo.

THE ESTE

Ferrara: Castle

This imposing castle, with its massive ramparts and moat, stands at the centre of Ferrara and was built by Niccolò II d'Este in 1385 but enlarged and rebuilt in the sixteenth century. It possesses a fine Renaissance courtyard, and many frescoed rooms including the private chapel of Renata, the French wife of Ercole II d'Este.

Ferrara: Palazzo Schifanoia

Now within the city, this was the country pleasure house of the Este family, ironically called the 'palace of boredom'. The frescoes of scenes from the life of Borso d'Este and the marvellous set of allegories of the months are by relatively unknown painters from Ferrara but count among the finest frescoes of the second half of the fifteenth century.

Corso Ercole I d'Este

This street was the central axis of the so-called 'Addizione Erculae', which Ercole I built towards the end of the fifteenth century, a masterpiece of town planning which made Ferrara one of the first modern European cities. The many palaces and gardens still evoke the elegance and grandiosity of this project, which doubled the size of Ferrara in a few years.

Ferrara: Palazzo dei Diamanti

This palace, known as the 'Palace of Diamonds' because of the stones of the façade cut in diamond shape, was begun in 1492. It is the most elegant of the buildings of the 'Addizione Erculae'. Today it houses the Pinacoteca Nazionale of Ferrara.

Tivoli: Villa d'Este

A short distance from Rome, and cooler on summer evenings, the villa built by Cardinal Ippolito d'Este is the finest monument to this family. The villa itself has fine frescoes, but its glory is the landscaped garden with its fountains, grottoes, and pools which took twenty years to complete. The Oval Fountain and the Path of a Hundred Fountains are stunning even today, and although original features, such as the water organ and Fountain of the Owl and Birds — which alternately produced an owl screech and bird song — no longer work it is still a superb garden.

THE COLONNA

Near Rome

Many of the towns and villages near Rome have vestiges of Colonna power in ruined castles, towers, or palaces.

Palestrina, birthplace of the sixteenth-century composer of the same name, is one of the hilltop towns of the Alban Hills near Rome which still preserves something of a medieval atmosphere — although it was badly damaged by bombing in the last war. The medieval cathedral was rebuilt by the Colonna in the twelfth century, and was the see of the Colonna-sponsored Girolamo Masci who became Pope Nicholas IV in 1288. At the highest point of the town is Palazzo Colonna-Barberini, one of the original family seats, sold to the Barberini in the seventeenth century. It commands spectacular views across Rome to the sea, and today houses an excellent archaeological museum.

Beyond Palestrina is Paliano, a small fortified town which was home to the main Colonna line and from whence their princely title derives. Parts of the original castle survive, and early Colonna tombs may be seen in the church of Sant'Andrea.

Rome: Palazzo Colonna

The Palazzo Colonna stands just off Piazza Venezia, a massive much-rebuilt palace dominating the roads on three sides of it and ironically best identified by a wax museum which is housed in one corner. Only a few rooms are open to the public, and only on Saturday morning, but they suffice to evoke the life in such palaces.

Beside and within Palazzo Colonna is the Basilica of the SS. Apostoli, a sixth-century church which was completely rebuilt in the eighteenth century. This is the church where the funeral of Prince Aspreno Colonna took place in 1987, and which houses the recent tombs of the family. Behind the palace, in Via della Pilotta, are several arched bridges which lead directly from the palace over the street to the gardens which once stretched up the hill to the Quirinal hill.

Rome: Galleria Colonna

The family picture gallery, also open only on Saturdays, houses important portraits of Vittoria Colonna and Marcantonio II in addition to paintings by Poussin, Tintoretto, Veronese, and Annibale Caracci.

THE SFORZA

Milan: Castello Sforzesco

This became the principal Sforza residence when Francesco Sforza enlarged and modernized the existing Visconti castle from 1450, and was then decorated by Galeazzo Maria and Lodovico il Moro successively. The entire castle can be visited, and an idea of the extravagance of the Sforza gained, by touring the various museums now occupying the building. These include a sculpture museum (which contains Michelangelo's last work, the *Rondanini Pièta*), a fine Pinacoteca (with paintings by Mantegna, Filippo Lippi, Giovanni Bellini, and others), and museums of furniture, ceramics, musical instruments, coins, Egyptian archaeology, and the Trivulziana Library with a collection of illuminated manuscripts.

Milan: Ospedale Maggiore (The State University)

This hospital was founded by Francesco Sforza and his wife Bianca Maria in 1456. It was built as a series of cloisters grouped around a large internal courtyard by the Florentine architect, Filarete, who enlarged the castle for Francesco using the same red brick. Together with the castle it represents the height of Sforza monumental architecture in Milan.

Francesco Sforza himself lived mainly in Pavia at Visconti Castle there, and when in Milan resided at the old palace now replaced by the Palazzo Reale, beside the cathedral.

Milan: Santa Maria delle Grazie

This church was begun under Sforza sponsorship in the late fifteenth century and completed by Bramante, who built the lovely cloister. But its most important treasure is the *Last Supper* of Leonardo da Vinci, commissioned by Lodovico il Moro in the adjacent refectory. This was the favourite church of Beatrice d'Este, and her funeral was held here.

Milan: Brera Gallery

This gallery, one of the most important in Italy, houses the altarpiece attributed to Zenale with the most celebrated portraits of Lodovico il Moro and his wife Beatrice d'Este.

Pavia: The Certosa (Charterhouse)

This was begun by Gian Galeazzo Visconti as the projected family mausoleum, but completed and elaborated by Lodovico il Moro. Although they were not buried there, the central nave contains the monumental sculpted tombs of Lodovico il Moro and Beatrice d'Este. There are also contemporary frescoes, such as the Coronation of the Virgin with Francesco Sforza and Lodovico. It also contains the tomb of Gian Galeazzo Visconti.

Forlì: Rocca di Ravaldino

The fortress of Ravaldino, situated at the southern gate of Forlì, where Caterina Sforza defended the city against Duke Valentino in 1499 and tricked the attackers by allowing her children to be taken as hostages and then showing herself naked and pregnant to them. The Pinacoteca in the same city contains the portrait of Caterina Sforza by Palmezziani.

Pesaro: Palazzo Ducale

A fine Renaissance palace begun by Alessandro Sforza in 1450, with an elegant and imposing portico.

THE MALATESTA

Verucchio: the Castle

Verucchio was the place of origin of the Malatesta, inland from Rimini in a spectacular site with fine views. The original Malatesta fortress, restored by Sigismondo in 1449, stands precariously on the rock above the village and provides a good example of the size and site of many late medieval castles.

Rimini: the Malatesta Temple

The 'Tempio Malatestiano' built by Sigismondo is the principal surviving monument of the Malatesta, built 1147–1460. Alberti's façade is one of the most imposing structures of the Italian Renaissance, inspired by the concept of a Roman triumphal arch. Inside are Sigismondo's tomb, a separate chapel with the tomb of his third wife Isotta degli Atti, and the magnificent fresco by Piero della Francesca of Sigismondo on his knees before St Sigismond.

In nearby Piazza Malatesta are the restored ruins of Sigismondo's castle, built with Brunelleschi's advice just before the 'Tempio'.

Fano: Palazzo Malatestiano

This palace, now the town museum, was rebuilt by Pandolfo III Malatesta in the second decade of the fifteenth century. Pandolfo and his wife Paola Bianca were buried in the church of San Francesco, which was demolished earlier this century; his tomb was designed by Alberti, a simple, severe classical structure which can still be seen in the surviving portico of San Francesco.

Gradara: Castle

One of the best-preserved medieval castles and fortified villages, between Urbino and Pesaro, this is where Gian Cotto surprised his wife Francesca and brother Paolo. The room is open to visitors and the trapdoor he used can be seen. The castle is furnished with contemporary objects.

THE GONZAGA

Mantova: Palazzo Ducale

Rather than a palace, this building is a vast complex of castles, palaces, and apartments added to and rebuilt continuously between the fourteenth and eighteenth centuries. Perhaps no other single building provides such a vivid image of the exaggerated grandeur of the smaller Renaissance courts. The most interesting are the tapestry apartment, the ducal apartment, the Metamorphosis apartment with its frescoes based on the stories of Ovid, and the extraordinary dwarf's apartment where everything is scaled down. The normal guided tour, which goes quite quickly through some of the rooms, takes one and a half hours.

Isabella d'Este's favourite part of the palace was in the fourteenth-century Castle of St George. In one of the towers is the famous 'Camera degli Sposi' with portraits of Marquis Lodovico Gonzaga and his family by Mantegna.

The ducal palace forms part of a well-preserved and dramatic historic city centre, with the thirteenth-century Broletto, where the town government met, and Palazzo della Ragione. The church of S. Andrea, designed by Alberti for the Gonzaga, contains the tomb of Mantegna.

Mantova: Palazzo del Tè

This palace was once outside the city, and was built as a pleasure house for Federico II Gonzaga by the architect Giulio Romano in the sixteenth century. The frescoes of the Psyche Room and the Giants Room are impressive.

San Benedetto Po

This interesting monastery was founded in the tenth century, but later expanded with its present classical façade in the sixteenth century by Giulio Romano for the Gonzaga — whose native town lies fifteen kilometres south of San Benedetto. The Gonzaga first appear in history as recipients of land grants from the monastery. Today, only the church survives.

THE FARNESE

Rome: Palazzo Farnese

Palazzo Farnese is the most impressive of all Roman palaces, with its massive façade and extraordinary upper storey added by Michelangelo. Started by Alessandro Farnese, later Pope Paul III, in 1514, it was completed only in 1589. Its many features include the vestibule, the bridge designed by Michelangelo to cross the Tiber to the Villa Farnesina on the other side, and, above all the Caracci gallery with its walls and ceilings frescoed with scenes from Ovid's Metamorphosis.

Rome: the Farnesina

Across the Tiber from Palazzo Farnese, the Farnesina was originally built between 1508 and 1511 for Agostino Chigi by Baldassare Peruzzi. It is not properly part of Farnese patronage, since the frescoes of the Loggia of Psyche by Raphael were painted for its previous owner. But it is interesting to contemplate the grandiosity of Michelangelo's project to link it to the palace across the river.

Caprarola (near Viterbo): Villa Farnese

Seventy kilometres north of Rome, Villa Farnese was built by Vignola for Alessandro Farnese between 1559 and 1575. It dominates the town, and is approached by a triumphal flight of steps. The courtyard and internal helicoidal staircase are important examples of sixteenth-century architecture, while the allegorical frescoes in the halls and rooms illustrate the history of the Farnese.

Parma: Palazzo del Pilotta

A huge, unfinished palace built by the Farnese dukes between 1583 and 1622, the Palazzo del Pilotta had a magnificent courtyard, and houses the National Archaeological Museum of Parma, with important objects from the Farnese and Gonzaga collections, and the National Gallery on the second floor with examples of painting from Parma, Ferrara, and other cities of Emilia Romagna.

Parma: Teatro Farnese

Inside the Palazzo del Pilotta, on the same floor as the National Gallery is one of the first permanent theatres built in Europe, and also one of the biggest. It was built in 1618, with movable scenery, and has recently been restored after bombing during the Second World War.

THE MEDICI

Florence: Palazzo Medici

Evidently the whole of Renaissance Florence is testimony to the grandeur and taste of the Medici. But Palazzo Medici, built by Michelozzo for Cosimo the Elder between 1444 and 1464, was the first Renaissance building in Florence designed as a family home. It was later sold and expanded, but the courtyard and family chapel bear the original stamp. In the chapel is a painting of the journey of the Wise Men to Bethlehem, with a portrait of Lorenzo the Magnificent and other family members.

Florence: La Biblioteca Laurenziana

Medici literary interests, literary friendships, and book collecting may be said to have culminated in this exquisite library. Designed by Michelangelo, who was responsible for the famous and breathtaking staircase, and conceived in sculptural terms which make it unique, it held the huge Medici collection of books and manuscripts which his predecessors like Cosimo the Elder and Lorenzo the Magnificent had made. The main reading room, with a wooden ceiling by Michelangelo, has manuscripts and books from the Medici collections on display.

Florence: the Medici Chapel

The Medici Chapel is in the new sacresty of the church of San Lorenzo, started by Michelangelo and completed by Giorgio Vasari. Unfinished like many of Michelangelo's ambitious projects, this chapel contains the simple tomb of Lorenzo the Magnificent and the two famous Medici tombs of Lorenzo, Duke of Urbino, and Giuliano, Duke of Nemours. The tombs of Lorenzo the Magnificent and his brother Giuliano, which were to complete the arrangement, were never built.

Florence: the Uffizi gallery

The Uffizi gallery was originally built by Giorgio Vasari for Cosimo I for administrative offices, and pàrt of it was used after his death for a sculpture gallery. Apart from the superb Medici collections housed in this museum, it also contains splendid portraits of members of the Medici dynasty: Pope Leo X by Raphael, Cosimo I by Vasari and Bronzino, Giovanni delle Bande Nere by Titian, many minor members, later dukes such as Cosimo II and Gian Gastone, and posthumous portraits of Lorenzo di Giovanni by Bronzino and Cosimo the Elder by Pontormo.

Near Florence: Poggio a Caiano

Of all the Medici villas in and near Florence, at Fiesole, Careggi, and Cafaggiolo, the finest is that rebuilt by Giuliano Sangallo at Poggio a Caiano for Lorenzo the Magnificent. Built within fortified walls, it included a farm and was the site of hunting, hawking, and banquets — the place loved above all others by Lorenzo. The main salon has excellent frescoes by artists including Andrea del Sarto and Pontormo.

Rome: Villa Medici

Now the French Academy in Rome, Villa Medici was bought by Cardinal Ferdinando de' Medici in 1580, having been built some forty years earlier. Near the Spanish Steps, it retains the original layout of the gardens, and commands a spectacular view over the city of Rome. Nowadays it is used for art exhibitions and, in the summer, concerts are sometimes given in the gardens.

INDEX

190